Educating for Peace through Theatrical Arts

This volume illustrates how theatre arts can be used to enact peace education by showcasing the use of theatrical techniques including storytelling, testimonial and forum theatre, political humor, and arts-based pedagogy in diverse formal and non-formal educational contexts across age groups.

The text presents and discusses how the use of applied theatre, especially in conflict-affected areas, can be used as an educational response to cultural and structural violence for transformation of relations, healing, and praxis as local and global peacebuilding. Crucially, it bridges performing arts and peace education, the latter of which is unfolding in schools and their communities worldwide. With contributors from countries including Northern Ireland, Denmark, Norway, the USA, Mexico, Japan, the Philippines, Pakistan, Burundi, Kenya, and South Africa, the authors identify theoretical and technical aspects of theatrical performance that support peace through transformation along with embodied and sensorial learning.

This book will appeal to scholars and students with interests in teacher education, arts-based learning, peace studies, and applied theatre that consider practice with child, adolescent, and adult learners.

Candice C. Carter is an educational researcher and consultant. Previously, she was an Associate Professor and Director of the Conflict Transformation Program at the University of North Florida, USA.

Rodrigo Benza Guerra is a director and researcher of performing arts, and Associate Professor in the Department of Performing Arts at the Pontificia Universidad Católica del Perú (PUCP).

Routledge Research in Arts Education
Books in the series include:

Making and Relational Creativity
An Exploration of Relationships that Arise through Creative Practices in Informal Making Spaces
Edited by Lindsey Helen Bennett

Engaging Youth in Critical Arts Pedagogies and Creative Research for Social Justice
Opportunities and Challenges of Arts-based Work and Research with Young People
Edited by Kristen P. Goessling, Dana E. Wright, Amanda C. Wager, and Marit Dewhurst

The Value of Drawing Instruction in the Visual Arts and Across Curricula
Historical and Philosophical Arguments for Drawing in the Digital Age
Edited by Seymour Simmons III

Perspectives on Learning Assessment in the Arts in Higher Education
Supporting Transparent Assessment across Artistic Disciplines
Edited by Diane Leduc and Sébastien Béland

Culturally Sustaining Pedagogies in Music Education
Expanding Culturally Responsive Teaching to Sustain Diverse Musical Cultures and Identities
Edited by Emily Good-Perkins

Addressing Issues of Mental Health in Schools through the Arts
Teachers and Music Therapists Working Together
Edited by Jane Tarr and Nick Clough

Educating for Peace through Theatrical Arts
International Perspectives on Peacebuilding Instruction
Edited by Candice C. Carter and Rodrigo Benza Guerra

Artist-Teacher Practice and the Expectation of an Aesthetic Life
Creative Being in the Neoliberal Classroom
Edited by Carol Wild

Educating for Peace through Theatrical Arts

International Perspectives on Peacebuilding Instruction

Edited by Candice C. Carter and
Rodrigo Benza Guerra

NEW YORK AND LONDON

First published 2022
by Routledge
605 Third Avenue, New York, NY 10158

and by Routledge
4 Park Square, Milton Park, Abingdon, Oxon, OX14 4RN

Routledge is an imprint of the Taylor & Francis Group, an informa business

© 2022 selection and editorial matter, Candice C. Carter and Rodrigo Benza Guerra; individual chapters, the contributors

The right of Candice C. Carter and Rodrigo Benza Guerra to be identified as the authors of the editorial material, and of the authors for their individual chapters, has been asserted in accordance with sections 77 and 78 of the Copyright, Designs and Patents Act 1988.

All rights reserved. No part of this book may be reprinted or reproduced or utilized in any form or by any electronic, mechanical, or other means, now known or hereafter invented, including photocopying and recording, or in any information storage or retrieval system, without permission in writing from the publishers.

Trademark notice: Product or corporate names may be trademarks or registered trademarks, and are used only for identification and explanation without intent to infringe.

Library of Congress Cataloging-in-Publication Data
A catalog record for this title has been requested

ISBN: 978-1-032-13047-7 (hbk)
ISBN: 978-1-032-13050-7 (pbk)
ISBN: 978-1-003-22738-0 (ebk)

DOI: 10.4324/9781003227380

Typeset in Goudy
by SPi Technologies India Pvt Ltd (Straive)

Contents

List of Figures	*vii*
List of Tables	*viii*
Acknowledgments	*ix*
About the Contributors	*x*

1. Introduction: Peacebuilding through Performance Art as Education   1
   CANDICE C. CARTER AND RODRIGO BENZA GUERRA

2. Culture, Performance, and Peace: How Performance Art and Intangible Cultural Heritage Help to Create Peace in Our World   13
   CHRISTOPH WULF

3. Aesthetic Resonance as Peacebuilding in Applied Theatre with Newly Immigrated Children in Germany   27
   SERAFINA MORRIN

4. Bridging the Classroom Divide in the US: Dialogical Pedagogy and the Healing Arts   41
   JAMES ALAN ASTMAN

5. From a Place of Not Fully Knowing: Devising Theatre with Young Adults in Austria as a Vulnerable Process of Elicitive Peace Education   71
   HANNE TJERSLAND

6. Teaching for Gender Equality as Peace Education through Theatrical Performance in Mexican Schools   91
   LUCÍA E. RODRÍGUEZ MCKEON AND NÁYADE SOLEDAD MONTER ARIZMENDI

7	Theatre Arts in Peace Education: The Praxis at the Mindanao Peacebuilding Institute in the Philippines KYOKO OKUMOTO, BABU AYINDO, AND DESSA QUESADA PALM	109
8	Storytelling in Burundi: Traditional and Theatrical Education to Support Peacebuilding WILLIAM M. TIMPSON, FULGENCE TWIZERIMANA, AND GODELIEVE NISENGWE	130
9	Desiderata: Dancing Social Cohesion in Cape Town GERARD M. SAMUEL AND CHARLOTTE SVENDLER NIELSEN	146
10	Peacebuilding through Testimonial Theatre in the United States and Northern Ireland JENNIFER BLACKBURN MILLER	159
11	Political Humor and Peace Education SYED SIKANDER MEHDI	181
	Conclusion CANDICE C. CARTER	201
	Appendix	206
	Index of Names	210
	Index of Terms	216

Figures

4.1	Fourth grade script writing session with teacher	55
4.2	Storyboard for *The Strong Ones*	55
4.3	Fourth graders vote on *Words Behind Bars*	56
4.4	Parents watching a strike scene in *The Strong Ones*	57
4.5	"Get outside of your fourth-grade selves"	60
4.6	Sixth graders reading their Eleanor Roosevelt books to kindergarteners	61
4.7	Art teacher guiding sixth grader while he sculpts his "hero"	62
4.8	Sixth grade sculptures of peace/human rights heroes: Mahatma Gandhi, Malala Yousafzai, Gloria Steinem, Frederick Douglas	63
4.9	Student explaining her homelessness booth to classmate	64
4.10	Student visitors to immigration booth	64
4.11	Students learning about LGBTQ booth	64
6.1	Performance: *The Street and the Stalking Vampires*	99
6.2	Performance: *Secondary School Warriors*	99
6.3	Gender mainstreaming in the classroom	105
7.1	The logo of the Mindanao Peacebuilding Institute Foundation Incorporated	114
8.1	Peace English Club meeting with Fulgence Twizerimana	136

Tables

7.1 Direct/structural/cultural violence and peace and negative/positive peace 116
7.2 Art, direct/structural/cultural violence and peace and negative/positive peace 124

Acknowledgments

This book expresses the hope and perseverance of everyone who contributed to it and their supporters during the second year of an ongoing pandemic that caused widespread illness with loss of family, friends, peers, and fellow activists in addition to a way of life. The development process illustrated how visions of and commitment to peacebuilding sustain action for its advancement in the midst of difficult circumstances.

About the Contributors

Editors

Candice C. Carter, Independent Educational Research and Consultant, USA

Candice C. Carter applies her Ph.D. in Education as an independent researcher of conflict and peace processes. She has been an administrator for international, national, and regional peace, education, and policy organizations as well as in universities. At the University of California, she examined aspects of intercultural communication and conflict while she taught peace education. In the University of North Florida, she co-founded and directed the interdisciplinary Conflict Transformation Program that students across five colleges joined. Her experiences as a directress in Montessori academies, teacher, and district mentor in public schools of California, along with instruction of abandoned children she adopted, provided insights on student-centered education. Her research, development of study abroad, Fulbright leadership, and administration of organizations has occurred across several world regions that have been afflicted with violence. In her lifelong service as well as her scholarship, she has worked to increase understanding and promote well-being between people and other members of their environment. Dr. Carter's publications in journals and books include a multitude of topics related to conflict and peace. The book she co-edited *Chicken Soup for the Soul, Stories for a Better World* (2005) illustrates how peace can be developed in many different contexts of conflict. The book *Peace Philosophy in Action* (2010) that she co-edited with Ravindra Kumar provides information about applied theories in peace initiatives around the world. *Conflict Resolution and Peace Education: Transformations Across Disciplines* (2010) that she edited illustrates applications of peace education across organizations, including discipline-based courses in university programs. *Youth Literature for Peace Education* (2014), which she co-authored with Linda Pickett, explains development of language, social, and artistic literacy with peace competencies. In *Social Education for Peace* (2015) she describes transdisciplinary instruction for visionary learning. *Teaching* *and Learning for Comprehensive Citizenship: Global Perspectives on Peace Education* (2021) that she edited forefronts critical analyses of instruction towards peace. It is part of the series Routledge Research in International and Comparative Education.

Rodrigo Benza Guerra, Associate Professor, Pontificia Universidad Católica del Perú

Rodrigo Benza Guerra is a director and researcher of performing arts, and Associate Professor of the Department of Performing Arts of the Pontificia Universidad Católica del Perú (PUCP). He has a Master in Theatre from the Universidade do Estado de Santa Catarina (UDESC) in Brazil and a Bachelor of Performing Arts from the PUCP where he serves as director of cultural affairs. He has developed various intercultural theatre projects with indigenous and mestizo youth from the Peruvian Amazon and was a member of the nucleus for the training of facilitators in community theatre (FOFA) of the UDESC. Among his most outstanding scenic projects are the creation of the work *La gran fiesta de la democracia real (The Great Party of Royal/Real Democracy)* (2017), *Ausentes—Proyecto escénico (Absents—Scenic Project)* (2016) and *Proyecto Empleadas (Maids' Project)* (2009), winner of the Iberescena Prize. He has published articles in academic journals and books in Peru, Brazil, Cuba, Argentina, England, and South Africa, mainly about intercultural theatre, community theatre, documentary theatre, and Andean theatricality.

Authors

Náyade Soledad Monter Arizmendi, Ph.D. candidate, National Polytechnic Institute, México

Náyade Soledad Monter Arizmendi, Ph.D. candidate in the Department of Educational Research of the Center for Research and Advanced Studies in the National Polytechnic Institute México, is a gender specialist in education. She has a Master in Management of Coexistence at School from National Pedagogical University-Ajusco, basic level teaching credential, and diploma in "Sexualities: body, human rights and public policy," from the Center for Gender Research and Studies. Her research areas are gender, education, and coexistence and relevant publications include: "Genre and discourses on romantic love: Case study at Autonomous University of Mexico City, Cuautepec campus", co-authored with Ana Lara; and a brief outline of femicide in Mexico and the sociocultural construction of masculinity. She has participated in various conferences and symposiums related to education and gender studies.

James Alan Astman, Oxford University Faculty, Oakwood School Headmaster Emeritus, Sherman Oaks, USA

James Alan Astman is a Visiting Scholar in the Ethics, Law, and Armed Conflict Program at Oxford University's Blavatnik School of Government (2019–2022). He was a Visiting Fellow in Oxford's Department of Politics and International Relations (2014–2018). He serves as a faculty member in the Oxford Consortium of Human Rights, and is currently completing a book on the dialogical nature of teaching for human rights, titled *To Begin with the Children (From Cradle to Classroom to Community: Educating for Peace and Human Rights)*. In 2019, he led an inaugural Consortium Conference on Human Rights Education in Los Angeles, "Welcoming the Stranger: Educating for Human Rights." He served as Associate Adjunct Professor of Psychiatry at University of California at Los Angeles' Geffen School of Medicine from 1996 to 2019, where he taught child and adolescent development. He has been Adjunct Professor of Education at Claremont Graduate University and Visiting Scholar in the Graduate School of Education at Stanford University. He is Headmaster Emeritus of the Oakwood School, a K-12 day school in Los Angeles, California, known for its programs in the arts and humanities. Under his leadership, the school developed a signature program for peace and a human rights education program to inspire advocacy for human rights and to promote dignity, social justice, and activism.

Babu Ayindo, storyteller, educator, and researcher based in Nairobi, Kenya

Babu Ayindo is a storyteller, educator, researcher, and writer. In the past, he has served as Artistic Director of Chelepe Arts (Nairobi, Kenya), founding Artistic Director of Amani People's Theatre (Nairobi, Kenya) and instructor at the Nairobi Theatre Academy. As founding Artistic Director of Amani People's Theatre in the 90s, he led community-based creative and dialogical peacebuilding processes that drew from African Indigenous arts and Theatre of the Oppressed and Playback Theatre. Some of his publications include: *When You Are the Peacebuilder* (with Jan Jenner and Sam G. Doe) and *In Search of Healers*. Babu's doctoral research was entitled *Arts, Peacebuilding and Decolonization: A Comparative Study of Parihaka, Mindanao and Nairobi*.

Lucía E. Rodríguez McKeon, National Pedagogical University, México City, México

Lucía E. Rodríguez McKeon holds a Ph.D. in Education. She is a member of the National System of Researchers of México and faculty member at the National Pedagogical University (UPN) where she is presently the coordinator of the Graduate Program on Management of Coexistence at School, Violence, Human Rights, and Culture of Peace with the support of the official Human Rights Commission of the City of México. Her research interest focuses on themes such as diversity, human rights, culture of peace, and education for citizenship. She has coordinated the design of intervention programs on contexts of cultural differences and migration, including the Intercultural Educational Model for Agricultural Migrant Children with UNICEF.

Among her recent publications include "Las vías de lo escolar en tiempos violentos. Una reflexión desde la alteridad" (The Ways of the School in Violent Times. A Reflection from Alterity) in *Revista Murmullos Filosóficos* (2016); "Violencia, Escuela y Gramáticas de la Convivencia" (Violence, School and Grammars of Coexistence) in Anzaldúa, Raúl, *Entramados sociales de la violencia escolar*, (UPN México 2017); "From Indifference to Withdrawal: Teaching Ethos and Processes of Change in Civic and Ethical Education" in Oser et al., *The International Handbook of Teacher Ethos* (Springer 2021).

Syed Sikander Mehdi, Director Academics and Projects, Malir University of Science & Technology, Karachi, Pakistan

Syed Sikander Mehdi of Pakistan was educated at Dacca University, Bangladesh, and Australian National University, Canberra, Australia. He is the former chairperson of the Department of International Relations in the University of Karachi and he is a leading peace scholar. He has taught courses on peace education, peace culture, and peace movements at universities in Pakistan, Austria, and Spain. He has also worked as visiting scholar at the International Peace Research Institute in Oslo, Norway, the Henry Stimson Centre in Washington DC, USA and in Ritsumeikan University of Kyoto, Japan. He is a board member of the International Network of Museums for Peace and a former member of International Peace Research Association's Council and the executive body of its Peace Education Commission. His most recent publications are "Freedom and Security in the Changing Times" in *Strategic Thought* (2019) and "Memory, Freedom, and Power" in *Strategic Thought* (2020).

Jennifer Blackburn Miller, D.Ed. Candidate, The Pennsylvania State University, USA

Jennifer Blackburn Miller is a dual-title D.Ed. candidate in Lifelong Learning and Adult Education, and Comparative and International Education, at The Pennsylvania State University. She has a BA in Philosophy and Religious Studies with Minors in Music and International Studies from Radford University and an MA in Teaching English as a Second Language from The Pennsylvania State University. Jennifer is interested in conflict transformation, trauma healing, and peacebuilding through the arts. Her dissertation research is about a social justice testimonial theatre program in Philadelphia, Pennsylvania USA and Derry/Londonderry, Northern Ireland. Her preliminary research on this program has been published in the *Canadian Journal for the Study of Adult Education* in an article titled "The Transformative and Healing Power of Theatre of Witness" (2018). She has also published an article titled "Transformative Learning and the Arts: A Literature Review" in, *Journal of Transformative Education* (2020).

Serafina Morrin, Research Associate, Catholic University of Applied Sciences Berlin, Germany

Serafina Morrin is a pedagogical scientist and childhood educator with many years of experience as an actress and theatre educationalist. Her Ph.D. dissertation is availing of this experience and exploring the connections between aesthetics and education. Her research activities focus on childhood research, performative learning, teaching and research, as well as on theatrical-aesthetic education.

Godelieve Nisengwe, Branch Manager, Society for Women Against AIDS in Africa, Ngozi, Burundi

Godelieve Nisengwe is a coordinator of Society for Women Against AIDS in Africa. She is a Ngozi Rotary Club member and a committed peacebuilder. Godelieve graduated from the University of Burundi in the Institute for the Applied Pedagogy, English Department. She also has Master in Public Health. Since 2008, she has been a teacher of adult in evening classes and she is a teacher at the University of Muyinga in the faculty of public health. Godelieve is a representative of Future School that she created. She was an educator and teacher in a secondary school and a teacher of English in International Care and in MSF Hollande. She made the health center that she leads a "Center Friend of the Young."

Kyoko Okumoto, Professor, Osaka Jogakuin University, Vice Chair of Northeast Asia Regional Peacebuilding Institute, Osaka, Japan

Kyoko Okumoto is a researcher, facilitator, educator, writer, and citizen artist. Kyoko holds a Ph.D. and an MA in the Arts and Literature from Kobe College Graduate School of Letters in Japan, and an MA in Peace Studies from Lancaster University in the UK. She is a Professor of Peace Studies, Conflict Transformation, and Arts-based Approaches to Peacebuilding at Osaka Jogakuin University, a women's university. Her research fields are: conflict transformation, nonviolent intervention, facilitation and mediation, the arts including literature and drama/theatre, and the relations among the areas. She facilitates peace training workshops in several places at all levels—from high school, to university to elderly communities. With NGOs/CSOs, including academic associations such as Peace Studies Association of Japan, Transcend-Japan, Transcend-International, Nonviolent Peaceforce-Japan, ACTION-Asia, Northeast Asia Regional Peacebuilding Institute and Mindanao Peacebuilding Institute, Kyoko tries to explore ways to connect with other Asian—Northeast, Southeast and South Asian—communities, and beyond to build more peaceful societies where people can have creative dialogues among themselves and with their neighbors and communities.

Dessa Quesada Palm, Youth Advocates Through Theater Arts, Artistic Director, Silliman University College of Performing and Visual Arts, Faculty, Dumaguete City, Philippines

Dessa Quesada Palm has had more than 40 years of performing and theatre practice as artist–teacher–organizer–leader, performing and leading workshops locally and internationally. Dessa spent many years with the Philippine Educational Theater Association (PETA), that has pioneered theatre for development and in education. She was educated at the University of the Philippines School of Economics, and later pursued her Master in International Relations at the New School for Social Research in New York as a Fulbright scholar. Now based in Dumaguete City in central Philippines, she works as faculty at the Silliman University and is the founder/Artistic Director of the Youth Advocates Through Theater Arts, a 2008 recipient of the Ten Accomplished Youth Organizations. She served as head of the Committee on Dramatic Arts of the National Commission for Culture and the Arts from 2017 to 2019 and is the Vice President of the Women Playwrights International—Philippines. Dessa has facilitated trainings on the nexus of arts and peacebuilding at the Mindanao Peacebuilding Institute, at the Canadian School of Peacebuilding, and at the African Peacebuilding Institute.

Gerard M. Samuel, Associate Professor, University of Cape Town, South Africa

Gerard M. Samuel is an Associate Professor in the University of Cape Town (UTC), Centre for Theatre, Dance and Performance Studies and the Head of CTDPS Dance Section. He is the Convener: Post Graduate studies in Dance, Editor: *South African Dance Journal*, and Chair of *Confluences* a biennial, international dance conference hosted by UCT. During the Apartheid era he performed with the NAPAC Ballet Company and The Playhouse Dance Company in Durban. He held senior management posts for The Playhouse Company, until 2006. His notable choreographies include *Prabhati* and *The Man I Love*. He received the Durban Theatre Awards in 2006 for *The Sound of Music*. Gerard has produced *Place of Grace*, a dance film in 2011. He is an advocate of disability arts in South Africa and in Denmark. He obtained his Ph.D. for a thesis entitled Dancing the Other in South Africa from UCT, in 2016 in which it was announced that "Gerard Samuel's thesis makes a highly significant intervention in Dance and Performance Studies in terms of its original argument about how the category of 'age' is used [as] part of 'othering' process… coining the term 'body-space' as a theoretical tool to observe bodies and dancing as states of becoming."

Charlotte Svendler Nielsen, Associate Professor, University of Copenhagen, Denmark.

Charlotte Svendler Nielsen Ph.D. is Associate Professor in Educational Studies focusing on Dance and Head of Studies at the Department of Nutrition, Exercise and Sports, research cluster Embodiment, Learning and Social Change University of Copenhagen, Denmark. She is co-editor of *Dance Education around the World* (2015), *Dance, Access and Inclusion* (2017), and *Dancing across Borders* (2020), all forming part of the book series Perspectives on Dance, Young People and Change published by

Routledge UK. She is also Executive Board member of Dance and the Child International and Chair of the European Observatories of Arts and Cultural Education. Charlotte has together with Gerard M. Samuel co-led the educational research project Red Apples Green Apples-Arts-Integrated and Intercultural Learning in Multi-Cultural Schools in South Africa 2017–2020. She is also involved as collaborator of Nordic research projects Embodied Language Learning through the Arts—a Finnish-based research project (2021–2024), Empowering Student Teachers as Agents of Change in Cross-Sectorial Collaborations using The Cultural Schoolbag in Norway as a Learning Platform (pARTiciPED) led by the College in Østfold, Norway (2021–2023), and Arts as Public Service-Strategic Steps towards Equality (ArtsEqual) led by the University of the Arts Helsinki (2015–2021).

William M. Timpson, Emeritus Professor, Colorado State University, Fort Collins, USA

William M. Timpson Ph.D. is an Emeritus Professor from the School of Education at Colorado State University in the USA. Three of his relevant books include *Learning Life's Lessons: Inspirational Tips for Creating Peace in Troubled Times* (2019), *Teaching and Performing* (2002), and *Teaching and Learning Peace* (2002). He has focused on the education of difficult topics, i.e., peace and reconciliation, sustainability and diversity. Along with numerous articles, chapters, and grants, he has written or co-authored 19 books including original titles as well as new editions. From 1981 to 1984 he was the recipient of a Kellogg National Fellowship to study international conflicts and their implications for education. In 2006 he served as a Fulbright Specialist in peace and reconciliation studies at the University of Ulster's UNESCO Centre in Northern Ireland and again in 2011 at the University of Ngozi in Burundi, East Africa, where he continues to work with Rotary Foundation Global Grants to promote sustainable peacebuilding. In Spring 2014 he served as a Fulbright Teaching Scholar at Kyung Hee's Graduate Institute of Peace Studies in South Korea. He conducted study tours to areas of conflict that include Israel–Palestine in 2017, Ukraine–Russia in 2019 and the US–Mexican border also in 2019.

Hanne Tjersland, Director, Peace in Movement, Hurdal/Oslo, Norway

Hanne Tjersland is a Ph.D. candidate in International Studies in Peace, Conflict and Development at the Universidad Jaume I, Castelló de la Plana, Spain. She holds a Master of Arts in Peace, Development, Security, and International Conflict Transformation from the University of Innsbruck, Austria, and a Bachelor of Arts in Drama/Theatre from the Norwegian University of Science and Technology (NTNU), Trondheim, Norway. In both her research and work, Hanne focuses on arts-based and embodied approaches to peace education and conflict transformation, particularly theatre and conscious dance and movement. She is writing her Ph.D. dissertation on the conscious dance and movement practice Open Floor and facilitates different groups through her initiative Peace in Movement (www.peaceinmovement.com) where she uses theatre and conscious dance and movement to practically engage dynamics of peace. Her recent co-authored article "Identity, Diversity, and Inclusion on the Dance Floor" explores the practice of embodied self-reflexivity in relation to how teachers of conscious dance and movement practices can invite more authentic possibilities for diversity and inclusion on to the dance floor. She has also published an article titled "The Dancing Body in Peace Education" in the *Journal of Peace Education* as well as co-edited a special issue on "Transrational Perspectives in Peace Education" in the same journal. During autumn 2021, Hanne commences a three-month research stay at the Tampere Peace Research Institute at the University of Tampere, Finland.

Fulgence Twizerimana, Teacher, Hope Fountain School

Fulgence Twizerimana is an educator and teacher at Hope Elementary School. He has a bachelor's degree in Applied Pedagogy, English teaching from the University of Burundi. Fulgence is a fervent peacebuilder who inspires and empowers others, especially the youth. In 2012, while he was studying in the university, with two other friends he founded IKIREZIWACU, which is a youth organization that promotes peace and reconciliation through cultural events. In 2014, he worked as a volunteer for PARCEM, a local NGO committed for peace, awareness raising, human rights advocacy, and dismantling corruption. He works to address local and global challenges related to peace and environment changes. Fulgence is a Rotarian, an alumni of World Beyond War and Youth African Leaders Initiative (Yali) organizations. He is also a member of Environmental Peacebuilding Association (EnPax) and a volunteer in many local organizations. In 2019, with William M. Timpson, he initiated Peace English Clubs, in which he teaches students and others in the community English through the study of peace.

Christoph Wulf, Professor, Free University of Berlin, Germany

Christoph Wulf Ph.D. is Professor of Anthropology and Education and a member of the Interdisciplinary Centre for Historical Anthropology, the Collaborative Research Centre "Cultures of Performance" (SFB, 1999–2011), the Cluster of Excellence "Languages of Emotions" (2007–2012), and the Graduate Schools "Body Staging" and "InterArts" at Freie Universität Berlin (Free University of Berlin). His books have been translated into 20 languages. He is currently the Vice President of the German Commission for UNESCO. His research areas include: historical and cultural anthropology, educational anthropology, rituals, gestures, emotions, imagination, intercultural communication, mimesis, aesthetics, and epistemology. Christoph Wulf is editor, co-editor, and member of the editorial staff of several international journals. He has published over 20 books in multiple languages.

1 Introduction

Peacebuilding through Performance Art as Education

Candice C. Carter and Rodrigo Benza Guerra

This compilation is about theatrical performance as a catalyst for peace. It features the processes and roles of arts production that have comprised a mosaic of performative peace education. The described instructors and learners advanced knowledge and skills in performance creation, preparation, production, interaction, and reflection that support several types of peacebuilding. Teaching, learning, creating, physically enacting, sensing, and thinking about a performance can develop and strengthen several capabilities for peace advancement in and beyond the performance's context. Peacebuilding education through learning performing arts happens where there is a goal for advancement of interactions and knowledge that support peace. The book's chapters spotlight the intersectionality of performance education that occurs through interdisciplinary and transrational learning. The vignettes of and research on performance's role in personal, social, and political peace presented in this book forefront and rationalize the advancement of performing arts as crucial education in several contexts with regional as well as shared ideologies.

Educating for Peace

This book's foundation holds peace as a process as well as an instructional goal with performance education as a means of preparation for advancement of that condition. While peace takes its own meaning in each context, culture, mind, and interpretation, the notion of peace as a condition of individual and collective well-being generally characterizes its construal. Processes that can contribute to well-being include response to conflict without violence, power-sharing, anti-oppression, intercultural harmony, compassionate communication, healing of physical and social wounds, restorative justice, enactment of culture with protection of human rights, protection and representation of nature, along with sharing of peace visions, which is a precursor to their pursuit. Enactment of local, traditional, and new means of learning about and pursuing peace in a context constitutes peace education. Additionally, peace in the learning process is a goal of peace education. The goals include learning

DOI: 10.4324/9781003227380-1

for peace, by peace, and of peace (Galtung, 1996). The latter goal, which includes concepts and processes in different world regions, advances diversity as well as vocabulary for description and understanding of peace. Ethical traditions, such as *ahimsa*, which translates to do no harm, express values that comprise the foundation of peace education (Joshee & Shirvell, 2021). The protection of the community's well-being is another traditional value that collectivist cultures teach. *Ubuntu* in African communities, for example, is a tradition that expresses that value (Marovah, 2021). Peace education is clearly value-based.

Instruction as well as the official and hidden curriculum of education convey values. The messages of the unofficial curriculum are 'hidden' yet very influential, and a source of student resistance where there is not an enacted value for democracy in the learning context (Yüksel, 2006; Oseroff-Varnell, 1998). Values expressed in neoliberal education are accountability, efficiency, productivity, competition, and economic advancement, among others, that support capitalism. Values promoted in peace education are relating, caring, interdependence, harmony, inclusion, and fairness. Education in dominator-style instruction that modern schools commonly feature has been a challenge for teachers of peace education who work with both sets of values. Cultivation of peace education's values optimally occurs through horizontal interactions of shared power in a prosocial milieu of learning together (Eisler & Miller, 2004). Facilitation in the learning context of processes that aim for collective as well as individual well-being, such as praxis in comprehensive citizenship for creation of solutions to local and global problems, is prosocial. Performances that show or cause cessation of violence are peacemaking, and peacebuilding involves fortification of peace.

The performing arts provide opportunities for transmitting and enacting peace-oriented values, skills, knowledge, and processes. Artists value creativity as much as peacemakers and peacebuilders do, regardless of their goal differences. The ability to create is a core skill of making a means of bringing about peace where it has been lost as well as where peace needs to be built stronger for its durability. Performances have creatively disrupted and halted battles, communicated messages that would otherwise be censored, connected ostensible "enemies," revealed conflict sources, inspired and facilitated peace movements, and advanced understanding of needs, while they addressed and sometimes relieved the wounds of violence. Expression of imagination is another value-based process of peace education that the arts enable. In "Education and Disarmament" Maxine Greene (1982) pointed out how one's imagination fostered through arts with value consciousness can construe alternative realities with moral constraints that exclude violence and injustice. Herbert Read (1943, 1949) called for peace brought about with collective as well as individual imagination stimulated by the senses in aesthetic education. As a battlefield survivor of a world war, he thought that healing and collective cooperation for problem-solving without violence were learning goals. The effects of a world war stimulated Maria Montessori's *Education for*

Peace (1972), which involves sensorial learning, as arts education enables. She believed that learners should know about world regions and the interconnections people have, to form international-mindedness (Duckworth, 2006). Her enduring pedagogy stimulates learners' knowledge and sense of interdependence with the Clock of Eras that shows the small amount of time that humans have had on earth. That clock and the Timeline of Life in the Montessori curriculum emphasize the significance of all life on earth, before and during the Anthropocene. Throughout the twentieth century, humanity's continual engagement in violence of several types has sustained initiatives for peacebuilding education.

The articulation of secular, versus faith-based, peace education, due to the official separation of church and state in the constitution of many countries, including our own countries of Peru and the United States, increased throughout the twentieth century. Meanwhile, peace education has expanded worldwide in several types of schools, most notably in conflict zones where war and direct violence between contesting groups have occurred. Research on many aspects of peace education and scholarly publications with that topic informed the field of education and its policies during the second half of the twentieth century. When the movement to standardize instruction began and peace was not articulated as a goal or learning process, researchers responded. Researchers of peace education from several world regions collectively developed the Standards for Peace Education (Carter, 2006, 2008). The Standards for Peace Education (SPE) include goals for student learning, teaching, teacher preparation, and school administration. The SPE feature the learning domains of knowledge, skills, and dispositions that have been common strands in other sets of education standards. The chapters included in this book describe instruction that aligns with several of the SPE goals. The enactment of performing arts in education includes processes that were of recommended for peace education.

Performing Arts in Education

Inclusion of performing arts in education augments human development and enables cultural expression in ways that literacy and computational-based learning lack unless they integrate aesthetic experiences through performance. However, the integration approach, which Candice has used for three decades in childhood through adult education, does not include all of the benefits that students have reaped in comprehensive learning of performing arts. Creation and production of, along with reflection on, performance is comprehensive. In his explanation of the interdependence of aesthetics and experiential learning Dewey (1958) emphasized that no intellectual and practical experience has unity unless it has an esthetic quality. In agreement that arts and the intellect need partnership in education, Eisner (2005) advanced awareness of how arts education can have "ancillary outcomes" (1999) that advance learning objectives in several other disciplines. There are several types of benefits of sensory activation for knowledge, skill, and disposition development that experiential learning of performing arts have provided. These developments occur across the human age span.

Education that includes experience with performing arts has variably enhanced student participation motivation, communication within an "alternative reality" of a performance context that is a bridge between participants' different backgrounds, where new perspectives can form (Hawes, 2009), interaction confidence, intercultural connection and experience (Carter, 2003; Hunter, 2005; Pruitt, 2011), relationship building (Cabedo-Mas, 2015), co-creative expression, and engagement in other subject areas (Colley, 2012). Performing arts in education has enabled analysis of and embodied experience with peace-oriented responses to conflict (Cohen, Varea, & Walker, 2011; Malm & Löfgren, 2007). Aesthetics stimulates "expressive ways of knowing" that may not result from instruction that lacks sensorial experience (Yorks & Kasl, 2006). Aesthetic performance in education has been therapeutic for disaffected and traumatized students (Karkou, 2010; Thompson & Neimeyer, 2014), especially through clarification of their emotions. Performance has been a means of emotional expression, healing, and personal transformation (Lance, 2012). Active, whole-body participation infused across a curriculum that includes performing arts and other kinetic experiences is a goal of holistic peace education (Noddings, 2012). As Montesorri and others have demonstrated, it is optimal to start in early childhood with activation of sensorial, cognitive, and physical experiences for accomplishment of that goal (Keskin, Keskin, & Kirtel, 2019).

Common Goals of Performance Arts and Peace Education

Performing arts and education for peace can have the same goals, such as the choice of artists to touch the subject of violence from a critical perspective, to the explicit use of performance methodologies in educational processes for, through, and about peace.

Once, when Juan Ibarra, a former member of the performance collective *La Pocha Nostra*, was asked why his performances were so violent, why they hurt their bodies so much, Juan's response was "to show the absurdity of violence in the world."[1] The members of *La Pocha Nostra* violated their bodies to challenge the audience so that they could question the violence around them.

Violence has always been a theme in the performing arts. We find it in the Greek tragedies, the Elizabethan theatre, in the writings of Antonin Artaud and in a long et cetera. Perhaps one of the most present aspects of it, until today, is a war and its consequences, that are important triggers for theatrical creation in their midst and afterwards (Thompson, Hughes, & Balfour, 2008). Plays and projects that present this topic—contrary to what happens with Hollywood films—tend to do so from a critical perspective in an effort to seek and promote a culture of peace. Starting in the 1990s, for example, war was a recurring topic in theatrical creation in Croatia. According to Nikolina Židek (2021, p. 131), one of these "was the difficulty of former combatants to reintegrate into peacetime life" as seen in Ivan Vidić's play *Big White Rabbit* in which "soldiers coming back from the warfront were also unable to find their place in society" (Židek, 2021, p. 131).

Another example of this can be found in the play *Minefield* by the Argentinian Lola Arias that "is a project that reunites Argentine and British veterans from the Falklands/Malvinas war to explore what is left of it in their heads 34 years later" (Arias, 2016). Gathering on stage and in a process of performance creation ex-combatants who were on opposite sides, who were enemies, who possibly had killed each other, allows us to see that these "enemies" can have many things in common and show the absurdity of war.

Although the aforementioned experiences do not necessarily present an explicit intention to serve for peace education, their pedagogical potential is undeniable and can be very valuable to question us about violence and its consequences and, even, to propose alternatives for the construction of a peaceful coexistence.

On the other hand, various performance experiences that, in addition to promoting entertainment, based on the aesthetic experience, propose to generate a positive impact on communities and individuals. The names and lines of work of these experiences are varied and diverse; however, perhaps the most "accepted" term today to encompass this type of practice, although it is not free from questioning, is that of applied performance. According to Tim Prentki and Ananda Breed, in these practices "performance is applied to social realities in order to criticize them, debate them and move them into the realm of public discourse. Where possible and appropriate, performances are used to suggest alternatives to prevailing sociopolitical conditions" (2021, p. 1).

If we speak specifically of theatre, for Phillip Taylor, "it is an applied theater because the art form becomes a transformative agent that places the audience or participants in direct and immediate situations where they can witness, confront, and deconstruct aspects of their own and other actions" (2003, p. xx). Tim Prentki and Jane Preston add that:

> applied theatre usually works in contexts where the work created and performed has a specific resonance with its participants and its audiences and often, to different degrees, involves them in it… Those practices existing (some rather reluctantly) under the umbrella of applied theatre might include: community theatre, community performance, theatre for social change, popular theatre, interventionist theatre, drama in education, theatre for integrated rural development, participatory performance practices, process drama/theatre, prison theatre, theatre in health/education, theatre for development, theatre for conflict resolution/reconciliation, reminiscence theatre and so on.
>
> (apud Prentki, 2015, pp. 14–15)

We can see then that performative or theatrical experiences that have the goal of developing an education for peace can be considered as applied performance. Now, how can the methodologies developed in performing arts contribute to build an education for peace? First, in the performing arts we work from and with the body. It is the body that receives and exercises violence and, therefore, it is in the body that we must find the ways of peace.

Colombian choreographer Ana Carolina Dávila developed a dance project in which she worked with former FARC guerrillas. The project sought a way to "recover" the bodies of these ex-combatants through dance. According to Dávila:

> if the world of a human being is forced with violence, his body beaten, wounded, raped, mutilated or displaced, trauma will break the spirit; maybe it can be relieved, reconciled, consoled, comprehended and accepted through another reading of the body, a body-being that is not alone in pain and sorrow, a body that returns to its territory through dance.
> (2021, p. 237)

The author adds that "the challenge was to propose to them through the experience, the idea of the body as a territory of peace" (Dávila, 2021, p. 238).

It is through the body, through the senses, that we interact and this is perhaps the main value of projects such as that of Dávila, who adds that:

> the reason why this approach seems to work, even in the cold institutional framework of a government office, is that it is based on the senses: the body is taken as an epicenter of meaningful experiences which are conducted through music and dance, and seek above all the reassignment of the body itself from tools of war or battlefield to persons of peace.
> (Dávila, 2021, p. 239)

Another relevant element to address peace education from the performing arts, as we already mentioned, is the dialectical relationship that exists between reality and imagination. If we are immersed in a violent reality, it is only through imagination that we can aspire to a peaceful environment, and it is that imagined reality, the experience of fantasy, that can lead us to build a different world in our concrete reality. Augusto Boal, creator of the Theater of the Oppressed 2000), said that the theatre is not the revolution, but a rehearsal of the revolution. In this sense, the fact that our bodies experience imagined realities, in some way can be a rehearsal that helps to modify reality.

On the other hand, there are experiences that are so painful or traumatic that they cannot be expressed rationally and/or through articulated discourse. Working with fantasy allows us to express things that, perhaps, we don't even know we want to express. According to Hellen Nicholson:

working in the 'imaginary space' of drama enables participants to juxtapose different narrative perspective, to fictionalize life as it is experienced and, conversely, to make the imaginary world of fiction tangible and 'real'. Conceptualized and practiced in this way, drama becomes a place to explore the ethical gap between description and prescription, hypothesis and factuality.

(2005, p. 64)

The places of conflict that can lead to violence are deeply marked by the misunderstanding of the other, by the lack of empathy, by the reductionism of identity and power asymmetry. It is in this sense that education for peace also requires taking into account the critical interculturalism approach that, in addition to promoting the encounter and exchange between people of different cultures, seeks to highlight injustices and generate the conditions for subalternized cultures to be integrated into modern society without losing their original characteristics (Tubino & Flores, 2020). Theatre and performing arts are very suitable to develop this intercultural encounter for several reasons, including the presence of play (games), the use of different languages, and the appreciation of the irrational:

> The notion of play, that is an activity with rules whose ultimate goal is fun, is transversal to different cultures. And since the game is the basis of the theater, we then find that this is also natural to the human being and transverse to cultures. On the other hand, the theater uses various means of communication such as the physical, the sound, the image and also, of course, the verbal. This allows that, in the intercultural context, more effective communication spaces can be established than we would have if only verbal/rational language is developed. This is another relevant point, the assessment of both the rational and the non-rational, of thought as well as feeling and emotion.
>
> We find that the best way to get to know the other – fundamental to build interculturalism and therefore to develop an intercultural education based on the encounter of different people – is coexistence which, if it has a common goal, generates a permanent negotiation space that (…) is not free of conflict, but it allows for an intense coexistence that leads to a true knowledge of the other. The fact that the common objective is the construction of a theater play created from the interests, movements, sounds, words, sensations of the participants themselves, enhances the relationship because the product is made up of a part of each of them.
>
> (Benza & Tubino, 2021, pp. 15–16)

We can find that this approach presented by Benza and Tubino oriented to intercultural education can be illustrative of education for peace, when taking into account the values of relating, caring, interdependence, harmony, inclusion, and fairness.

The performing arts per se, whether in the encounter between artists and spectators or training spaces, do not necessarily generate a culture of peace; however, if these performance experiences have a dialogical approach in the sense proposed by Paulo Freire (1970, in which a meeting of subjects that together, in collective and respectful learning, seek to improve a context and increase well-being there, then performance can become a natural path for education for peace.

Overview of Chapters

In Chapter 2, Christoph Wulf accounts for how performative arts and intangible cultural practices contribute to humanity's capacities for peacebuilding. He elucidates how working together for a culture of peace must include a society's performativity because the arts activate people's imaginations and senses. The ability to imagine is crucial for transformation and the creativity that enables change. Emotions stimulated by aesthetic and social experiences of performance production and audience response to it facilitate more than rational awareness. The sensorial awareness that performance enables is holistic learning. In Chapter 3 Serafina Morrin examines the facilitation of children's imagination during their theatrical experience. She analyzes the effects on the thinking of an aesthetic lesson in a new language with young refugees of different identities, cultures, and types of trauma. Those realities impeded their sense of belonging and rendered ambivalence in their new situation. Imaginative theatre play stimulated the children's cognitive resonance in the midst of their ambivalent living and learning spaces. In Chapter 4 James Alan Astman analyzes dialogical pedagogy in performing arts and then illustrates how two school programs enacted it. He describes the intersubjective communication and vulnerability in the teaching–learning relationship that enabled healing as well as embodied learning in arts-based social studies, which the students and teachers co-created. The limelight of Chapter 4 is how learning through applied arts in school advanced children's moral agency for enacting peace. In Chapter 5, Hanne Tjersland describes elicitive peace education wherein the performers construed and created their production together. Her chapter is a reflection on the collaborative, relational, and vulnerable process of teaching out of a place of not fully knowing what will result from that facilitation. With diversity as the theatrical theme of the created performance, she describes intercultural knowledge, identity, and skills in performance generation. Lucía E. Rodríguez Mckeon and Náyade Monter Arizmendi present two case studies in Chapter 6 of how deliberation and critical thinking of students in different schools enabled their problematization and transformation in theatrical performances of harmful gender relationships. One case entailed storytelling performances with representation of extant gender relations followed by a second performance with conversion of inequities represented in sexism, hegemony, sexual harassment, and other conflictual interactions. The second case, which involved student performance of documented gender violence in their region, presents their reflections and heightened awareness that femicide and other forms of gender violence can be changed. The chapter concludes with several recommendations for equalization of gender in the formal and informal curriculum of schools. Kyoko Okumoto, Babu Ayindo, and Dessa Quesada Palm explain in Chapter 7 how they integrate arts from several world cultures in the annual program of the Mindanao Peacebuilding Institute. During reflection on their praxis in aesthetic peacebuilding they point out how peace and art are dynamic processes that can reveal conflict and create peacebuilding responses to it. They also incorporate Indigenous customs of treating art as an aspect of everyday life and cultural expression. While all of the contributors to this book wrote their chapters in the midst of an ongoing pandemic, these authors point out that a crisis highlights the artistic capabilities of humans. They identify how theatre arts awakens senses and intuition while it enables storytelling as pedagogy through performance. In Chapter 8 William M. Timpson, Fulgence Twizerimana, and Godelieve Nisengwe discuss uses of storytelling to address trauma from past violence as well as harmful responses to current conflicts. They describe peacebuilding in two community contexts that facilitated storytelling: (1) a club for English acquisition and (2) the health trainings for youth with HIV. The chapter contributors confirm the tradition of storytelling as a traditional means of educating, responding to conflict, repairing harm, and its current uses as a multidisciplinary performance pedagogy. Gerard M. Samuel and Charlotte Svendler Nielsen Chapter illuminate in Chapter 9 a project that integrated dance with visual arts in Cape Town's former 'Coloreds only' primary schools. They let the participants speak for themselves to illustrate their thoughts during and responses to the project. In the midst of structural and direct violence, the children valued their opportunities for aesthetic interactions in formal education. They mentioned that the encouragement they received in the project boosted their confidence and self-esteem. The project facilitators point out that culturally sensitive and embodied pedagogies enhanced their understanding of the children's realities. Jennifer Blackburn Miller illuminates in Chapter 10 her case study of community theatre in two world regions where members of outgroups collaboratively performed and connected as audience. She elaborates a theory of perspective transformation and identifies how participation in documentary theatre contributed to that process. Her study highlights how audience witnessing of the transformative process can foster their empathy for the "other." In addition, she identifies several aspects of the performance production that comprise peacebuilding in divided and contesting communities. Syed Sikander Mehdi describes in Chapter 11 how performance of political humor has had a role in peacebuilding. He describes uses of humor and research on those applications in theatre, identity clarification, professional communication, stress relief, conflict resolution, and creative cooperation with outgroups, as well as politics. After he identifies limits peace education has had, he recommends its expansion with instruction in theatrical and political uses of humor. Learning how to make political jokes for disruption of a power imbalance as a response to political oppression is one of the humor strategies that he recommends for inclusion in peace education. His chapter offers several examples of such usage possibilities.

Note

1 Informal conversation with Rodrigo Benza in 2003.

References

Arias, L. (2016). *Minefield*. Lola Arias Company. Retrieved at https://lolaarias.com/minefield/

Benza, R. & Tubino, F. (2021). Educación intercultural y teatro: un aporte desde la experiencia peruana. [Intercultural education and theater: A contribution from the Peruvian experience]. *Revista Brasileira de Edducação do Campo [Brazilian Journal of Rural Education]*, 6, 1–19. doi: 10.20873/uft.rbec.e12472

Boal, A. (2000). *Theatre of the oppressed*. London: Pluto Press.

Cabedo-Mas, A. (2015). Challenges and perspectives of peace education in schools: The role of music. *Australian Journal of Music Education*, 2015(1), 75–85.

Carter, C. C. (2003). Prosocial music: Empowerment through aesthetic instruction. *Multicultural Perspectives*, 5(4), 38–40.

Carter, C. C. (2006). *Peace education standards*. Research Gate. Retrieved at https://www.researchgate.net/profile/Candice-Carter

Carter, C. C. (2008). Voluntary standards for peace education. *Journal of Peace Education*, 5(2), 141–155. doi:10.1080/17400200802264347

Cohen, C., Guteiérrez Varea, R., & Walker, P. O. (2011). *Acting together Vol 1: Performance and creative transformation of conflict: Performance and the creative transformation of conflict*. Oakland, CA: New Village.

Colley, B. M. (2012). Teaching social studies through the performing arts. *The Educational Forum*, 71(1), 4–12.

Dávila, A. C. (2021). Dance as a tool for the construction of peace and identity. In: T. Prentki & A. Breed (Eds.) *The Routledge companion to applied performance*. Vol. 1. London: Routledge.

Dewey, J. (1958). *Art as experience*. New York: Capricorn Books.

Duckworth, C. (2006). Teaching peace: A dialogue on the Montessori method. *Journal of Peace Education*, 3(1), 39–53, doi:10.1080/17400200500532128

Eisler, R., & Miller, R. (2004). *Educating for a culture of peace*. Portsmouth, NH: Heinemann.

Eisner, E. (1999). Getting down to basics in arts education. *The Journal of Aesthetic Education*, 33(4), 145–159.

Eisner, E. (2005). Opening a shuttered window: An introduction to a special section on the arts and the intellect. *Phi Delta Kappan*, 87(1), 8–10.

Freire, P. (1970). *Pedagogy of the oppressed*. New York: Seabury.

Galtung, J. (1996). *Peace by peaceful means: Peace and conflict, development and civilization*. London: Sage.

Greene, M. (1982). Education and disarmament. *Teachers College Record*, 84, 128–136.

Hawes, D. (2009). *Why art matters: Artists and peacebuilding*. Düsseldorf: VDM Verlag.
Hunter, M. (2005). Of peacebuilding and performance: Contact Inc's 'third space' of intercultural collaboration. *Australasian Drama Studies, 47*, 140–158.
Joshee, R., & Shirvell, S. (2021). Slow peace and citizenship: The experience of one classroom teacher in Canada. In C. C. Carter (Ed.), *Teaching and learning for comprehensive citizenship: Global perspectives on peace education* (pp. 46–57). Milton: Taylor & Francis Group. doi:10.1057/9780367548049.
Karkou, V. (2010). *Arts therapies in schools: Research and practice*. London: Jessical Kingsley.
Keskin, Y., Keskin, S. C., & Kirtel, A. (2019). Sociocultural education and empathy in early childhood: Analyzin the battle of Gallipoli. *Social Behavior and Personality, 47*(3), 7440.
Lance, K. M. (2012). Breakin' beats and building peace: Exploring the effects of music and dance in peacebuilding. Unpublished thesis American University UMI 1507128.
Malm, B., & Löfgren, H. (2007). Empowering students to handle conflict through the use of drama. *Journal of Peace Education, 4*(1), 1–20. doi:10.1080/17400200601171164
Marovah, T. (2021). Using the capability approach to assess the value of Ubuntu: Comprehensive citizenship in Zimbabwean higher education. In C. C. Carter (Ed.), *Teaching and learning for comprehensive citizenship: Global perspectives on peace education* (pp. 95–113). Milton: Taylor & Francis Group. doi:10.1057/9780367548049.
Montessori, M. (1972). *Education for peace*. (H. R. Lane, Trans.). Chicago, IL: Regnery.
Nicholson, H. (2005). *Applied drama: The gift of theatre*. New York: Palgrave Macmillan.
Noddings, N. (2012). *Peace education: How we come to love and hate war*. Cambridge, UK: Cambridge University.
Oseroff-Varnell, D. (1998). Communication and the socialization of dance students: An analysis of the hidden curriculum in a residential arts school. *Communication Education, 47*(2), 101–119.
Prentki, T. (2015). *Applied theatre: Development*. London: Bloomsbury.
Prentki, T., & Breed, A. (Eds.). (2021). *The Routledge companion to applied performance*. Vol. 2. London: Routledge.
Pruitt, L. (2011). Creating a musical dialogue for peace. *International Journal of Peace Studies, 16*(1), 81–103.
Read, H. (1943). *Education through art*. London: Faber and Faber.
Read, H. (1949). *Education for peace*. New York: C. Scribner's Sons.
Taylor, P. (2003). *Applied theatre: Creating transformative encounters in the community*. Portsmouth, NH: Heinemann.
Thompson, B. E., & Neimeyer, R. A. (Eds.). (2014). *Grief and expressive arts: Practices for creating meaning*. New York: Routledge.
Thompson, J., Hughes, J., & Balfour, M. (2008). *Performance in place of war*. London: Seagull.
Tubino, F. & Flores, A. (2020). *La interculturalidad crítica como política de reconocimiento. [Critical intervulturality as a policy of recognition]*. Lima: Pontificia Catholic University of Perú.
Yorks, L., & Kasl, E. (2006). I know more than I can say. A taxonomy for using expressive ways of knowing to foster transformative learning. *Journal of Transformative Education, 4*(1), 43–64. doi:10.1177/1541344605283151

Yüksel, S. (2006). The role of hidden curricula on the resistance behavior of undergraduate students in psychological counseling and guidance at a Turkish university. *Asia Pacific Education Review*, 7(1), 94–107. Retrieved at https://files.eric.ed.gov/fulltext/EJ752331.pdf

Židek, N. (2021). Giving voice to the voiceless: Raising awareness and spurring debate on the Homeland War (1991–1995) in Croatian theatre. In T. Prentki & A. Breed (Eds.) *The Routledge companion to applied performance*. Vol. 1. London: Routledge.

2 Culture, Performance, and Peace

How Performance Art and Intangible Cultural Heritage Help to Create Peace in Our World

Christoph Wulf

Culture of Peace as a Challenge

While performative arts and intangible cultural practices contribute to the preservation of peace, there is a need for initiatives to procure it. Extensive efforts bring about peace and people's as well as societies' capacities for developing and sustaining peace. It is only when many people in all areas of society work together that living conditions can be created in which violence between people, to oneself, and towards nature can be reduced and for achievement of more justice in society (Wulf, 2022). Hence the importance of educating people as widely as possible with the knowledge, skills, and dispositions that support peace (Carter, 2008). Peace education describes efforts in and across many contexts and disciplines where there are goals for developing the capacities of peace. It enacts the goal of cultivating a culture of peace through individual and group interactions that comprise nonformal as well as formal education.

For many years now emphasis has been placed on the need to create a culture of peace (Obrillant et al., 2017). Social structures are beginning to change, and people's actions are becoming geared towards the values of non-violence and peace, especially through peace education. In this complex process performative arts and intangible cultural practices play an important role. It is not enough to define the values and concepts of non-violence and peace. It is equally important to understand what culture means and what role performative arts and intangible cultural practices can play in this context. Culture is a general term that encompasses many heterogeneous aspects. Heritage takes expression in the intangible cultural practices such as traditions expressed in performances, communication, and crafts. A culture of peace is defined as a set of values, attitudes, modes of behavior and ways of life that reject violence and prevent conflicts by tackling their root causes to solve problems through dialogue and negotiation among individuals, groups, and nations (United Nations, 1998).

Clearly, in this broad field of culture the performative arts and intangible cultural heritage contribute to education and to the reduction of violence. This approach is not based purely on cognition and rationality; it offers sensual

DOI: 10.4324/9781003227380-2

and emotional experiences that comprise holistic learning (Kress et al. 2021; Michaels, & Wulf, 2014) through embodied participation related to the development of peace-oriented interactions (Glenberg, 2008). The arts provide aesthetic experiences and are important ways of shaping people's imaginaries (Huppauf & Wulf, 2013; Wulf, 2021). Imaging peace is a crucial foundation on which it has been built (Carter & Kumar, 2010). The arts are closely linked to questions of individual and collective identity and human rights, with the potential to provide people with insights into the identity and self-image of their own and other societies. When the encounter with them also takes place in a space free of constraints, such as political and economic agendas for expression, people have aesthetic and social experiences that are not bound to language and rationality. Being experienced by the senses, they influence and change people's emotional worlds (Michaels, & Wulf, 2012). The arts are a crucial component of holistic education. Performativity with goals of advancing cognitive, emotional, and physical development, along with propensities for building up peace, is a needed opportunity, everywhere.

Applied Theatre as Peace Education

Performativity's role on the stage of learning exists worldwide where humans are affected by performance and intangible cultural practices. Learning occurs through observation of, responses to, and experience with processes performed. The arts foster creativity that enables design of new processes borne of imagination and ingenuity. Teaching performance can involve stimulation of those capacities and demonstration of their applications. Creativity is a core strategy in development of problem solutions. The ability to think and act creatively in response to a challenge is a crucial skill in work for peace and other developments (Galtung, 2004). Consequently, cultivation of creativity is a requisite learning objective in peace education. The use of multiple senses in performativity optimizes awareness, which maximizes perceptions and comprehension. Maria Montessori, who studied human brains and then created sensorial instruction in her pedagogy, clarified (1995) how understanding and skill development advance through activation of multiple senses. She recognized learners' needs for direct experience with application of new ideas. Children need to observe, then physically and sensorially do, the skill that they see performed. Maria Montessori also recognized the need for aesthetics in human development. Theatrical instruction implements these pedagogical techniques of peace-oriented education that Montessori advocated (1949). After her experiences in a world war, she called for education that would build human connections and their capacities for problem solving. Almost a century later now, she would be pleased to see how activation of the senses and performativity in problem solving occurs through peace education in applied theatre. She would likely be intrigued by the games and theatrical techniques developed by Augusto Boal (2002), especially the direct experience with the audience through their response to and participation in the theatrical performance. Maria

Montessori's pedagogy has an offspring in applied theatre as peace education. Performance-based learning that involves support of a director and peers in the instructional process, along with self-assessment of the learning experience, characterizes both pedagogies. Additionally, several types of applied theatre share with Montessori the goal of cultivating social capacities such as intercultural understanding and cross-cultural connection. Diverse cultural expressions and collaborations in theatrical performances foster those capacities.

The arts lead to encounters with the foreign. In a dialogue between members of different cultures, characterized by respect and tolerance, in which the richness of diversity is taken as a starting point, the importance of art, literature, music, and intangible cultural practices for a non-violent intercultural understanding can hardly be overestimated (Wulf 2006a, 2016). In a non-violent dialogue people's world views are expanded and enriched by the encounter with performative arts and intangible cultural practices. Often experiences of alterity are generated, inviting a playful interaction from which there are no fixed or expected outcomes. The performing arts and the intangible cultural practices permit a ludic treatment of difference and diversity, which leads to new experiences, perceptions, and insights. Sometimes the result is fascination and rapprochement, sometimes restraint and distancing. Both practices are non-violent and the result of free decisions. In the face of difficult political and economic conditions, in particular, the great potential of the arts and intangible cultural heritage to contribute to intercultural understanding still needs further exploration (Wulf 2006a, 2013, 2016). This viewpoint is also supported by the two conventions of the United Nations Educational, Scientific, and Cultural Organization (UNESCO) on *intangible cultural heritage* (UNESCO, 2003) and on the *protection and promotion of the diversity of cultural expressions* (UNESCO, 2005).

Examples of Performative Arts and Intangible Cultural Practices

There now follow three examples from the fields of performing arts and intangible cultural practices, which show the power performing arts have in confronting violence and conflicts in a non-violent way. The first is an art performance by Marina Abramovic. The second is the performative art work of Niki de Saint Phalle. The third is a performance not of one single artist, but of thousands of Baltic people who met to sing traditional religious and folk chants to assert their cultural identity and stage the "Singing Revolution."

The Jewish Badge

Two women's hands open a pair of trousers; they expose a cisgender female belly; it belongs to the same body as the hands; a slightly arched curve. The hands take a razor blade and cut lines into the skin; blood swells, drips, and runs down the light curve of the belly. A cut makes the scene disappear again: a snapshot from a video recording of a performance by Marina Abramovic.

What is this performance about? A performance artist uses a razor blade to cut a Jewish star into the skin above her stomach. Blood gushes out. Marina Abramovic inflicted this injury on herself in front of the audience who came to this performance. It is a self-inflicted injury to the place in the female body where new life is created. The performance points to the vulnerability of the body, but above all to the vulnerability of the bodies of the Jews, who have been abused, tortured, and destroyed for centuries. The persecution of the Jews through anti-Semitism, pogroms and the Shoah becomes present. The suffering of the Jewish people is condensed in this action. Those who have seen it will not forget it. It inscribes itself into the imaginary, into memory. In a moment it brings together what the violence of anti-Semitism has created in terms of suffering and injustice. The emotional identity of this scene is created by the fact that it causes the aesthetic scene of a performance to overlap with the terrible images of suffering in the concentration camps and gas chambers. The mutual interpenetration of these images is inevitable.

Destruction and Self-destruction as an Aesthetic Challenge

In the second example too, the work of Niki de Saint Phalle, the vulnerability of the body is the central theme of the artistic performances. In her "Tir" performances in the 1960s, the artist shot at images of herself, thus addressing human violence and destructive energy, and making the female body the central theme of her work. In some of her works, the depictions of the female body are gigantic. In "Nanas" and her metamorphoses, the artist was concerned with the power of the maternal body. Female bodies with the names "brides," "births," "prostitutes," "witches," "goddesses" were created. Architectural projects followed, and variations on the female body, which was threatened by disfiguring forces against which the vitality and will to live had to assert themselves, were created again and again. The human body and its symbolizations have always been one of the central themes of the visual arts. From an anthropological perspective, the broad spectrum of figurations of the human body can be understood as an expression of human beings' continuous search for themselves and a life free of violence.

The violence to which their bodies are exposed plays a central role in the performances of the two artists. They subjugate, hurt, and overwhelm their bodies. The aesthetic experience of these performances allows the audience to witness violent actions and experiences of violence without being harmed by them. Marina Abramovic performs the act of violence and at the same time experiences the pain of its effect. The artist's body is injured but not destroyed as it was in many anti-Semitic atrocities. The emotional impact of the scene—and also of the performances by Niki de Saint Phalle—is a consequence of the contradiction inherent in it. The artists injure their bodies voluntarily in order to make us aware of the extent of involuntary violence. The pain of injury in an act of "as if" is the center of the aesthetic experience. Its contradiction cannot be resolved. It creates helplessness and makes it impossible to resist the intensity of the performance.

The Performance of Collective Singing as Political Resistance

In contrast to the two performances described above, which were staged as artistic performances and which focused on the aesthetic treatment of manifest violence, the following describes the singing demonstration of tens of thousands of people as an artistic performance whose goal is to change social conditions. They sing in order to eliminate the structural violence inherent in the political system of the Baltic countries. Over decades of involuntary membership of the Soviet Union, the singing of church and national songs in Lithuania, Latvia, and Estonia contributed to keeping alive a cultural and national sense of identity, which helped people to resist being robbed of their cultural self-image. Many singing traditions in Lithuania and Latvia were closely linked to Catholicism. But in Estonia, too, the predominantly Protestant singing traditions helped to keep cultural identity alive. The importance of singing together was articulated particularly clearly in the performative political-musical demonstrations of the "Singing Revolution," which helped the people regain political self-determination and freedom in 1990/1991. During this period, many people met regularly to sing together and thus perform and maintain their cultural identity. In these demonstrations they showed their feelings of togetherness and solidarity.

To this day, these traditions have led to more than 20,000 people in Latvia and Estonia meeting every five years to sing together and reaffirm their traditions and togetherness through singing. These singing festivals, which are attended by choirs from all parts of their countries, take place over a long weekend in summer at the Singers' Field in Tallinn or the Forest Park in Riga. There are also choirs in many smaller towns and villages, in which young and old participate. Parallel to the singers' festivals, dance festivals have also been held since Soviet times, with thousands of dancers in their regional costumes coming to the capital cities to demonstrate their local identity. These singers' festivals came into being as early as the second half of the nineteenth century, when Estonians and Latvians tried to find and express their cultural identity after the abolition of serfdom, Even under Soviet rule, their cultural traditions were considerably curtailed. Patriotic songs that had become national anthems in 1918, such as "Mu isamaa, mu önn ja rööm" (My fatherland—my happiness and joy) in Estonia and "Dievs, sveti Latviju" (God, protect Latvia!) in Latvia, were not allowed to be sung at the singing festivals. In each of these singing festivals a "collective body" was created. In this "body" the feelings "flow" and put the demonstrating singers into a state of happiness. In this harmony all feel connected, so that a social and cultural community is created. These countries have subsequently included these aesthetic practices of the fight against structural violence on the UNESCO list of representative world heritage sites, thus giving the concept of the "Singing Revolution" a place among the cultural traditions of Europe.

As previous examples have shown, the spectrum of performative arts and their handling of violence is wide. It ranges from the staging of performances by individual artists to the development of artistic practices by larger groups of people with the aim of non-violent enforcement of political goals. The performative practices of art contribute to a culture of peace, which comprises practices from a plethora of different cultures. These practices play an important role in the cultural identity of human beings. But the spectrum of violence-reducing practices extends further. It includes practices from the UNESCO Convention for the Safeguarding of the Intangible Cultural Heritage of 2003, which comprises not so much performances in which a direct confrontation with violence takes place, but rather those in which there is a development of meaningful cultural and social relations. These practices come from the following areas: (1) oral traditions and expressions, including language as a vehicle of the intangible cultural heritage; (2) performing arts; (3) social practices, rituals, and festive events; (4) knowledge and practices concerning nature and the universe; (5) traditional craftsmanship (UNESCO, 2003). All aim to reduce violence in general and to enable people to lead a fulfilled life. In some areas, this is achieved through direct confrontation with violence. In most areas, participants take part in meaningful cultural practices and thereby develop psychologically and socially, which helps them to deal constructively with violence. Participants have the opportunity to engage in cultural practices in which they find meaning and fulfilment and develop as self-determined, responsible individuals. This will increase their resistance to violence.

Performativity, Mimesis, and Aesthetics

The performative arts and the intangible cultural practices create bridges between people and initiate aesthetic and educational developments on many levels (Wulf, 2021). They promote inter-human processes of mediation and initiate educational and aesthetic developments on many levels (Wulf, 2021). To understand how these practices work and what contribution they can make to non-violent behavior, it is important to identify and analyze the following key aspects: (1) the human body as a medium, (2) performing arts as practices of communication and interaction, (3) mimetic learning and practical knowledge, (4) the performativity of cultural practices, (5) producing culture and generation order, and (6) difference and otherness.

The Human Body as a Medium

In contrast to architectural monuments, which are arguably more easily identified, it is much more difficult to identify performing arts and cultural practices for peace. While architecture produces tangible cultural objects, *the human body is the medium* of the performative arts and cultural practices which foster peace. If we wish to grasp their specific character, we need above all to reflect upon the fundamental role which the human body plays as the medium that conveys them.

This has several consequences. Bodily practices are determined by the passage of time and the temporality of the human body. They depend on the dynamics of time and space. The *mise en scène* and the performance of arts and cultural practices are not completely fixed. They are subject to processes of transformation linked to social change and exchange. Interlaced with the dynamics of life, they are characterized by the fact they are processes.

As they are staged performances of the body, they tend to have greater social weight than mere discourses. For with their bodily presence, the artists invest the community with "something extra" in addition to the spoken word. This "extra" is rooted in the materiality of the body and thus the human being's very existence, with their bodily presence and vulnerability (Wulf, 2013).

Performing Arts as Practices of Communication and Interaction

Many of the practices of performing arts like the singing festivals in the Baltic countries are performed on "stages"; this staging and performing creates non-violent forms of cohesiveness and intimacy, of communal solidarity and integration. Communities are distinguished not only by a collectively shared symbolic knowledge but also by aesthetic actions, in which they stage and perform such knowledge.

Human beings communicate and interact in cultural practices and performing arts. These practices are bodily, performative, expressive, symbolic, rule-based, non-instrumental, efficient; they are repetitive, homogenous, playful, public, and operational; in them collectively shared knowledge and collectively shared practices of action are staged and performed and our projection and interpretation of the self is reaffirmed. Performing arts and intangible cultural practices have a beginning and an end and thus a temporal structure of communication and interaction. They take place in cultural spheres which they in turn help shape in a non-violent way; they have a pronounced character, they are conspicuous and determined by their respective framing (Goffman, 1986).

We need not so much theoretical as practical knowledge if we are to succeed in our actions. Intangible cultural and aesthetic practices contribute considerably to the development of practical knowledge. Practical knowledge is what enables people to act in accordance with the respective requirements in various social spheres, institutions, and organizations. Such practical knowledge is acquired largely in mimetic processes, through which the actors integrate images, rhythms, schemes, and movements of patterns into the world of their imagination. Mimetic processes are the conduits for staging and performing the aesthetic or cultural action that new contexts require. Mimetic acquisition engenders a practical knowledge within the protagonists which can be transferred onto other situations. Consequently, the practical knowledge that has been acquired mimetically is practiced, developed, and adapted through repetition (Resina, & Wulf 2019). Practical knowledge, thus incorporated, is historical and cultural in character and as such intrinsically open to change (Wulf, 2006b, 2013).

Mimetic Learning and Practical Knowledge

As the examples of *performing* cultural and aesthetic practices in the Baltics show, they are largely appropriated in mimetic processes, in which the practical and aesthetic knowledge necessary for their staging and performance is acquired (Bell, 2009; Butler, 1997; Sahlins, 1978). These learning processes take place first and foremost when people participate in aesthetic *mises en scène* and performances, in which mimetic processes unfold as processes of creative imitation (Gebauer, & Wulf, 1995, 1998). These processes of mimetic alignment, or making oneself similar, differ from one person to the next and depend on one's way of relating to the world, to other persons and to oneself. People take an "imprint" of the aesthetic arrangement and in so doing make it a part of themselves.

The importance of mimetic processes for the transfer of non-violent knowledge can hardly be overestimated. These processes are sensual; they are tied to the human body, they relate to human behavior and seldom unfold consciously. Through mimetic processes, human beings incorporate images and patterns of performing arts and cultural practices, which subsequently become part of their inner world of images and imaginations. Thus, mimetic processes contribute to an aesthetic enrichment of this inner world and broaden it, furthering human development and education. The aesthetic knowledge necessary for the staging and performance of cultural actions is acquired. This culturally diverse knowledge develops in the context of the staging of the body and plays a special role in the creation of cultural practices in a modified form. As an aesthetic form of knowledge, it is a result of a mimetic acquisition of performative behavior, which develops out of a bodily form of know-how. Wulf, 2010, 2013 Wulf, 2004b). Gebauer & Wulf, 1998.

Aesthetic and intangible cultural practice does not produce a mere copy of previous actions. Each performance of an intangible cultural practice is based upon a new *mise en scène*, which leads to modifications of prior actions. Between the past, present, and future of intangible cultural practices a mimetic relationship exists, within which new actions are produced with reference to previous ones. In mimetic processes, a relationship to an existing cultural world is established, frequently based upon a link of likeness: a likeness of occasions, of protagonists, or of the social functions of the cultural actions. What is important, however, is not the likeness itself but producing a relationship to the other world. When an intangible cultural practice is linked to a previous one and performed in a way that is like it, a wish exists to do something like the protagonists to whom this relationship refers, to liken oneself to them. This wish is rooted in the desire to become like the others, but at the same time to differentiate oneself from them. Despite the desire to become alike, a desire for difference and autonomy persists. Many practices of intangible cultural heritage tend, simultaneously and with equal urgency, towards repetition *and* difference, thus setting free energies that drive the staging and performance of intangible cultural practices. While maintaining continuity, they offer scope for discontinuity and enable the negotiation of the relationship between continuity and discontinuity.

Cultural and aesthetic practices synthesize past and future—they embody social memories and communal projections of the future. The life of a society is structured by time patterns. They also determine the temporal sequences of cultural practices. In this way, these artistic and cultural practices encourage certain memories and make others gradually disappear. Through their repetitive structure, many practices signify durability and immutability and thus produce and control social memory. Cultural and artistic performances bring past events into the present and make them accessible to present experience. They form a connection between the present (that is in danger of being forgotten) and a past that is meaningful, as tradition and history. Cultural and aesthetic practices evolve because they can never be performed as an exact reproduction. Rather, they are always mimetic, and in these mimetic processes, their creative potential, through repetition, is an integral part (Gebauer & Wulf, 1995, 1998).

Since aesthetic knowledge, mimesis, and performativity are interlinked, for example in the cases of rituals, dances, or gestures (Wulf, & Fischer-Lichte 2010), repetition of the aesthetic practices plays an important role. Artistic competence only develops in cases in which behavior that is part of the social norm is repeated, and in being repeated, modified. Without repetition, without the mimetic rapport to something non-violent, present, or past, it is difficult for non-violent behavior to come into being (Resina & Wulf, 2019).

The Performativity of Performing Arts

First, the performativity of performing arts and cultural practices is the result of staged *bodily performance*. This involves the arrangement of scenes, in which the artists fulfil different functions. The interaction between speaking and doing produces aesthetic scenes. The works of art and literature may be construed as the outcome of cultural practices.

Second, the *performative quality of language and singing* is of crucial significance, as is clear, for example, in the Baltic singing festivals in which the words and songs during the performance contribute substantially to the creation of a new cultural reality. The same is true for artistic practices in which the relation of the sexes to one another is staged.

Third, performative arts and cultural practices also have an aesthetic dimension inherent in *the performances*. This aesthetic perspective shows that artistic and cultural performances cannot be seen purely in functional terms. They are far more than this.

We often notice important differences in the way artistic performances and cultural practices are staged. Among the reasons for this are the general historical situation, cultural, and social conditions as well as the fact that the actors are unique. The interplay of all these factors gives staged cultural performances their performative quality. At the same time, we see how unpredictable artistic practices are when we take into consideration that they are unique, one-off events and also processes. The style of the performance is important. There is a difference between what is consciously intended and the actual effect created, which can have many layers of meaning, depending on the scenic arrangement of the performing bodies. The performative quality of artistic acts invites many different interpretations and readings, which in no way make them less effective (Schechner, 1977; Tambiah, 1981; Turner, 1982). On the contrary: performances are often so effective precisely because they can be read in different ways. This is in no way detrimental to the magic of their performance.

Producing Culture and Generating Order

Aesthetic practices and intangible cultural performances help to create communities. The symbolic content of many forms of interaction and communication, and the performative processes of generating interaction and meaning, in particular, result in a feeling of coherence and stability within a community. Many performative arts and intangible cultural practices transform, by their specificity, non-determined into determined behavior. The techniques and practices associated with this transformation serve the staging of aesthetic and cultural enactments.

Communities are distinguished not only by the common sphere of a collectively shared symbolic knowledge, but also through aesthetic and artistic interaction and communication, in which and through which they stage symbolic and aesthetic knowledge. Such staging can be understood as a community's way of contributing to the integrity of the aesthetic and cultural order and the way it portrays and reproduces itself. Many performative arts and intangible cultural practices create the community on an emotional and symbolic level—they are performances and as such are stage-like, expressive actions, in which the participants, via mimetic processes, reciprocally attune the worlds of their perception and imagination to one another.

As cultural templates for action, performative arts and cultural practices develop their own rules, conventions, and correctness. It is impossible to determine which comes first—do aesthetic and cultural practices arise from the social order or is the social order actually generated by cultural and aesthetic actions? The performative arts and the cultural practices are body-based, which determines how they are experienced, perceived and remembered. For that reason, they generate a special form of reality. The fact that there is a "correct" way for a community to behave means that the actors can decode the symbolic content of a situation according to the specific rules of performative arts and cultural practices. These ensure that the community behaves in a well-defined way.

Difference and Otherness

The performing arts help people to develop a sensitivity to what is "other." If we are to avoid reducing aesthetic difference to sameness, i.e. homogenizing aesthetic diversity completely, then we need to develop a sensitivity to heterogeneity, i.e. to what is different or other. Only by fostering an understanding of otherness can we avoid standardizing aesthetic experiences. This results partly from the homogenizing processes of globalization (Bhabha, 2004; Said, 1978). Both experimental and fresh artistic performances as well as the more routine practices are of central importance for the experience of difference and otherness.

Over recent years we have come to realize that we were wrong in thinking, as was sometimes the case, that difference and otherness are bound to gradually disappear. In order for people to be aware of the importance of cultural diversity, they need new-to-them experiences, where they can perceive otherness. This encounter puts them in a position to be able to think about what is different and feels foreign to them, when they may develop an interest in things unlike themselves and their culture. Individuals are not self-contained entities; they consist of many contradictory and fragmentary elements. Rimbaud coined an expression for this experience, which remains as valid as ever: "I is someone else." Freud's observation that the ego is not the master of its own house points in the same direction. Internalizing those elements of subjective individuality that are not part of our own self-image is a precondition for us to be able to take in and respect difference perceived as otherness. Only if people are able to recognize themselves as others are they capable of perceiving the otherness of different people, and of coming to grips with it. If we succeed in perceiving what is other in our own cultures, we can begin to take an interest in the distinct aspects of other cultures, and hopefully learn to value them. To do so, we need to learn to be able to think first from the point of view of the other person and try and see ourselves through the eyes of others, i.e. learn to think heterologically.

If we are to win people over to an appreciation of cultural diversity and the importance of protecting and promoting performative arts and intangible cultural heritage, in today's world we need inter- and trans-cultural projects and perspectives more than ever before. Presently, many people belong not to just *one* culture, but are part of various cultural traditions. Intercultural or trans-cultural education as part of citizenship education is a means of supporting people in dealing with the cultural differences inherent within themselves, in their immediate surroundings and in encounters with others (Bernecker & Grätz, 2018; Carter, 2021; Cloete, Dinesh, Hazou, & Matchett, 2015). The development of social citizenship involves instruction that fosters intercultural cooperation in the educational site, its community and across nations (Carter, 2015). Since identity cannot be conceived of without otherness, intercultural education involves making relationships and connections between the disconnected parts of the self and many forms of otherness. Hybrid forms of culture are becoming increasingly important. If understanding others relates to understanding oneself and vice versa, then the process of intercultural education is also a process of self-learning, of educating oneself. It establishes that it is fundamentally impossible to understand the other without awareness and analysis of the self. Given the demystification of the world and its decrease in cultural diversity, the danger arises that all over the world people may only encounter themselves and their own products; this lack of otherness will dramatically reduce the richness of experiencing oneself and the world. Because the reduction of cultural diversity threatens the richness of human life, it is essential that education takes on the task of saving and promoting accommodation of cultural diversity (Wulf, 2016). Cultural and intercultural learning needs to involve far more than simply teaching how to work together across social, economic, regional, and political divides. Rather, education today is an intercultural task in all parts of world society and groups in one's own region in which encountering and coming to terms with different cultures, with the otherness of one's own culture, and with the other inherent in oneself are of central importance.

Literature, the arts, and performing arts are important areas where these experiences are made and peace education occurs (Carter, 2003; Carter & Pickett, 2014). This was particularly evident with Marina Abramovic and Niki de Saint Phalle, whose performances are frightening and astonishing, and which convey experiences of the foreign, of the other. These experiences call into question the strategies of egocentrism, logocentrism, and ethnocentrism by means of which Europeans have repeatedly reduced the foreign to what is familiar to them. They are closely intertwined, and as strategies of transforming the other they mutually reinforce one another. Their shared objective consists in destroying otherness and replacing it with something familiar. The obliteration of the diversity of cultures is the consequence. People have only been able to survive by accepting and taking on the culture of the victors. A tragedy lies in those cases where the annihilation of local and regional cultures ensued.

Outlook

Performative arts and intangible cultural practices are an important area of education for peace. Their spectrum ranges from a direct confrontation with violence to practices that bring meaning and joy to our lives and what we do and thus contribute to our society, world, and human development. In these processes, forces are created that enable people to master the impulse to behave violently. Because they are embodied, performing arts and intangible cultural practices affect us not only on a cognitive, but also a physical and sensual, i.e. aesthetic, level. Therefore, they educate people in a deeper psychological way and stimulate emotions. Such holistic peace education, which involves the senses and feelings, cultivates resistance towards violent attitudes evidenced in exclusion and marginalization, racism, and xenophobia. The performativity inherent in these artistic and cultural practices ensures their multimodal effects. In contrast to many other social behaviors, aesthetic performances and most intangible cultural practices can be sustainable when they have no negative impact on nature or on the development of peace. In so far as they bind human activities in a non-destructive way, they even contribute to the development of peacebuilding behaviors. Developing this dimension is an important task of the performative arts and intangible cultural practices. This is all the more important since the destructive actions of human beings, in the age termed the Anthropocene, and the attempts to reduce their destructiveness, are among the major tasks today of education for peace and environmental protection (Wulf, 2022; Wallenhorst, & Wulf, 2022).

References

Bell, C. M. (2009). *Ritual theory, ritual practice*. New York: Oxford University.
Bernecker, R, & Grätz, R. (Eds.) (2018). *Global citizenship: Perspectives of a world community*. Göttingen: Steidl.
Bhabha, H. K. (2004). *The location of culture*. London: Routledge.
Boal, A. (2002). *Jeux pour acteurs et non-acteurs*, 2nd ed. [*Games for actors and non-actors*]. London: Routledge.
Bourdieu, P. (1972) *Esquisse d'une théorie de la pratique: Précédé des trois études d'ethnologie kabyle*. [*Outline of a theory of practice: Precede by the three studies of Kabyle ethnology*]. Genève [Geneva]: Librairie Droz.
Butler, J. (1997). *Excitable speech: A politics of the performative*. New York: Routledge.
Carter, C. C. (2003). Prosocial music: Empowerment through aesthetic instruction. *Multicultural Perspectives*, 5(4), 38–40.
Carter, C. C. (2008). Voluntary standards for peace education. *Journal of Peace Education*, 5(2), 141–155.
Carter, C. C. (2015). *Social education for peace. Foundations, curriculum, and instruction for visionary learning*. New York: Palgrave Macmillan. doi: 10.1057/9781137534057
Carter, C. C. (Ed.). (2021). *Teaching and learning for comprehensive citizenship: Global perspectives on peace education* (*Routledge research in international and comparative education*). Milton: Taylor & Francis Group. doi: 10.1057/9780367548049
Carter, C. C., & Kumar, R. (Eds.). (2010). *Peace philosophy in action*. New York: Palgrave Macmillan. doi: 10.1057/9780230112995
Carter, C. C., & Pickett, L. (2014). *Youth literature for peace education*. New York: Palgrave Macmillan. doi: 10.1057/9781137359377
Cloete, N., Dinesh, N., Hazou, R. T., & Matchett, S. (2015). E(Lab)orating performance: Transnationalism and blended learning in the theatre classroom. *Research in Drama Education: The Journal of Applied Theatre and Performance*, 20(4), 470–482. doi: 10.1080/13569783.2015.1065723
Frazer, J. G. (2009). *The golden bough: A study in magic and religion (Reissued)*. Oxford: Oxford University.
Galtung, J. (2004). *Transcend and transform*. Boulder, CO: Paradigm.
Gebauer, G., & Wulf, C. (1995). *Mimesis: Culture, art, society*. Berkeley: University of California.
Gebauer, G., & Wulf, C. (1998). *Spiel, ritual, geste: Mimetisches Handeln in der sozialen Welt*. [*Game, ritual, gesture*]. Reinbek, Hamburg: Rowohlt.
Glenberg, A. M. (2008). Embodiment for education. In P. Calvo & A. Gomila (Eds.), *Handbook of cognitive science: An embodied approach* (pp. 355–372). Amsterdam: Elsevier.
Goffman, E. (1986). *Frame analysis: An essay on the organization of experience*. Boston: Northeastern University.

Huppauf, B., & Wulf, C. (2013). *Dynamics and performativity of imagination: The image between the visible and the invisible.* Milton: Taylor & Francis Group.

Kress, G., Selander, S., Saljö, R., & Wulf, C. (Eds.) (2021). *Learning as social practice: Beyond education as an individual enterprise.* London: Routledge.

Michaels, A., & Wulf, C. (Eds.) (2012). *Emotions in rituals and performances: South Asian and European perspectives on rituals and performativity.* London: Routledge.

Michaels, A., & Wulf, C. (Eds.) (2014). *Exploring the senses.* London: Routledge.

Montessori, M. (1949). *Education and peace.* (H. R. Lane, Trans.). Chicago: Henry Regerny.

Montessori, M. (1995). *The absorbent mind.* New York: Henry Holt and Company.

Obrillant, D., Wulf, C., Saint-Fleur, J. P., & Jeffrey, D. (Eds.) (2017). *Pour une éducation à la paix dans un monde violent.* [For an education towards peace in a violent world] Paris: L'Harmattan.

Resina, J. R., & Wulf, C. (Eds.). (2019). *Repetition, recurrence, returns.* Lanham: Lexington Books/Roman & Littlefield.

Sahlins, M. (1978). *Culture and practical reason.* Chicago: University of Chicago.

Said, E. (1978). *Orientalism.* New York: Pantheon.

Schechner, R. (1977). *Essays on performance theory, 1970–1976.* New York: Drama Book Specialists.

Tambiah, S. J. (1981). *A performative approach to ritual.* London: British Academy.

Turner, V. W. (1995). *The ritual process: Structure and anti-structure.* New York: Aldine de Gruyter.

United Nations. (1998). *Resolution A/RES/52/13: culture of peace.* New York: Author. Retrieved from www.un-documents.net/a52r13.htm

United Nations Educational, Scientific, and Cultural Organization. (2003). *Convention for the Safeguarding of intangible Cultural Heritage.* Paris: Author.

United Nations Educational, Scientific, and Cultural Organization. (2005). *Convention on the protection and promotion of the diversity of cultural expressions.* Paris: Author.

Wallenhorst, N., & Wulf, C. (Eds.) (2022). *Handbook of the Anthropocene.* Basingstoke: Springer Nature.

Wulf, C. (Ed.) (1974). *Handbook on peace education.* Frankfurt/M. and Oslo: International Peace Research Association.

Wulf, C. (2005). *Zur Genese des Sozialen: Mimesis, performativität, ritual.* Bielefeld: Transcript.

Wulf, C. (2006a). *Anthropologie kultureller Vielfalt.* Interkulturelle Bildung in Zeiten der Globalisierung. Bielefeld: Transcript.

Wulf, C. (2006b). Praxis. In J. Kreinath, J. Snoek, M. Stausberg, & M. Leiden (Eds.), *Theorizing rituals: Issues, topics, approaches, concepts* (pp. 395–411). Amsterdam. Brill.

Wulf, C. (2013). *Anthropology: A continental perspective.* Chicago: The University of Chicago Press.

Wulf, C. (Ed.) (2016). *Exploring alterity in a globalized world.* London. Routledge.

Wulf, C. (2021). *Human beings and their images: Mimesis, imagination, performativity.* London: Bloomsbury.

Wulf, C. (2022). *Education as human knowledge in the Anthropocene: An anthropological perspective.* Milton: Taylor & Francis Group.

3 Aesthetic Resonance as Peacebuilding in Applied Theatre with Newly Immigrated Children in Germany

Serafina Morrin

Ambivalent Living and Learning Situations of Children Newly Migrated to Germany

People flee and migrate for the most various of reasons. As is the case whenever people abandon their current living environment, fleeing is accompanied by changes and rearrangements. Leaving loved ones and familiar places behind, as indeed encountering war and devastation, can lead to traumatization, and this is not unusual in the context of fleeing. Upon arriving in a new living environment, experiences of being foreign or different, of alienness, become relevant; and that for both those who newly arrive, as well as for those who meet and encounter the new arrivals and who already seem to be familiar with the existing structures. Spaces of hopes and expectations can arise. Yet encounters with the unknown alien also contain the potential for disharmony or crises. Educational settings, in which children with the most diverse experiences come together, constitute jointly used spaces of diversity where inner images and perceptions can also become relevant, but which are not yet related to shared imaginary knowledge.

This chapter explores which roles aesthetic–theatrical education and applied theatre can play in order to negotiate realities in such glocalized spaces (Engel, Göhlich, & Möller, 2019), as well as to facilitate the enhancement of well-being and harmony, which provides the basis for peace education. Taking an example of a videographed play of a magic trick with a ritual character from the author's planned Ph.D. dissertation, the intention is to reveal which relevance the power of imagination and aesthetic experiences can have in this regard.[1] Initially, the ambivalence of the living and learning situation is examined, so as to understand the extent to which this could be relevant. Following this, there is an empirical example of the play with enchantment elements, in order to then, on the basis of this example, be able to answer the question of how belonging can arise and how to handle the ambivalent alien or further discrepancies. In relation to this example, the intention is to then rudimentarily explore to what extent imagination and aesthetic experiences as a resonance chamber can contribute to the shaping and structuring of an (alien) world. Presented next is an examination of the educational aspiration for harmony, with respect to its topicality, in order to be able to understand aesthetics and the potential promises linked to this, as well as to also open the view to irritations. The concluding part considers the significance of ambivalent interspaces, the liminal difference situations, and the negotiations of meaning with regard to the possibilities of peace education in applied theatre.[2]

In order to have a better understanding of the living and learning situations of the newly migrated children and be able to subsequently interpret the empirical example presented, it is important to clarify in advance upon which ambivalences these living and learning situations can be based.

The 'temporary living' (in refugee homes) and the 'temporary learning' (in language-learning classes) is regulated in Germany by the German Federal Asylum Law and the Education Acts in the German Federal States.[3] In fact, these forms of temporary living and learning are quite ambivalent:

For instance, Scherr (2019) ascertained that children living in refugee homes are offered little privacy and no secure or sheltered atmosphere can develop. Refugee homes are ambivalent places that do provide a protective space to sleep after an exhausting journey, but they do not represent a home as such. The bringing together of people who do not know each other and who do not have a common language, and who have differing daily rhythms and must share sanitary facilities, provides occasions and reasons for conflicts in a space threatened by uncertainty and deportation (Scherr, 2019).

Likewise, the gesture of welcome linked to the so-called welcome classes or language-learning classes is similarly ambivalent. That which is intended as a protective space can, depending on how it is effected, also become a space of exclusion that does not really satisfy the desire for social participation (for details, see Morrin, 2021). The classes can—just like the refugee homes—be understood as transitional places, as they are only intended for a limited time period. As places of transition, they may also be comprehended as heterotopic spaces in a Foucauldian sense (1992).[4]

Not only is the heterotopic space ambivalent; the encounter with alienness is too. Waldenfels (2020) has already pointed out that the alien is regarded per se as unknown and non-graspable, and thus eludes each and every conceptualization. The unknown within one's own self and world relationship cannot assume a symbolic form, and for that cannot provide any inner images. It is the present absentee (Kokemohr, 2015). As long as refugee homes and welcome classes as "a place without a place" (Foucault, 1992, p. 39) represent a heterotopic space, they also remain alien spaces as "non-spaces" (Waldenfels, 2020, p. 26). Alienness may also be understood as not belonging to an us (Waldenfels, 2020).

With this background in mind, the question arises of how a feeling of belonging and of well-being can develop in such ambivalent spaces between protection and uncertainty, between a place and a non-place. How can the ambivalent alienness and the conflicts that potentially arise be handled and peace education thus enabled?

The Play with Magic—an Empirical Example

This question is explored by taking as a basis a videographed exercise of perception that occurred in the context of an applied theatre project in a refugee reception center in Germany. The aim in this regard is not to provide formulaic knowledge. Instead, the example of a ritual play with enchantment aspects should illustrate in which way and manner aesthetic resonance spaces can arise with the help of applied theatre. Moreover, the intention is to show to what extent these resonance spaces can offer a framing for dealing practically with the ambivalences mentioned above and how realities can be reflected, evoked, or even negotiated by the participants in this regard. For the drama practitioner, this example can potentially provide inspiration for their own work.

Pedagogical settings with children newly arrived in Germany often seem to be marked by a certain unrest. What is striking about the scene selected is that a movement from great unrest to apparent concentration on a shared, common matter was possible.[56]

The videographed situation comes from a one-week applied theatre project in a refugee reception center. At the start of the learning unit, the drama practitioner and four children (Achmet, Selina, Tamara, and Hasan)[7] aged 6–11 are playing with a plastic rod containing a glittering liquid. They call it a "magic wand." After completing some exercises, the situation becomes loud and animated. The drama practitioner now holds up the plastic rod in her hand and positions herself next to five chairs forming a semi-circle. With that, the children also gather around the chairs. The practitioner quickly tips the rod on each child's shoulder, one after the other. Three of the children start sitting down on the chairs immediately. Hasan, who is initially kneeling on a chair, only sits down after being touched by the rod. The situation calms down somewhat. Speaking in a low tone, Achmet says: "A magic trick." The drama practitioner holds up the plastic rod demonstratively and announces: "Okay, when I touch you now again with the magic wand, you will close your eyes." She slowly touches Tara's shoulder a second time with the rod, at which Tara closes her eyes. And after she taps Selina on her shoulder with the rod once again, Selina closes her eyes as well. Both girls keep their eyes closed—except for short blinks—while Achmet and Hasan are also touched a second time with the plastic rod on their shoulders. Hasan emits a short whistle, and the practitioner whispers: "Quiet." Achmet and Hasan now close their eyes as well. When Selina touches her face, the practitioner says in a gentle voice: "And leave your eyes closed, Selina."

After tapping the children a second time with the glittering plastic rod, although more slowly this time, the practitioner takes a cloth out of her trousers' pocket. Hasan lets out another whistle. Tara observes the practitioner as she now begins to let the cloth glide across Tara's face. Tara smiles. Selina leans her head back and smiles as the practitioner touches her face with the cloth as well. Now Tara lets her body relax and slides down on her chair. When the drama practitioner approaches Achmet's face with the cloth, he responds with a smile: "That's not a magic trick." To which the practitioner answers: "Yes, because you're opening your eyes." Achmet reiterates his comment: "That's not a magic trick." He begins again: "That's not..." But, on being touched with the cloth, Achmet cannot stop himself giggling: "That tickles." The practitioner whispers that he should close his eyes again, and now she glides the cloth over Hasan's face. It is apparent that the situation has become calmer by now – even Hasan's whistling has stopped.

After all the children have been touched with the rod and the cloth, the drama practitioner returns the cloth to her pocket and sits down between the children. Achmet remarks: "That wasn't a magic trick." The practitioner turns to him and enquires further: "That wasn't a magic trick? Okay." She smiles, wanting to know from Achmet what it was then? Achmet retorts: "That... is a scarf." Yet again the practitioner asks whether it was not a magic trick. Shaking his head, Achmet responds: "You did that, that and that to us." Doing so, he brushes his hand across his forehead, to which the practitioner replies: "It was a pretend magic trick. But we're ready now. I've already enchanted you so we can play out our stories from yesterday one more time." The children look over to the practitioner; Hasan again emits a brief whistle. And now they all move their chairs closer to the drama practitioner. A new exercise begins. When the children are asked during the subsequent feedback session what they enjoyed most that day, Achmet answers: "The magic tricks."

Taking this exercise-of-perception example as a starting point, the focus hereunder is on how a feeling of belonging can be generated in ambivalent spaces and how any discrepancies that arise can be confronted.

Equilibration of Liminal-Difference Situations in Spaces of Aesthetic Resonance

Imagination and the aesthetic experiences they invoke can also play a role when developing meaning and experiencing discrepancies, becoming possible due to "Weltoffenheit" (Scheler, 1947, p. 37) and the eccentric positionality (Plessner, 1965), as explained hereunder.

People's lack of instincts can be seen in connection with their design of the world, for which the ability to imagine is relevant. The cosmopolitanism or "Weltoffenheit" (Scheler, 1947, p. 37) described by Scheler enables it whenever the human is lacking information to develop meaning in order to design the world with the help of imagination. For Scheler understands by Weltoffenheit that the human is—thanks to their spirit—themselves capable of generating a cultural world. According to Scheler's theory, the word spirit includes, among others, thinking in ideas or "Ideendenken" (Scheler, 1947, p. 35), as well as a specific kind of contemplation. This ability to contemplate, to have a sensory-receptive perception, which Scheler regarded as an intellectual ability, can also be grasped as an ability of imagination.

In the empirical example provided above, this sensory-based design of the world becomes clear when the participants know exactly on an explicit level that this does not concern magic, but rather their being touched by an object (a rod or a cloth). On an implicit level, this touching is filled with meaning and framed as being pleasant. For a moment, the children succumb to this magic and have their eyes closed, as the drama practitioner had "prophesized" ("Okay, when I touch you now again with the magic wand, you will close your eyes").

By means of the ability to contemplate, aesthetic experiences can be elicited. Imagination is capable of evoking aesthetic processes and enables the human to shape and design these with such cosmopolitanism. In this sense, imagination can be understood as a "conditio humana" (Wulf, 2018, p. 133).

With the example mentioned above, this means that the term "magic trick" is connected to certain perceptions that can be envisioned with their respective phantasy and imaginativeness. In this way, an initiation ritual can be associated with the touching of the shoulder by the plastic wand, potentially even the ritual act of a knighting. In this case, memories enable the association with a depicted ritual that the children may have seen in a film or already even re-enacted themselves.

The imagination that is linked to the slowness of the movement and the drama practitioner's celebratory manner also seem essential for the creation of a ritual in this performative action. Every single child is important, every single child is intended and receives dignified attention through the touching. In this way, a ritual truth is produced with the help of the imagination that is connected to the action.

With imaginative theatre play, a further anthropological aspect becomes relevant, which is based on eccentric positionality (Plessner, 1965). This, for example, permits the ability to distance from one's own physicality (ibid.) to be understood. The equilibration of the bodily expansion, "Sphäre der Ausdehnung" (ibid., p. 43), and the manner in which a body appears, "Sphäre der Innerlichkeit" (ibid.), allow the human to have experiences of the ambivalence between being and semblance (Zirfas, 2018).

In the empirical example, these two spheres then become clear when the practitioner holds the wand in such a way that it is visible for everyone and takes center stage. Because the position of the professional (*Sphäre der Ausdehnung*/bodily expansion) then recedes behind the wand, she becomes the conveyor or facilitator of the situation (*Sphäre der Innerlichkeit*/bodily appearance). The children sit down on the chair at the latest after the drama practitioner has touched them with the wand, as though it were a familiar ritual and everyone knows what is going to happen now. The being-touched with the wand leads like an invisible force to everyone becoming quiet. In the example, both spheres are present at the same time. Even if it is clear to the children that it concerns a plastic rod or a scarf, there is still a connecting level, on which the children grant the practitioner some trust for a moment and delight in succumbing to an illusion.

These experiences of ambivalences create aesthetic resonance spaces that are relevant for imaginative theatre play. Because, due to the ability to design and structure Weltoffenheit (Scheler) and the eccentric positionality (Plessner), liminal-difference situations can be evoked as an interspace experience, a "betwixt and between" (Turner, 1967, p. 93 et seq.), a social situation—in which any prior structures seem to be nullified (Morrin, in press). Imagination enables the experience of liminal difference situations to be designed. In this sense, liminal or aesthetic experiences can be characterized as situations, in which opposites are nullifiable, with the opportunity to become involved and remain distanced at the same time (Zirfas, 2018). For an aesthetic experience means being torn out of the space, the time, and the causality (Zirfas, 2004), and thus out of the "Sphäre der Ausdehnung" (Plessner, 1965, p. 43). Hence, prior symbolic figurations or inner images can be questioned with the help of Weltoffenheit and the eccentric positionality, and potential new ones arise at the same time (Morrin, in press).

In the example, this difference experienced reveals the possibility of a simultaneity of opposites in Achmet's smiling and the closing of his eyes—enjoying the situation on the one hand— and the parallel verbal negation of that which is being enacted as a magic trick on the other hand.

The dialectic of aesthetic experiences becomes clear here. They entangle the human in sensuous–emotional facts and distance themselves from them to an equal extent (Zirfas, 2018). Liminal spaces and discrepancies that are construed by imagination permit a handling of dissent, with the simultaneities of opposites possible like they can occur in ambivalent learning and living environments, as also described at the start of the paper. Applied theatre is capable of evoking aesthetic resonance spaces because aesthetic processes can be embodied in theatrical play situations and experienced in the form of practices of the imagination.

This shaping and structuring of aesthetic resonance spaces becomes relevant especially when dealing with and handling the alien. Alienness is only determinable through the manner and form of its accessibility (Kokemohr, 2015). But as the alien cannot become accessible as such, as already mentioned above, it requires an imaginary space. Mimetic processes play a role in the accessibility of (alien) worlds. In this regard, the accessible outer world is perceived and felt bodily by means of practices. And reality becomes experienceable in a creative process, in which the outer and inner interrelate with each other (for details, see Gebauer & Wulf, 1998). Mimesis offers the possibility of creatively overcoming contradictions experienced with the help of actions, through which aesthetic experiences can become possible.

For the example above, this means that the children have cultural knowledge and their own perceptions of what a magic trick means for them. They connect the touching experience by the practitioner and the significance of the plastic rod with their self and world relationship to date, with what has been experienced up to now—which can also be an associated knighting from a film they once saw. In this way, the children and the drama practitioner are attempting to connect the accessible outer world and the inner world with the help of practices. In this process, the plastic rod becomes a magic wand, and the practitioner becomes a magician. Borders become opened up and a harmless touch is linked to the transition to a different state of being. The scenery or setting becomes a magic place.

Thus, it may be summarized that ambivalences can be incorporated in liminal resonance spaces, in which opposite are dissolved and Weltoffenheit can be shaped and structured. In an aesthetic resonance space, in which the available structures are shifted or disempowered, new inner images and references can be evoked (Morrin, 2021). In this way with the help of aesthetic experiences, places of belonging arise as structured and structuring places, in which imagination and inner images that are based on experienced, desires, and fears play a role.

Aesthetic Education and Its Promises—Harmony and Resistance

But what relevance can applied theatre have in ambivalent living situations? When we focus on the enhancement of well-being and harmony and the accompanying process of (aesthetic) *Bildung*, we immediately find ourselves considering a German classic in the theory of education. For Willhelm von Humboldt (1851), the education of the human is understood to be the formation to become a harmonic whole. In this way, the inner powers of the human should not be considered singularly, with them instead jointly working together or facilitating the formation of a harmonic unit. This striving for harmony can also be found in a German contemporary of Humboldt. Friedrich Schiller (1795) understands the harmonic whole as a balance between several human driving forces. He regards the play drive as a means of reconciliation to balance out the formal drive (the rational nature of the human) and the sensuous drive (the sensory existence of the human) with each other. Thus according to Schiller, the human only become a 'whole' human through play.[8] With Schiller's Letters On the Aesthetic Education of Man (1795), aesthetics with its potential to create harmony gained a pedagogical–educational moment. Play and the aesthetic perception connected to this is regarded as the enabling of the beautiful or morally good.

In the context of the empirical example provided above, this means that all the participants know that it concerns a shared play of a magic trick. They are all aware of this as-if situation of the play. By the drama practitioner grasping the plastic rod and through the children succumbing to the suggested touching with the cloth or the rod, the aesthetics are able to develop their potency. The play can offer a balance between the various needs of the children and the practitioner, as well as with the knowledge of their reasonable action in this situation. The ever-increasing concentration on a shared matter can potentially indicate the seeking for harmony, with which Schiller also associated a moral character. It can be ascertained accordingly in the example that a common we is found in which the formal drive and sensuous drive merge, in that it becomes quieter over the course of the exercise, that the children—despite the occasional blinking—abandon themselves to it, and that the practitioner says at the end: "It was a pretend magic trick. But we're ready now." and the children move up closer to her. Finally, after the formal drive and the sensuous drive are united in harmony by the play, a new shared task can begin and the practitioner can also put the "magic materials," such as the cloth and the magic wand, back in her pants or aside.

This, however, does raise the critical question of whether play, as understandable in the sense of Schiller, can of itself be able as such—in the sense of peace education—to set aesthetic processes in motion and thus create more harmony. Does aesthetic play and applied theatre in the context of fleeing and migration have a pedagogical effect per se and thus also always create an enhancement of well-being? Because applied theatre is often associated with the promise of healing (Ehrenspeck, 1998) and the acquisition of key competencies. Especially in the context of fleeing and migration, theatrical play is accorded the possibility of confronting and analyzing that which seems alien to us. For instance, Sting (2018) points out that intercultural theatre education as a training of perception and expression of heterogeneity imparts a productive handling of diversity and difference as a social and aesthetic practice (Sting, 2018). But how should this productive handling be understood? Especially in postmodernism, aesthetics may no longer merely be comprehended as the sublime and the beauty in the sense of Kant (1790) and Schiller (1795), but rather aesthetics can in a postmodern understanding also be viewed as the ugly, or even the unknown or unfamiliar. Which in turn questions the striving for harmony. Aesthetics and aesthetic education could potentially also develop an irritating or even destructive effect or be utilized in the form of manipulation.

Regarding the example mentioned above, might the argument not also be posed that the practitioner could be pursuing a disciplining and manipulative purpose with the exercise, and she would like to subdue the children? The practitioner is the person permitted to hold the rod so that it looks like an extension of an admonishing forefinger and thus potentizes the pointing pedagogical forefinger. By the practitioner placing herself in front of the row of chairs (she is bigger than everyone else) and holding up the rod, her position of power as a rod-holder becomes visible. It can, however, also be argued contrary to this manipulative view that already at the beginning of the period, the children looked at the plastic rod with great curiosity and they announced their interest in it of their own volition. The practitioner takes up this impulse from the children later on. The looks that the children then direct to the practitioner when she holds up the rod accord her an active power to shape or create. In this way, the children are actively participating in this situation. All of the players give the drama practitioner the space, in that they sit down, lean back, and abandon themselves.

In order to not only pursue the question of striving for harmony in light of this disciplining or even manipulation background, a reference to Koller (2018) seems helpful. Koller proposes in regard to the challenges of postmodernism to reconsider the term "education." He describes it as being necessary due to the much-diagnosed plurality and heterogeneity of languages and mindsets so as to consider a theory model that is more powerfully oriented to dissent than to a harmonious addition (Koller, 2018). In this regard, Peukert (2015) also warns about having a half-education that, in the sense of classic theory of education (Humboldt, 1851), conducts artistic–aesthetic projects without overcoming situations of estrangement, divisiveness, and division (Peukert, 2015), so as to be also able to actually initiate changes to deep structures of the complete consciousness (ibid.). Accordingly, one should not solely seek the production or creation of harmonies but also keep an eye on the handling of dissent.

If we understand aesthetics to not only be the sublime, but also the unfamiliar, a view can be accorded of the resistances by the children in the empirical example. For instance, Hasan utters antithetically through his whistling that he can barely understand the German language—and is thus verbally disempowered. For him, this represents a possibility to "have his say," to articulate himself. He utilizes a means of expression that does not require verbal language. In this way through his whistling, Hasan also remains a protagonist in this situation. But because he stays seated on the chair, the whistling cannot be interpreted as an oppositional attitude, with which he is taking a direction different to the group orientation. The magic "atmosphere" is not really interrupted by his whistling.

By contrast, Achmet's skepticism is far more clearly resistant when he questions the "magic powers," and thus is capable of preventing the transition from the real to the imaginary world. His resistance indicates the ambivalent structure of this situation, which Achmet exposes and makes explicit. And which the practitioner does ultimately also actively follow up. By her asking: "Was it not a magic trick?" and "Then what was it?" she opens space for negotiations. Achmet accepts this call to respond and points to the instrument used, the "magic object," which he describes as a "scarf." Likewise, by brushing his hand across his forehead, he materially describes the physicality of how the practitioner lets the cloth glide across the children's foreheads by mimicking how she moves the cloth. In this way, he clearly separates the real and material world from the world of imagination. A resistance becomes visible here that, however, is not only articulated, but also leads to a situation where negotiating of realities is possible. The drama practitioner permits this resistance and responds to it by her admitting that the trick was just pretended, but that now everyone has already become enchanted. In this example, the resistance leads to the negotiating of a shared reality. The doubts articulated by Achmet are especially relevant because he emphasizes at the end of the applied theatre project that he liked the magic trick most of all in the whole period. In this way, the objection articulated by him indicates once more the ambivalence of this liminal difference situation.

Thus, it may be ascertained that for the enhancement of well-being and harmony in the sense of Koller (2018), not solely the seeking of harmony, but also having an orientation to the dissent and the resistances can be of importance. Hence, processes that shift borders especially for the undermining of orders as seen from a critical migration–research perspective are relevant in order to break open binary structures (Mecheril, 2012). By applying this dissent orientation to applied theatre, it can contribute to questioning and scrutinizing existing orders. Aesthetic experiences are embedded in cultural and political contexts and refer to such contexts, for which reason with their potential for irritation they are also linked to socially important themes (Mecheril, 2012), which can make them relevant for peace education.

Applied Theatre as Peace Education—Ambivalences and the Possibilities of Experiencing Change

Peace education is also always accompanied by experiences of change. Especially whenever a grasping through the role (Zirfas, 2018) occurs and aesthetic resonance spaces arise, this enables applied theatre to evoke processes of alienation through performance. As illustrated by the empirical example, the practical designing and shaping of aesthetic resonance spaces can, with the help of imagination, enable the embracing of ambivalent structures, as well as facing and thematizing them on an explicit level. This is relevant especially in view of the heterotopic living and learning worlds of the children. Newly migrated children live and learn in ambivalent and insecure structures. A high level of fluctuation prevails in the refugee homes and school classes as the pupils often do not remain there for long. The uncertain situation necessitates always "being ready to move." Aesthetic experiences, in which the perception of time permits pausing for a moment (Zirfas, 2004), are capable of embracing this unrest in the living situations and ambivalent searching movements. In this regard, the searching for a shared imagination in play, that at the same time wants to find a connection with one's own inner images and perceptions, has the aim of making the shared imaginary noticeable and visible in performative practice. In such performative processes, self-initiative is required of all the participants; applied theatre necessitates and enables such active participation. Through the search for meaning and the mimetic touching of a world influenced by one's own inner images, relevant themes can be performatively addressed for all the participants, which would not arise otherwise, and which are also not necessarily intended.

In this regard, the practice of magic seems to inherently have a universal character that is capable of also embracing potential diversities. The conjuring in this empirical example concerns the handling of ritual content that—especially when the verbal ability to communicate is limited due to differing language competencies—seems to be connectable for all those present, because this situation is framed as being exclusive by the participants. In a manner similar in religious education under the term "mystagogical learning" (Schambeck, 2000) for being mindful of divine experiences in everyday life, this provides access to an experience of unavailability and transgressing borders. Children should also perceive life within its limits and test out once what it could mean to overstep the present world and thus develop a sense of the possible and even the utopian (Schambeck, 2000). Although a deeper contextual meaning or divine experiences do not play a role in the empirical example, for that the reference to exteriority and to overstepping the existing world is a given in play. This overstepping can lead to alienation. The experiences of difference that become possible through aesthetic processes have the potential of being able to evoke a change in deep structures of the consciousness. To that extent, aesthetic experiences are of significance for peace education. They enable the performative embracing of differing perspectives—and even ambivalences. In liminal difference situations, the imaginary can be named and then also negotiated, even if it only remains imaginary. A pedagogical orientation to resistances that is able to transform the implicit into a verbal dimension not only facilitates the experiences of irritations, but also a shared reflection on this. With this orientation on difference, the formal drive and the sensuous drive in liminal situations become united in the sense of both Koller (2018) and Schiller (1795). While no true consensus is achieved in the example about what constitutes a magic trick, the idea of a shared we that is "ready" does arise. This becomes possible because contradictions are given space and thematically addressed. When the practitioner admits that it was about a "pretend magic trick," the imaginary dimension does indeed not achieve a consensus, but it does—due to the resistance to and negotiations of it—still permit something new to arise; namely the readiness for the next exercise. The imaginary idea of a shared we. The feeling of belonging to an imaginary community can arise through a desire for a collective identity (Castoriadis, 1987). But as this community only ever remains imaginary, ambivalences can also continue to exist.

As this empirical example is capable of showing, the possibility of experiencing dissent, addressing it thematically and also letting something communal arise from it can be significant. Contradictions as experienced in liminal difference situations can be embodied in practices and thus be processed performatively in an aesthetic resonance space. They also have the potential to effect a negotiation and thus to lead to conscious reflection. Liminal difference situations can—as in the case of Hasan's whistling—be interpreted as an articulation and possibility to participate, or be considered as the trigger of a negotiation, as in the case of Achmet's skepticism.

Encounters with the alien can evoke irritations or crises. In the search for harmony, these crises demand changes that can be experienced in liminal spaces of applied theatre. The processing and the negotiating of differences in aesthetic resonance spaces permits change processes to become experienceable, and thus constitute a basis for peace education and the enhancement of well-being. However, it may also be mentioned in this regard that the creation of harmony can only ever be a process that refers to a continuous searching movement.

Notes

1 For the dissertation, projects of applied theatre with children in refugee reception centers and in temporary classes for children without prior knowledge of German were videographed in order to pose the question of which social and culture orders are invoked by this and which role the imagination plays doing so. The project is being supported by the Catholic University for Applied Sciences in Berlin, Germany (duration: 2018–2023).

2 The liminality term stems from the ethnologist Victor Turner (1982) and describes the phase of a transition in the context of ritual theory.
3 In Germany, the asylum law stipulates that minor children and their parents or custodians for whom an asylum application has been submitted are obliged to live in an admission facility (Sec. 47 Para. 1 Sentence 1 German Asylum Law – AsylG) until a decision is taken on their application. The schooling and education of children who have newly migrated to Germany is treated different in the various German Federal States, but all of the Federal States have established temporary learning groups (so-called welcome classes or language-learning classes). They all have the aim of facilitating the children's transition into regular school classes (Tangermann & Hoffmeyer-Zlotnik, 2018). The pupils attend the classes for a specific time period that should, however, not last longer than one year.
4 Foucault understands a heterotopia to be places beyond all places (Foucault, 1992) that, in the form of a counter placement, represent the real places of culture. In this way, they are an actually realized utopia (Foucault, 1992). They enable the creation of an illusion space (Foucault, 1992) because they are, for instance, characterized by the idealistic perception that after attending welcome classes, children and youth will have a sufficient command and knowledge of German and are entitled to and capable of participating in the German educational system.
5 The abridged videographed scene, as well as the empirical reconstruction and the analysis, are provided in Italics to give a better overview.
6 The abridged videographed scene is from the author's planned Ph.D. dissertation project entitled "(Neu-)Ordnungen und Imagination im Spiel. Empirische Ergebnisse und erziehungswissenschaftliche Reflexionen zu theaterpädagogischen Settings mit 'neu zugewanderten Kindern.'"
7 All names pseudonymized.
8 "Denn, um es endlich auf einmal herauszusagen, der Mensch spielt nur, wo er in voller Bedeutung des Worts Mensch ist, und er ist nur da ganz Mensch, wo er spielt." (Schiller, 1795, p. 88)
"For, to say it once and for all, Man plays only where he is in the full sense of the word a Man, and he is only wholly Man when he plays."

References

Castoriadis, C. (1987). *The imaginary institution of society*. Cambridge: MIT Press.
Ehrenspeck, Y. (1998) *Versprechungen des Ästhetischen: Die Entstehung eines modernen Bildungsprojektes [Promises of the aesthetic: The emergence of a modern education project]*. Opladen: Leske + Budrich.
Engel, J., Göhlich, M., & Möller, E. (2019). Interaction, subalternity, and marginalisation: An empirical study on glocalised realities in the classroom. *Journal Disaspora, Indigenous, and Minority Education 13/10*, pp. 40–53.
Foucault, M. (1992). Andere Räume [Of other spaces]. In K. Barck, P. Gente, & H. Paris (Eds.), *Aisthesis: Wahrnehmung heute oder Perspektiven einer anderen Ästhetik* (pp. 34–46). Leipzig: Reclam.
Gebauer, G., & Wulf, C. (1998). *Spiel, Ritual, Geste: Mimetisches Handeln in der sozialen Welt. [Play, ritual, gestures: mimetic acts in a social world.]* Reinbek: Rowohlt.
Humboldt, W. (1851). *Ideen zu einem Versuch, die Gränzen der Wirksamkeit des Staats zu bestimmen [The limits of state action]*. Breslau: Trewendt. Retrieved from: www.deutschestextarchiv.de/book/show/humboldt_grenzen_1851
Kant, I. (1790). *Critik der Urtheilskraft [Critique of judgment]*. Berlin: Lagarde und Friedrich. Retrieved from www.deutschestextarchiv.de/book/show/kant_urtheilskraft_1790

Kokemohr, R. (2015). Bildung als Welt- und Selbstentwurf im Anspruch des Fremden: Eine theoretisch-empirische Annäherung an eine Bildungsprozesstheorie. [Education as a design of the world and the self within the claims of the alien]. In W. Marotzki, O. Sanders, & H.-C. Koller (Eds.), *Bildungsprozesse und Fremdheitserfahrung* Vol. 7 (pp. 13–68). Bielefeld: Transcript.

Koller, H.-C. (2018). *Bildung anders denken: Einführung in die Theorie transformatorischer Bildungsprozesse* (2nd ed.) *[Thinking education differently: Introduction to the theory of transformative educational processes.]* Stuttgart: Kohlhammer.

Mecheril, P. (2012). Ästhetische Bildung: Migrationspädagogische Anmerkungen [Migration-Pedagogical Comments on Aesthetic Education]. In ifa (Institut für Auslandsbeziehungen) (Ed.). *Kunstvermittlung in der Migrationsgesellschaft/Reflexion einer Arbeitsgagung-2011* (pp. 26–35). Berlin/Stuttgart: German Institute for Foreign Relations.

Morrin, S. (2021). Die Paradoxien der Sprachlernklassen [Paradoxes of separated language-learning classes]. In U. Binder, & F.-K. Krönig (Eds.), *Paradoxien (in) der Pädagogik*. Weinheim: Beltz Juventa.

Morrin, S. (in press). Play practices of the imagination – reconstruction of a magic trick. In M. Martens, B. Asbrand, T. Buchborn, & J. Menthe (Eds.), *Dokumentarische Unterrichtsforschung in den Fachdidaktiken*. Wiesbaden: Springer.

Peukert, H. (2015). Über die Zukunft von Bildung [On the future of education]. In O. John, & N. Mette (Eds.), *Bildung in gesellschaftlicher transformation* (pp. 319–334). Paderborn: Schöningh.

Plessner, H. (1965). *Die Stufen des Organischen und der Mensch* (2nd ext. ed.) *[Levels of organic life and the human]*. Berlin: de Gruyter.

Schambeck, M. (2000). Mystagogisches Lernen: Aufmerksam werden für Gotteserfahrungen [Mystagogical learning: Becoming mindful to the experience of god]. In Ludwig-Maximilian-University Munich (Ed.), *Münchener Theologische Zeitschrift*, 51/3, (pp. 221–230).

Scheler, M. (1947). *Die Stellung des Menschen im Kosmos [The human place in the cosmos]*. Munich: Nymphenburger Verlagshandlung.

Scherr, A. (2019). Flüchtlingsheim [Refugee home]. In J. Hasse, & V. Schreiber (Eds.), *Räume der Kindheit: Ein Glossar* (pp. 58–63). Bielefeld: Transcript.

Schiller, F. (1795). Über die ästhetische Erziehung des Menschen. [2. Teil; 10. bis 16. Brief.] [Letters on the Aesthetic Education of Man]. In F. Schiller (Ed.). *Die Horen* (pp. 51–94). Volume 1, 2nd part. Tübingen. Retrieved from www.deutschestextarchiv.de/book/show/schiller_erziehung02_1795

Sting, W. (2018) Theater [Theatre]. In I. Gogolin, V. Georgi, M. Krüger-Potratz, D. Lengyel, & U. Sandfuchs (Eds.) *Handbuch interkulturelle pädagogik* (pp. 417–420). Bad Heilbrunn: Klinkhardt.

Tangermann, J., & Hoffmeyer-Zlotnik, P. (2018). *Unbegleitete Minderjährige in Deutschland. Herausforderungen und Maßnahmen nach der Klärung des aufenthaltsrechtlichen Status: Fokusstudie der deutschen nationalen Kontaktstelle für das Europäische Migrationsnetzwerk (EMN) [Unaccompanied Minors in Germany. Challenges and measures after clarification of residential status]*. Nürnberg: German Federal Agency of Migration and Refugees.

Turner, V. (1967). *The forest of symbols: Aspects of ndembu ritual*. Ithaca: Cornell University.

Turner, V. (1982). *From ritual to theatre: The human seriousness of play*. New York: PAJ Publications.

Waldenfels, B. (2020). *Topographie des Fremden: Studien zur Phänomenologie des Fremden I* (8th ed.) [*A topography of the other: Studies on the phenomenology of the other*]. Frankfurt a. M.: Suhrkamp.

Wulf, C. (2018). Bildung durch ästhetische Figurationen in Literatur und Fremdsprache: Imagination, Mimesis, Imaginäres [Education through aesthetic figurations in literature and foreign language: Imagination, mimesis, the imaginary]. In R. Mattig, M. Mathias, & K. Zehbe (Eds.), *Bildung in fremden Sprachen? Pädagogische Perspektiven auf globalisierte Mehrsprachigkeit* (pp. 125–137). Bielefeld: Transcript.

Zirfas, J. (2004). Kontemplation—Spiel—Phantasie: Ästhetische Erfahrungen in bildungstheoretischer Perspektive [Contemplation—play—imagination: aesthetic experiences within the perspectives of educational theory]. In G. Mattenklott, & Rora, C. (Eds.), *Ästhetische Erfahrung in der Kindheit: Theoretische Grundlagen und Empirische Forschung* (pp. 77–97). Weinheim/Munich: Beltz.

Zirfas, J. (2018). Ästhetische Erfahrung [*Aesthetic experiences*]. In G. Gödde, & J. Zirfas (Eds.), *Kritische lebenskunst: Analysen—orientierungen—strategien* (pp. 134–142). Stuttgart: Metzler.

4 Bridging the Classroom Divide in the US

Dialogical Pedagogy and the Healing Arts

James Alan Astman

Introduction

A much-beloved performing arts teacher, and an avowed pacifist, once described the theatre in which she taught: "a bare, ugly, empty space."[1] Created from a converted meeting hall that once belonged to the Veterans of Foreign Wars, the walls were painted flat black, a light bar was strapped across a large wood support beam, and plastic folding chairs provided uncomfortable seating for the parents, teachers, and peers of the student performers.

Notwithstanding the makeshift nature of the theatre, student actors and audience members alike considered the room magical. For the teacher, it was a sacred space.

> This space—which once stood for war and now stands for peace—is the most wonderful thing in the world to me. It is my home, my reason for being. This space—with its three black walls, splintered floor, cluttered ceiling.

That the theatre stood for peace was not a sentimental observation; it was an apt description of her work with young people. She invited her students as working collaborators; pushed them to find their unique voices; challenged their understanding of the characters they played; called them to rise above themselves—to cultivate greater empathy, to combat self-absorption; and engaged them intensely and continuously in dialogue. Not surprisingly, she, herself, drew inspiration from Augusto Boal's "Theater of the Oppressed": in effect, she sought to disturb the peace in order to seek it.

To be sure, *all* good teaching requires disturbing the peace: introducing uncertainty and, at times, discomfort, for the sake of growth and critical awareness—akin to what Piaget called *equilibration* and Freire called *conscientization*. The purpose of "unsettling" students is not to undermine but to *strengthen* their confidence, and to cultivate positive change. "It is vital," writes Rachel Rhoades, "for applied theater practitioners and educators to nurture critical hope…" (2021).

DOI: 10.4324/9781003227380-4

The teacher who revered her makeshift theatre nurtured hope concretely by devoting herself to the young people who filled it. Little wonder that multiple generations of students carry the memory of her intensely attentive and receptive presence, her contagious theatrical imagination, and her moral clarity. Reciprocally, the teacher carried the memory of her students' lives in that transformative space:

> Often I come all alone to sit and look at my space, and if I squint my eyes and stare very hard I can see Anne and Peter chasing each other across the attic [*The Diary of Anne Frank*]. I see poor... Charlie hopelessly trying to beat his friend Algernon, the mouse [*Flowers for Algernon*]. My Antrobus rushes in, exalted because he has just discovered the wheel [*The Skin of Our Teeth*]. Tevye with his strong walk comes on and sings and dances "To Life" with a breathless abandon [*Fiddler on the Roof*]. I squint my eyes a little harder; and Pantalone and Isabella romp in old Commedia del'Arte clothes, and I hear roars of laughter greeting them. Juror #8 states his case for justice [*Twelve Angry Jurors*]. Cothurnus again calls for Edna St. Vincent Millay's words to "play the play," and Aria da Capo begins its tragic game. This space is more mine than anything else I have ever owned. I think this is true because year after year I give part of it away to those who come to play the play in it, for those who watch through that invisible fourth wall.

By the time each of these productions was mounted, the teacher made certain that the student actors appreciated the often-challenging contexts that endowed the plays with purpose. For instance, preparatory to *The Diary of Anne Frank*, she enlisted the social studies department to introduce students to the German occupation of the Netherlands during WWII and arranged for a survivor of the Bergen-Belsen concentration camp (where Anne ultimately died from typhus) to meet with the cast. Before rehearsals began for *Flowers for Algernon*, she brought a psychologist in to talk about the ethics of measuring intelligence; subsequently, a person with a cognitive impairment spoke about feeling judged and misunderstood.

Dignity, integrity, human rights, the resolution of conflict, and the pursuit of peace were explicit or implicit themes of virtually every production, whether tragic or comedic or both. They also informed the teacher's pedagogy, which proceeded from a keen sensitivity to the young people she taught.

> For teenagers, who have many doubts about their physical being, acting offers the opportunity to be freed from any hang-ups they have about their own looks. In other words, in the creation of a character, they become someone else, so their looks belong to the character. They grow from seeing parts of themselves develop into whole characters; it pushes their limits as a person.

Those teenagers, now adults, bear witness to her continuing impact. An alumnus who graduated over 30 years ago still chokes up as he describes his theatre teacher's impact on him. His role as Charlie in *Flowers for Algernon* came at a pivotal moment, as he wrestled with his own sense of adequacy and aloneness. He told me tearfully: "I learned that I was special because of her. She gave me a place in the world."

An alumna still carries the vivifying memory of her opening performance in Lanford Wilson's *The Hot L Baltimore*. Many years after the play, she wrote the teacher in gratitude:

> That night for the first time I experienced what it was truly like to be an actor. You gave me more than you'll ever know. I felt that magic you always talked about. I created something. Thank you for letting me into your space. Only a very special person could ever have a place like that. And only a very special friend could be so willing to share it.

Although she was an extraordinarily gifted performing arts teacher, my intent is not to lionize her. Instead, I mean to introduce, through her particular example, the work of theatre educators in promoting healing, growth, friendship, citizenship, and peace. The teacher's curriculum decisions deepened students' exposure to great works of literature and engaged them in serious conversations about moral conflicts, about human rights, about our higher and lower angels. Her pedagogy, which was inseparable from her curricular choices, invited her students into a genuine dialogue. Like Augusto Boal, she understood that "when dialogue becomes monologue, oppression ensues. Theater then becomes an extraordinary tool for transforming monologue into dialogue" (Paterson, 1995[2]).

Applied Theatre as Peace Education

In her zeal to transcend the traditional barriers of educational theatre, she also sought to promote peace. Like many of her colleagues in the performing arts, she embraced the role that Boal once termed *dificultator*: "undermining easy judgments, reinforcing our grasp of the complexity of a situation, not letting that complexity get in the way of action" (Jackson, 1994, pp. xix).

In fact, when young people are exposed to past and persisting inequities, their experience is, to borrow Freire's powerful notion, *problematized* (1985, pp. 52, 86). They can no longer understand or experience the world as they once did—unaware of, and without outrage toward, conditions that dehumanize others and/or themselves.[3] In essence, this is the work of applied theatre, as well as the goal of all peace education: to reveal the wounds carried unknowingly in the body, or the body politic, is to multiply the possibilities for healing and hope.

> [T]here is no genuine hope in those who intend to make the future repeat their present, or in those who see the future as something predetermined. Both have a domesticated notion of history: the former because they want to stop time, the latter because they are certain about a future they already "know." Utopian hope, on the contrary, is engagement full of risk.
>
> (Freire, 1985, p. 58)

Like peace education, applied theatre is utopian in its quest to confront injustice, promote dialogue, and resolve conflict nonviolently. Notwithstanding its sweeping range of practice, *all* applied theatre aims to cultivate agency and champion social change. By fostering empathy, it also bridges the divide between self and others.

Applied theatre practices—here, again, like peace education practices—vary greatly depending on the circumstances they serve. Gavriel Salomon wrote extensively about the significant differences between peace education efforts in relatively tranquil settings and those in areas of intractable conflict or intense inter-ethnic tensions (Salomon, 2006, 2021). Similarly, applied theatre practices are frequently used by those who work with impoverished and victimized populations. However, as the curricular and pedagogical examples in this chapter attest, applied theatre principles are powerfully pertinent for *all* students, regardless of background or circumstance. "Through applied theater, anyone can participate in envisioning, modelling, rehearsing, and demanding a more just world" (Rhoades, 2021, p. 339).

"Anyone" includes students at an elementary school where the performing arts are integrated with social studies curricula oriented around peace and human rights challenges. Later in this chapter, I will describe two values-driven programs—one in the fourth grade, one in the sixth—that promote understanding of historical injustices and the pursuit of peace and well-being. These achievements become possible because their teachers—very much like the gifted theatre educator I described in the introduction—employ a pedagogy that is inseparable from their curricular choices and which invites their students into dialogue. The *features* of pedagogical dialogue are important to understand, not simply as a prelude to the students' dramatic presentations of social justice challenges, but also as a means of bridging the classroom divide between students and teachers.

Positive Peace and Dialogue

If applied theatre relies on a "dialogue of equals" (Kotin et al., 2013), so does "positive peace"—Johan Galtung's term for a generative and just peace. Galtung's well-known distinction between positive peace and negative peace provides a unique means of understanding dialogical pedagogy and, therefore, the impact of the performing arts on students and the life of a school.

Negative peace is the absence of overt conflict; it can provide the means for groups in heightened tension to live in peace. But such a peace is an inherently uneasy one, since it does not address or resolve structural violence, which endemic poverty, injustice, and racism constitute. No society, and certainly no school, can thrive in conditions of negative peace, which requires force, coercion, and/or vigilant monitoring to maintain. Negative peace neither invites nor is hospitable to the interpersonal mutuality at the heart of dialogical pedagogy and inherent in the teaching of performing arts.

Positive peace does. Positive peace is the ongoing co-creation of a society characterized by justice, equity, and trust (Galtung, 1985). By confronting and seeking to repair the inequities of privilege and power that arise in daily life, and by empowering voices otherwise silenced, positive peace promotes healing. For Betty Reardon, positive peace—Reardon preferred to say "authentic peace"—gives rise to "a transformational peace education… that is life-affirming, oriented toward the fulfillment of human potential, and directed to the achievement of maturation" (Snauwaert, 2012, p. 49). Positive peace enables human beings to flourish: to know as we are known, to care and be cared for, to grow and to cause to grow (Palmer, 1993, Noddings, 1984). These are prerequisites of well-being. They enable young people to prosper in schools that are equitable and just, and in teaching-learning relationships that are nurturing and trusting.

Yet in the expansive body of literature on peace education, relatively little has been written about the human interactions at the heart of teaching. This deficit is not surprising given our culture's epistemological "bias toward an 'isolated brain' and a 'one-person psychology'"(Schore, 2003, p. 212). That is to say, like therapeutic progress, growth and development are commonly viewed as *individual* achievements. Educational parlance reflects a similar view—hence "teacher-centered" or "child-centered"—where the focus is on the individual person who steers the learning process.

Although child-centered approaches are generally favored by peace educators, since they emphasize active, self-directed learning, the experience of young people does not always correspond to the progressive pedagogical language used in many educational settings. John Dewey, himself, pointed this out in 1938: "It is not too much to say that an educational philosophy which professes to be based on the idea of freedom may become as dogmatic as ever was the traditional education which it reacted against" (1973, p. 22).

Teacher-centered approaches, reinforced by inflexible curricula as well as culturally entrenched habit patterns, require the adult to direct the learning process. Whether done with warmth and pleasure, or with authoritarian rigidity, this form of "education is suffering from narration sickness," Paulo Freire noted, where the teacher's "task is to 'fill' the students with the content of his narration" (1974, p. 57).

If monologue is at the root of "narration sickness," pedagogical dialogue is its antidote. Dialogue, which can only emerge *in relationship*, is the cornerstone of positive peace. It takes place in "dyadic synchrony" (Schore, 1994; Siegel, 1999). The act of teaching young people is a mutual one, a two-way exchange among learners—students *and* teachers—that depends on risk-taking and trust building, and that promotes joy and well-being.

Pedagogy is the determinant of human relationships in the educational process. It is itself the medium of communication between teacher and learner, and that aspect... which most affects what learners receive from their teachers.

(Reardon, 1993, p. 102)

For teachers of the performing arts, Reardon's words are resonant, although incomplete: reciprocal relationships mean that pedagogy affects what learners and teachers receive *from each other*. Disciplines like drama, music, and dance, engage students' whole being, inviting them to be partners in the learning process and co-creators of performance art. In other words, performing arts education relies on a dialogical pedagogy.

Dialogical Pedagogy and the Performing Arts

Three interrelated features of dialogical pedagogy highlight the seminal role of the performing arts in cultivating young artists *and* in fostering the moral agency on which positive peace depends. These features—the unmediated nature of human presence in dialogue; the engagement of the whole person, including the body; and the work of repair and change at the core of teaching—underscore the capacity for the performing arts to serve as *healing* arts.

The relational core of teaching and learning does not obviate the need for strong curricular content. To the contrary, dialogical pedagogy enables such content to be brought to life, as the elementary school projects described in this chapter will exemplify. "Teaching," Maria Harris writes, "is the incarnation of subject matter" (1991, p. 41). Students experience curriculum and pedagogy as inseparable.

The work of dialogical pedagogy is as daunting as it is rewarding: to sensitize young people to the experience and circumstances of others and, in the process, to foster a moral seriousness of purpose. We teach them dignity by treating them with dignity. We elicit wholeheartedness with wholeheartedness.

Human Presence

In many ways, teaching mirrors parenting. Notwithstanding differences in power and maturity, engaged teachers and students, like loving parents and children, learn from one another, are vulnerable to one another, and have the capacity to change one another. Nothing in these interactions is passive; in fact, teachers and students—again, like parents and children—are frequently adjusting to each other's cadences, temperaments, and needs (Stern, 2004). The living features of the relationship consist precisely in those moments when two human beings (parent–child, teacher–student) are *present* to one other.

Human presence, according to Martin Buber, is manifest in the immediacy of an "I–Thou" relationship, which embraces and transcends differences

(1970). Two human beings *meet*, not as a subject and an object, but as *two subjects*. Buber called this "genuine dialogue"

> —no matter whether spoken or silent—where each of the participants really has in mind the other or others in their present and particular being and turns to them with the intention of establishing a living mutual relation between himself and them.
>
> (1965, p. 19)

Buber recognized that I–Thou moments are impermanent, and that our predominant mode of relating to the objective (natural and human) world is what he termed "I–It." For instance, the fact that I can experience being fully present with a fellow human being does not preclude my thinking objectively of that very person as "my student" or "my teacher." "I–It" does not have the same character of immediacy or authenticity as "I–Thou," but it is a necessary aspect of relating to others. Buber described, largely without judgment, humans' dependence on this objective ("I–It") mode in their quotidian lives. He was considerably less dispassionate about what Freire called "narration sickness," which Buber considered to be:

> monologue disguised as dialogue, in which two or more men, meeting in space, speak each with himself in strangely tortuous and circuitous ways and yet imagine they have escaped the torment of being thrown back on their own resources.
>
> (1965, p. 19)

Describing the relevance of Buber's "classroom," Kenneth Kramer writes that "[o]ne becomes fully human only in I–Thou relationships; only these types of relationships bring about a person's unique wholeness" (2013, p. 5). Kramer's observation has an important corollary: wholeness is *not* an individual achievement. Rather, we locate ourselves and others in dialogue. "All real living is meeting," Buber famously wrote. ("Teaching," Parker Palmer quips, "is endless meeting" [1998, p. 16].) Thus the ecology of well-being is relational and its challenge is moral: *to be fully present.*

In the Genesis story, Adam hides from the first invitation to dialogue. In response to God's question—*Where are you?*—Adam confesses, "I was afraid because I was naked." Hiding, the story tells us, is safer than being seen. Thomas Mann once wryly observed that the Genesis myth is "a story about the way things never were, but always are" (as cited in Jech, 2013, p. 18). It is a human propensity to hide from being present, from meeting in dialogue.

In schools, "hiding" enables us to avoid conflict, to sidestep naming an uncomfortable truth, or to spare ourselves emotional fatigue. Presence in teaching requires courage (Palmer, 1998): to be fully attentive and receptive; to trust another person's capacity to grow in the face of difficult or challenging truths; to be caringly truthful and, at times, vulnerable to another person's truth.

The *experience* of presence cannot be defined adequately because it is, to use Daniel Stern's phrase, "a *lived story*" (2004, p. 55). When one is fully present one has no sense of time's passage: the intersubjective dialogue is, by its nature, *in the moment*. Hence for students who are not engaged, the clock moves with glacial speed. For engaged students, an hour seems but a minute.

To be clear: pedagogical dialogue *is not the goal of teaching performing arts*. Rather, it is the precondition. In being present to a student, the teacher must keep what John Dewey called "the end in view" (1966, p. 105). Learning outcomes for the performing arts—the knowledge students gain, the skills they develop, the work product they perform, the sense of self they acquire—are uniquely "open-ended outcomes." They help "to establish a relationship of trust and mutual exploration" between the teacher and the taught (Atkinson, D. in Kotkin, A. et al., 2013, p. 197).

The psychiatrist Robert Coles helps illuminate the nature of trust in relationship. Coles distinguishes between the role of theory and the role of story (1989). Using theory, he could organize his observations of his patients into tidy diagnostic categories. But even skillful theorizing did not help him help his patients. Only by listening to his patients' stories could Coles come to *know* them and thereby *help* them. Their stories "penetrated" him and created a human connection between doctor and patient that constituted the only reliable path to healing.

A similar truth obtains in teaching. The performing arts teacher may know in great detail *about* a student—their level of artistic skill and accomplishment, for example, or their recent educational history or even their psychological profile—without genuinely *knowing* the student. Surely all of us have felt convinced that we knew someone *very* well only to be surprised and humbled by a dimension of the person we had not previously even imagined. We reach the students we teach when, to use Buber's language, an "It" becomes a "Thou."

But with an important caveat. Teaching, Buber stressed, necessitates "a one-sided experience of inclusion" (1965, p. 99). To meaningfully teach a student, the teacher must, to the extent possible, become aware of—*be present to*—the *student's* experience. Nel Noddings describes this vital "leap" in perspective[4]:

> In "inclusion," the teacher receives the student and becomes in effect a duality. This sounds mystical, but it is not. The teacher receives and accepts the student's feeling toward the subject matter; she looks at it and listens to it through his eyes and ears. How else can she interpret the subject matter for him? As she exercises this inclusion, she accepts his motives, reaches toward what he intends, so long as these motives and intentions do not force abandonment of her own ethic. Inclusion as practiced by the teacher is a vital gift.
>
> (1984, p. 177)

Embodied Learning

Throughout these long pandemic months, grief has been an all-too familiar visitor. Many school communities lost members to COVID but were unable to offer the solace of human contact. Those who longed to offer consolation had to do so from afar. Even in families where everyone was healthy, children frequently wrestled with feelings of grief because they, themselves, lost the things they depend on: in-person friendships, relationships with teachers, the rhythm of a normal school year.

Grief, loss, missing: we experience these profound feelings in our bodies as much as in our thoughts. As feminist writers have long observed, and as performing arts teachers intimately know, our bodies are the ground of our deepest experiences (Ruddick, 1995; Harris, 1991; Grumet, 1988). When we say "she gave a touching performance" or "I was moved by the music" or "I was laughing so hard it hurt," we underscore the participation of our bodies in our responses to the arts.

In his essay, "The Thinking of the Body," William Butler Yeats wrote:

> Art bids us touch and taste and hear and see the world, and shrinks from what Blake calls the mathematic form, from every abstract thing, from all that is of the brain only, from all that is not a fountain jetting from the entire hopes, memories, and sensations of the body.
>
> (Yeats, 1952, pp. 106–107)

Our epistemological heritage, "from Plato onward, has effectively separated mind from body, privileging the former over the latter" (Gallagher, et al., 2017). Not surprisingly, then, schools focus on cognitive achievement and prize "objectivity," devaluing the profound experiences of the body—including not only what we feel but how we *know*. As a result, art courses are viewed as counting less, and are often consigned to extracurricular offerings or sacrificed altogether when budgets are cut (Nathan, 2020).

Yet there is a still more significant cost: we cannot teach the whole human being without taking the body into educational account. "It is not that we have a body," Ashbrook observes, "but that we *are* a body" (1971, p. 58). This ineluctable truth has increasingly drawn the attention of applied theatre scholars, who recognize the extent to which "[t]he body is implicated in… pedagogical practices that [not only] shape personal and educational experience, but also… cultural, social, and political change" (Gallagher et al., 2017). Pedagogy, writes dancer and peace educator Sherry Shapiro, must:

> begin with the body—the body understood as at once the most public and the most intimate material inscribed by cultural values and experiences, and the vehicle for transcending our limited social identities to a wider shared experience.
>
> (2002, p.149)

The absence of the body in education is a moral problem for several reasons. First, it constitutes a form of implicit violence. Eliminating the arts or play (including playground) time or the opportunity in school simply to rest—such acts constitute an assault on the fundamental rights of children as recognized in the Convention on the Rights of the Child (Article 31). They also compromise human dignity. Engaging and respecting the whole child through dialogical pedagogy means recognizing the embodied nature of learning.

Second, the body constitutes the changing ground of children's experience in the world and a determining factor in their self-image and social relations. Body size and shape are charged with cultural meaning. The erotic and destructive impulses that change with growth can and must be enlisted, especially through the arts, to serve positive and creative ends. After all, as Picasso remarked, "Every act of creation is first of all an act of destruction" (as cited in May, 1976, p. 60).

Third, the exuberance that attends impassioned interest, discovery, humor, meaningful and energetic activity, and competence, itself, is an expression of full and joyful bodily engagement. "Exuberance is a bounding, ebullient, effervescent emotion" (Jamison, 2004, p. 4). It is palpably evident in all young people, and a seminal feature of play and creativity, whether in the schoolyard or the classroom. In the absence of exuberance, young people's education cannot be fully human.

Fourth, the capacity for intuition, trust, and knowledge, itself, grows out of the body: we feel certain or uneasy or encouraged *in our bodies*. Teachers of the performing arts will recognize this capacity, since they know what it means to be attuned, as well as *misattuned*, with their students, to carry a moment-to-moment awareness of the dynamics of the classroom, and to recognize rising tension in their own bodies. The feeling tone of a classroom is therefore a crucial dimension of dialogical pedagogy.

Fifth, the performing arts require fully engaging the senses and heightening receptivity to one's inner and outer worlds. As individual students experience themselves as part of a *community* of learners, they come to appreciate the impact of their own and others' contributions, and to discover the contours of their own identities. Through the lens of applied theatre, these achievements can be viewed as "experience[s] through which students may come to understand human interactions, empathize with other people, and internalize others' points of view" (Wagner, B. J. as cited in Garcia-Mateus, 2021, p. 110). As the performing arts uniquely demonstrate, true self-awareness does not spring full blown by itself; it emerges inseparably from young people's empathic awareness of others. We do not simply find ourselves; we are also *shown* ourselves.

Unfortunately, education remains inhospitable to the full-bodied presence of young people. If the absence of the body constitutes a moral problem, then performing arts education, which honors and engages the whole embodied person, is a moral response. "It is crucial," bell hooks reminds us, "that we learn to enter the classroom 'whole' and not as a 'disembodied spirit'" (1994,

p. 193). Through a dialogical pedagogy, teachers bring young artists into wholehearted, embodied presence.

> Peace education must seek to remind individuals of what we as humans share in common—nothing can bring us closer to this than our recognition of the body as the frail, vulnerable, but irreplaceable vessel for that mysterious presence we call life.
>
> (Shapiro, 2002, p. 154)

Repair and Change

A much-beloved graduate school professor once told me about his experience in a seminar Martin Buber gave in the mid-1950s in Chicago.[5] At one point, Buber asked participants to turn to the person sitting next to them and shake hands. "What did you feel," he asked, emphasizing that he wanted them to be as specific as possible. Without exception, people responded with exacting descriptions: "The person's hand was warm." "I felt pressure." "I felt a bit awkward." "It was nice to greet my colleague." After hearing several such descriptions, Buber asked: "Why do you imagine that no one in the room has described what everyone felt?" His question was met by looks of puzzlement, until he explained: *"You felt your own hand."*

A stunned silence overcame the participants, whose focus had been on everything *but* the intersubjective truth of their handshake. Buber's demonstration underscores the challenge of teaching for peace: *we are often spectators of our experience rather than actors in it*. How we develop moral agency in young people, without which peace-building is impossible, is therefore a critical question. Agency cannot be the outcome of understanding alone, even when curriculum is oriented around social justice and peace. It requires that schools make students active partners in their education. This is the role of dialogical pedagogy.

However, as Buber recognized, our natural orientation to the world is "I–It," not "I–Thou." The human moments of "meeting" come by grace and not by dictate. Dialogical pedagogy is therefore a teaching *practice*, not a guarantee of presence. It is above all a trust-building endeavor, which depends on integrity, reciprocity, and a willingness to be vulnerable for the sake of growth.

I recognize that the very idea of vulnerability can be antithetical to peace and therefore to peace education, especially to the extent that the word refers to those who are powerless, victimized, and otherwise unprotected. However, I am also mindful of the importance of vulnerability in a therapeutic setting, which can open a pathway to self-disclosure and healing. In an educational setting, vulnerability, which enables young people to take risks and to enter wholeheartedly into relationships, can lead to repair.

Positive peace underscores the importance of repair, without which neither individual students nor classrooms nor communities can achieve well-being. Well-being is *not* a state to be achieved (as is, for instance, high self-regard or "happiness"). Rather, it is a mode of living that confers meaning and worth.

Its foundation is healthy relationships. All such relationships are reciprocal; they also accommodate and generate growth. However, as family systems research demonstrates, when relationships get stuck in recurring and predictable loops (called "homeostatic patterns"), they interfere not only with the healthy functioning of the group but also with the healthy growth of the individual. The goal of family therapy, then, is to break the homeostatic pattern or, in Salvador Minuchin's memorable words, to "disrupt the dance" (1993).

Similar "dances" occur in schools, which is why even the most heated faculty meetings are seldom surprising, with various people playing predictable, recurring roles (Friedman, 1985). While generous acts of compromise or selflessness can reduce conflict by improving impaired communication and rebalancing freighted dynamics, it is only when relationships move into the present moment that meaningful repair can take place (Stern, 2004).

The theatre, dance class, and the music studio all function as family systems. When these classroom "families" become trapped in dysfunctional dynamics, the consequences are wide-ranging: tension, humiliation, boredom, blaming, silence. (The analogue is negative peace, the mere absence of overt conflict.) In these unhealthy circumstances, the question which confronts the performing arts teacher is how to bridge the divide: to repair the felt breach that separates student artists from their sense of purpose and work.

This is no small task. As Kathryn Dawson writes, "[e]ducation is not neutral or benign… [It] should begin at the lived experiences of its participants and unfold through an intentional process where teachers and students are invited to be co-creators of their own learning" (Dawson et al., 2011, p. 317). But such an invitation becomes meaningful *only* in the context of a highly functional "family system" that effectively constitutes a healthy classroom.

The capacity for repair is a feature of healthy schools (Lawrence-Lightfoot, 2000; 1983). Since learning moments are by nature vulnerable moments, they often involve uncertainty, conflict, and mistake-making. These, in turn, can lead to joyful engagement and stimulating discoveries—or to stultifying self-protectiveness and even rage.

A few years ago, I witnessed a high school junior, struggling with lines in a final dress rehearsal, bring the rehearsal to a standstill. This elicited not-so-muffled frustration from fellow actors. Responding to the dynamics rather than the mistake, the theatre teacher brought the cast together to say, "This is a good moment for us to talk about what makes this pivotal scene so challenging." After a brief but substantive discussion, the embarrassed student turned to her peers and said, "Yes, I understand! I was so focused on remembering my lines, I wasn't thinking about what my character was really saying!"

Once the dress rehearsal picked up again, I was struck by the improvement in the performance: *all* the actors seemed to live more fully in their characters. A moment that might have been humiliating became, instead, an opportunity for repair and healing, and a pathway to presence.

All relationships, in and out of the classroom, require periodic repair. Unfortunately, as I have noted, schools are too rarely places that prize the dialogical conditions—collaboration, risk-taking, reciprocity, and trust—that make repair possible. Instead, they assume that students need such extrinsic behavioral inducements as discipline, competition, and rewards to motivate them. (In my experience, the overworked phrase "classroom management" too often masks teachers' failure to richly engage their students.) This is why "[the] move away from a deficit model of education to an inquiry-based model, which believed in students' capacity and desire to learn, involves a significant paradigm shift for teachers" (Dawson et al., 2011, p. 334).

Dialogical pedagogy occasions risk-taking, growth, and change not only for students but for teachers as well. In being present for the young people we teach, we open ourselves to being changed by them. "I don't think [my students] can possibly know how gratifying it is when everything clicks," a music teacher told me. I asked her to explain what she meant by "everything clicks." "It's not just about their excitement, or mine, when the class works perfectly. It's that I'm teaching them and they're teaching me!" What are they teaching you? I asked. "They're teaching me how to teach them. They're teaching me about who they are. I guess they're teaching me about who I am, too."

The words of a high school senior, reflecting on his years in the theatre program, also underscore the mutual impact in the teaching relationship: "Can you imagine what it was like for me to know that my ideas were actually capable of inspiring my teacher?" I asked him how he knew his teacher was "inspired." "You could see his eyes light up. I mean, someone I respect so much found me worth listening to. It's changed the way I see myself." In dialogical pedagogy, the learner is a teacher and the teacher is a learner.

The German social philosopher Eugen Rosentock-Huessy once observed (following a heated exchange he had been carrying on with Franz Rosenzweig): "I respond although I will be changed" (Rosenstock-Huessy, 2011, p. 4). Vulnerability, which is a potential source of hurt and conflict, is nonetheless a precondition of growth. It makes repair and healing possible.

Attachment theory reminds us that even our most intimate relationships—beginning in the cradle and continuing in the classroom—fall out of attunement, and require repair, over and over again (Karen, 1994). Those restorative acts bridge the divide, and reestablish intersubjective *presence*.

Yet, as attachment psychologists have shown, learning and growth depend primarily on the experience of joyful, exuberant connection (Schore, 1994; Stern, 1985). Joy is at the core of well-being, and is palpably evident in the generative energy of the performing arts classroom and the celebrative rituals of a community. It gives rise to "the courage to create" that requires "a centeredness within our own being" (May, 1976, p. 3). As every performing arts teacher knows, if joy suffuses the pedagogical process, it will be manifest in the curricular product.

Integrating Social Studies and Performing Arts

Nel Noddings notes that, in educating for peace, "the sharp separation of disciplines has not served us well" (2012, p. 143). The programs I describe in this section—one in fourth grade and the other in sixth grade—embrace the cross-disciplinary approach Noddings endorses. Both feature dialogical pedagogy, combine social studies with the performing arts, and rely on applied theatre practices. They are offered at the Oakwood School, a K-12 coeducational independent day school in North Hollywood, California. (I served as Head of School between 1979 and 2019.)

Oakwood was founded in 1951, not long after the creation of the Universal Declaration of Human Rights and not long before the Army-McCarthy hearings. Both events helped shape the school's core values: a commitment to peace and human rights is basic to Oakwood's mission. The founders were expressly influenced by Herbert Read's Educating for Peace (1949), and by Read's conviction that "[t] here is a certain way of life which we hold to be good, and the creative activity which we call art is essential to it (p. 115)."

As a moral enterprise, educating for peace requires teachers to dignify and respect learners *and* to make meaningful and significant demands of them. As I have noted, dialogue is not the goal but it *serves* the goal, which is growth and mastery. Coupled with values-driven curricular choices, dialogical pedagogy also fosters ethical engagement in the life of the community. Engaging students seriously, as artists and intellects, makes it possible to introduce even the youngest children to the injustices and inequities that prevent peace and undermine human rights. In Sabell Bender's words:

> The Oakwood Theater has never turned its back on difficult issues. Indeed, facing issues and conflicts is the essence of theater and can be a powerful force for the student/actors to develop greater sensitivity to themselves and their fellow human beings.[6]

Fourth Grade: *The Strong Ones*

Each year, fourth graders spend three months in a creative process, guided by their teachers, which culminates in a school-wide dramatic presentation.[7] It begins with students deciding collaboratively to focus on an event or period in which an affront to peace and/or an egregious human rights violation occurred. Students storyboard and write a play (Figures 4.1 and 4.2); research and write parts for the historical characters they will enact; collaborate with music, dance, and fine arts teachers; design costumes with parent help; mount an elaborate musical theatre production; and, as a culmination to a two-month social action project related to the play's themes, travel to Sacramento to lobby their State Senator.

Bridging the Classroom Divide in the US 55

Figure 4.1 Fourth grade script writing session with teacher.

Figure 4.2 Storyboard for *The Strong Ones*.

The process of students deciding on their play's title is democratic and robust. In 2018, I was present for an energetic class debate over what to call a drama about free speech. Two final candidates were chosen from a much larger list of initial proposals. One student endorsed A *Clash of Perspectives*:

> If you look at perspective, that's really what the play's all about: Should we allow free speech or should we not allow free speech? People have

different perspectives on this case and that's what made this historical event. I vote for A *Clash of Perspectives*.

Another student campaigned for *Words Behind Bars* (Figure 4.3).

Words Behind Bars is exactly like what happened with freedom of speech. Their first amendment right is being blocked and they're not allowed to use it. It's like their words are in prison. So I vote for *Words Behind Bars*.

After considering their classmates' opinions, the students submitted ballots. The teachers quickly tabulated the results and announced: "So the title is [dramatic pause] … 'Words Behind Bars.'" The fourth graders, as befits 9- and 10-year-olds, erupted in energetic applause.

Here is a meticulously crafted curriculum brought to rich life through dialogical pedagogy. Owing to that pedagogy, including their teachers' attentive presence, the children experience themselves as co-owners of their work. Hence the care and respect with which students engage one another, the substantive nature of their debate, and the creative process in which they become deeply invested.

I had the opportunity to spend many hours with (and to photograph and videotape) the students as their teachers guided them through the process of creating an original play about an historic social conflict. In 2016, the students dramatized the rise of the United Farm Workers in a production they entitled *The Strong Ones*. (2016 marked the 50th anniversary of the UFW's march to Sacramento. The theme resonated with the ongoing feverish debates over immigration, economic equity, and disparities in privilege.)

Students conducted research about the exclusion of farmworkers from the National Labor Relations Act of 1935; about the 1965 Delano grape strike; about Caesar Chavez, Dolores Huerta, and the creation of the UFW; and about the courage, solidarity, and sacrifices that made the farmworkers' non-violent movement so consequential. In the course of their research, the fourth graders

Figure 4.3 Fourth graders vote on *Words Behind Bars*.

Bridging the Classroom Divide in the US 57

Figure 4.4 Parents watching a strike scene in *The Strong Ones*.

developed substantial understanding not only about the impact of the United Farm Workers but also about the power of peaceful resistance to inequity and injustice. "Learners need to know how people were ethical by interacting well with others in response to conflict," Candice Carter writes. "A hope for humanity is problem solving without violence" (2015, p. 2).

After their research was complete, the students composed the lines their characters would speak (Figure 4.4). They coordinated their parts in small-group writing teams and then as a whole class. Here are three brief script excerpts, reflecting three perspectives:

1.
REPORTER: Robert Kennedy has joined striking farmworkers as they complete the final days of their 340 mile walk to Sacramento. Senator Kennedy, what do you think about this March?
KENNEDY: I support the farmworkers' decision to unionize.
REPORTER: Why are you pro-Union?
KENNEDY: I believe all workers should work under a fair contract. Right now, without union recognition, farmworkers don't have a voice.
2.
REPORTER: How are you feeling about another union, the Teamsters, blowing your deal?
PICKETER #1: We're discouraged, but we've come so far, we're not giving up now.
REPORTER: Do you have a new plan?
PICKETER #2: Our picket lines were stopped by violence. But at least they brought publicity.

3.
UFW MEMBER: Hi. Can you help us by supporting our grape strike?
CITIZEN: I heard about this, but I thought it was just going on in California.
MEMBER 2: We're here in New York City asking people to stop buying grapes, too.
MEMBER 3: We're travelling across the country trying to get national support to put pressure on the farm owners since California grapes are sold all over the United States.
CITIZEN 2: Why the focus just on grapes?
MEMBER 2: If they focus just on grapes, the farmers who grow the grapes will feel the impact.
CITIZEN 2: Not buying grapes? That's simple enough to do! I can do that!
MEMBER 3: Thank you for your time
MEMBER 2: And support!

I wanted to gauge students' understanding of the conflict they were depicting. I asked the class about the plight of the family-run farms. One fourth grader explained:

> The family farms had to try and keep up with the agribusiness farms. Some of them [the family farms] wanted to give their workers more, but they needed the agribusinesses to give their workers more also, or else they couldn't compete.

What about the UFW's tense relationship with the teamsters? I asked. Several students responded, after which a classmate added:

> What everyone is trying to say is that, basically, the farm owners couldn't get their produce to the markets without the Teamsters. So their business couldn't run. So they had a tough decision to make.

I told the students how gratifying it was to hear them speak so thoughtfully about the history they were depicting. Then I wondered aloud if they felt *changed* by this experience.

- It's all made me realize that there's so much work to be done, and so much conflict, and I haven't done nearly enough.
- It's changed my way of thinking about the world, just how much we went through that I didn't know about... I'm just so grateful.
- After I learned about... all these things that the people went through, I felt like I wasn't really doing enough. With so much trouble in the world, things like this really make you want to do more.

Along with empathy and agency, the students evinced a sense of joy. These qualities were apparent whether they were discussing their research ("Nicola [their teacher] has *great* books!") or identifying with their characters. (When I asked a question about Jimmy Hoffa, one student proudly exclaimed: "I AM Jimmy Hoffa!") Their performance was infectiously joyful, and put their fourth-grade sense of humor on full display.

REPORTER: Why are you donating to this cause?
SUPPORTER: When the farmworkers are on strike, they don't make money. I'm here donating so they can support their families and keep their organization funded.
REPORTER: How is the money raised?
SUPPORTER: When we buy a ticket to this dance, the money goes to the UFW.
REPORTER: Why do you think they chose a dance?
SUPPORTER (WITH A BIG—AND IT SEEMED TO ME, UNREHEARSED—GRIN): It's good for everyone to have fun and it increases morale.
[To camera] It's not too late to get in your car and drive over here!
[The whole cast sings and dances "Twist and Shout."]

Watching a rehearsal, I felt stirred by the "marching strikers," who loudly sing (to the tune of "Glory Hallelujah"): "Solidarity forever! Solidarity forever! Solidarity forever! The Union makes us strong!" Several fiercely chant: "*Huelga! Huelga!*" (Strike! Strike!) As the song ends, students portraying strike-busters attack students portraying strikers. Then the teacher, noting the end of the scene, announces: "And the lights go out!" The students whoop and high-five, their exuberance equal to their understanding of, and their feeling for, the events they have enacted. I am struck by the power of the performing arts to enable nine-year-olds to participate actively and imaginatively in the history they are "living" and learning. Given the commitment of the teachers to raising awareness about human rights in collaboration with their students, and the fervor with which the students have come to care about social injustice and their role as change agents, it seems to me that I am witnessing, in a privileged elementary school setting, a powerful instance of applied theatre.

Just prior to the dress rehearsal, a co-teacher has the students lie down in a large circle on the floor in front of the stage, their bodies radiating outward, mandala-like. The teacher's calming voice calls them into silence, as she asks them to close their eyes. "Get outside of your fourth grade selves," she softly tells them, "and into the characters you're playing. You've researched them so much and you've come to know them so well. Now *be* them!" In her deeply respectful tone, the teacher is communicating a vital if implicit message: We hold you in high and affectionate regard as our students and our creative partners, and we are grateful for our trusting dialogue of mutual discovery (Figure 4.5).

Figure 4.5 "Get outside of your fourth-grade selves".

Sixth Grade: *Be the Change*

The performing arts also play a pivotal role in the sixth grade's year-long curriculum centered on peace and human rights.[8] Students study all 30 articles of the Universal Declaration of Human Rights (UDHR) and explore human rights violations, locally and globally. They reinforce their knowledge and engage the wider school by teaching and performing for younger children in the school. At year's end, they write and present a culminating dramatic performance for the entire school community.

Two "lessons" with which the sixth graders engaged their younger peers provided meaningful opportunities for mutual learning and growth. The sixth grade social studies teacher arranged for her students to teach the kindergartners about Eleanor Roosevelt, who led the international effort to forge the UDHR. Students worked in pairs to write and illustrate original "children's books" on Mrs. Roosevelt, which they subsequently read (in one-to-one pairings) to the captivated "kinders." The five and six-year-olds excitedly returned to their classroom with their new books in hand (Figure 4.6).

The following week, I met with the kindergarteners to ask what they remembered about Eleanor Roosevelt. One girl offered this animated explanation:

> Eleanor Roosevelt, she was the first lady, and she married the president, and she was like a good person. Mostly boys get to do something. They only can wear wigs. They can only vote for president. But she didn't allow that. So she made it so that girls can put makeup on, put on wigs, they can vote for the president. *She* made that happen!

Figure 4.6 Sixth graders reading their Eleanor Roosevelt books to kindergarteners.

When I shared this response and others with the sixth graders, they laughed but also expressed appreciation: "I'm so happy we really did teach them something," said one. I asked why kinders should learn about Eleanor Roosevelt in the first place. A sixth grade boy said: "So they can aspire to be someone like her."

The students were later tasked with teaching first graders about human rights violations. In preparation for these presentations, the sixth graders learned about the "Cyrus Cylinder." Written in cuneiform, this clay cylinder was the first "charter" of human rights, proclaimed by the Persian King, Cyrus the Great. Then they created their own cylinders, choosing to "inscribe" it with a modern human right.

The students worried about whether first graders were too young to understand concepts like "no discrimination" or "arbitrary arrest," or to learn about human rights violations. Unbeknownst to them, their teacher wrestled with similar questions for the sixth graders, themselves.

> It's very weighty material. [I work hard] to keep it age appropriate so that they're not going to be weighed down by it. I want them to take on these challenges in an inspirational way, but not to be burdened emotionally with material that's maybe too hard for them to grapple with. And to help them navigate that is a challenge…

In the teacher's presence, I asked a sixth grader if people *his* age were too young to learn about human rights.

I think it's too old. You should be introduced to human rights at the youngest you can be. Because at a young age, it's what comes naturally to you that you should do the right thing. You shouldn't have to relearn the right way to treat people.

Despite their initial "stage fright," the sixth graders were skillful and graceful with the first graders, who were energetically engaged by the Cyrus Cylinders presentations. The sixth graders were equally engaged by the first graders. (Their exchanges were not without humor. One first grader asked for clarification: "Is it Cyrus the Great or Cyrus the Grape?")

Through these cross-graded interactions, first graders learn small lessons about peace and human rights; they also experience themselves as being taken seriously. To use Daniel Siegel's evocative phrase, they "feel felt"—that is to say, worthy of respect (1999, p. 89). The sixth graders are thereby teaching, and also learning, about human dignity (Figure 4.7).

Dignity is, in essence, the theme, each spring, when the sixth graders collaborate on a culminating theatrical presentation. Its purpose is to educate students and parents about their year-long work on making the world a more humane, just, and peaceful place. In preparation, students choose a peace activist/human rights hero to portray. They work with their art teachers to sculpt or draw their heroes; at the year-end production, these artistic creations are displayed in the theatre where they perform (Figure 4.8).

With support and guidance from their teacher, the students decide on how to dramatize the conflicts and injustices they have spent the year studying. To contextualize their decision, I should note that they devoted considerable time earlier in the (2018–2019) school year grappling with Chimamanda Adichie's riveting TED talk, "The Danger of a Single Story." One of the teacher's follow-up questions was "What is a 'single story' that people might have about you?" This led to an in-depth discussion, and personal revelations, about the students' own experience of stereotypes (e.g., being female or male, gay or straight, Asian or Latino or Black). With their teacher's skilled assistance, they co-created, a dramatic video montage, "I Am not a Stereotype," in which each student deconstructed a personally relevant stereotype.

Figure 4.7 Art teacher guiding sixth grader while he sculpts his "hero".

Figure 4.8 Sixth grade sculptures of peace/human rights heroes: Mahatma Gandhi, Malala Yousafzai, Gloria Steinem, Frederick Douglas.

Through their conversation and their art, the students responded to their teacher's request to "consider times when people felt singled out because of a defining feature that turns them into a target." By mid-spring, they envisioned, as part of their culminating drama, a kind of street fair, filled with booths sponsored by peace and human rights activists. Citizens, played by various classmates, would serve as devil's advocates, questioning or challenging the activists behind the booths. Students would play *both* roles and, in that way, acknowledge multiple perspectives.

As the idea percolated, several students realized that they could write most effectively for themselves if they were able to sponsor a booth that was personally important to them. For example, a Mexican student wanted to address, and teach about, immigration. A girl who had recently come out wanted to sponsor an LGBTQ booth. "The arts," Elliot Eisner notes, "help us become aware of ourselves" (2002, p. 112).

Here are three sets of interactions, excerpted from the culminating production, *Be the Change*. (I have not used the students' real names.) (Figures 4.9–4.11)

Homelessness Booth

JASON: Have you heard that the Los Angeles area has one of the highest populations of chronically homeless in the country?
ERICA: No I haven't, but that's a big issue. Tell me more.
JASON: Well, homeless people are turned away from shelters because they don't have space for them. They have to sleep in cars, in tented communities, or under bridges. Sign this petition and together we can make a difference. We're trying to get our lawmakers to make more affordable housing in the Los Angeles area.
ERICA: Of course. I understand how important this is. Thank you for opening my eyes.

64 James Alan Astman

Figure 4.9 Student explaining her homelessness booth to classmate.

Figure 4.10 Student visitors to immigration booth.

Figure 4.11 Students learning about LGBTQ booth.

Immigration Booth

JAVIER: Excuse me sir. How many US immigrants are given citizenship each year?
KAI: Uh, I don't know. Like a million?
JAVIER: Good guess. But only 675,000 out of 42 million immigrants.
KAI: Do you have a flyer I could take a look at? I'm a teacher and I'd like to find ways to get my students interested in this cause.
JAVIER: Perhaps you'd like to read up on the American Immigration Council.
KAI: Thanks so much. I'll check it out.
MIA: Okay, I have a question. I see you don't want to build a wall, but don't immigrants steal our jobs? Honestly, don't you think we'd be better off without them?
JAVIER: Well, immigrants often take the jobs that Americans don't want…

LGBTQ Booth

OLIVIA: Hi, so my name is Olivia and this booth is all about LGBTQ issues and activism.
AGGIE: L…G…B… T… Q…?? What does that even mean?
OLIVIA: LGBT stands for people who identify as Lesbian, Gay, Bisexual, and Transgender. And if you add the Q, it will most likely mean Queer or Questioning.
AGGIE: But wasn't gay marriage legalized in America in 2015? That's the only real problem that LGBTQ people really have had to face. Right?
OLIVIA: Well, gay marriage was legalized in America. But not all over the world. In some places you can even be killed for identifying with a different gender than the one you were born with, or having a different sexual orientation.
AGGIE: Sounds like an interesting organization you have. Can you tell me more?
OLIVIA: I realize that not everyone comes out surrounded by loving, caring people to support them. I've heard of children whose parents claim that they weren't their real child and kicked them out. My organization builds safe homes for LGBTQ children across America.
AGGIE: Wow. That's amazing. Good luck with your charity.

Although these interactions were rehearsed, creating them was an act of courage for the student booth sponsors. On its own, the script does not hint at the vulnerability of the writer, or the students' personal connection to the topic. Nor does it make self-evident the dialogical pedagogy that established the trust necessary to encounter their subject matter, teacher, and peers. Each of these stories is an *embodied* story, requiring the willingness to be vulnerable. For many of these sixth graders, then, the performing arts also function as healing arts.

As I was appreciating their final performance, I was also watching their teacher watch them. Afterward, I asked what she was feeling. "I was everywhere with them—hoping they'd remember their lines, amazed at how far they've come, and realizing that I'm losing them to seventh grade. But I'm lucky," she continued:

> I get to teach a curriculum that matters so much to me, and I think the kids can feel that and sense that, and then they feed me and I feed them. It's everything you want a teaching relationship to be.

The reciprocity between teachers and students reflects the care, trust, and risk-taking at the heart of dialogical pedagogy. But it also reflects another central truth in what Paulo Freire called a *Pedagogy of Freedom*: "Whoever teaches learns in the act of teaching, and whoever learns teaches in the act of learning" (Freire, 2001).

Conclusion

"All educators," writes Nel Noddings, "must become keenly aware of their responsibility to promote moral awareness and a commitment to peace" (2012, p.150). But the exercise of that responsibility, as I have noted throughout this chapter, depends as much on dialogical pedagogy as it does on curricular arrangements.

Still, this is neither a conventional nor determinative view. According to a report from Save the Children (2008), 37 full peace agreements were signed between warring parties between 1989 and 2005. Two-thirds specifically included education provisions, and nearly all of those mandated curriculum changes. No peace agreement mentions pedagogy, much less the relational dialogue through which curriculum becomes most meaningful.

Positive peace depends on that dialogue, which honors the humanity of young learners and respects their capacity to become agents of change. These are among the primary objectives of applied theatre, and they are the central aims of the fourth and sixth grade programs I have described. Those programs integrate the study of peace and human rights with the performing arts. They rely on dialogical pedagogy, which animates values-centered curricula and brings the whole student into presence with the teacher and the subject matter. They educate students about, and involve them in, real-life moral challenges. They culminate in performances that engage and educate the school community.

Because performing arts education is intrinsically dialogical, it can serve morally transformative ends: the act of co-creation promotes dignity, equality, and community, and constitutes the ongoing work inherent in positive peace. As embodied forms of education, the performing arts thereby have the power to bridge the divide: to restore the wholeness of experience and to promote individual and institutional well-being.

Notes

1 The words I have excerpted in this introduction, with her son's permission, come from Sabell Bender's writing, from her personal collection of letters from her students, and from my own conversations with alumni. An inspired theatre educator, Sabell served for nearly two dozen years as Chair of Performing Arts at Oakwood School in North Hollywood, California. When she passed away in 2019, students from across the country came to pay their respects and express appreciation for her profound influence on them as artists and as human beings. My debt to her is enormous: she immeasurably enlarged my understanding of teaching and of theatre that promoted personal and social change. (The description of Oakwood School's theatre—the space and several productions mounted in it—first appeared in an article Sabell wrote in 1994 for the school's annual magazine. For a fascinating reflection on "the school play as a site of memory," see Mackay, 2012.)

2 While the original use of this excerpt appears in a 1995 essay by theatre educator Doug Paterson, the provenance of this quotation has proven difficult to determine. In correspondence, Professor Paterson told me that Boal, himself, was "probably the original source." This quotation appears without attribution on numerous websites (e.g. http://advdpdrama.weebly.com/augusto-boal.html). It appears *with* attribution in Shutzman, M. and Cohen-Cruz, J. (Ed.) (1993). *Playing Boal: Theater, therapy, activism.* London: Routledge. https://doi.org/10.4324/9780203419717.

3 After attending a compelling and disturbing session on menstruation and girls' education—part of an international conference of the UN Commission on the Status of Women—a student described to me the transformation in her understanding of the issue: "I see so clearly now I can't remember what I once saw."

4 The task of taking a "leap in perspective" *in relationship* belongs not only to teaching but also to theatrical acting, as my friend, Marta Kauffman has taught me. (Marta is an acclaimed comedy writer, director, and producer for television. She is also a gifted teacher of her craft.) I described to Marta my work on "presence." In response, she talked about her work with the famed acting teacher Sanford Meisner, which is well worth quoting at length. "Awareness of the other person is crucial [as opposed to focusing on one's own state of mind]," she explained. In Meisner's classes, "both actors were given circumstances that the other person didn't know. For instance, I know his cat has just died. He knows he's going to ask me to marry him. The circumstances are imaginary; the words are about what you're feeling. Some say these are 'objectives.' The characters want something. But you still have to be *present* on that trip. You have to be experiencing what's happening *right now*. So when you come into a scene when my cat has died, that's just the background. It's how you relate to the other person in the room. There is a backstory you hang everything on, and then there's what's happening in the moment. Every actor, to be credible to the camera and the audience, has to be alive in the moment." (I told Marta that I believed an analogous truth obtained for educators: Awareness of the other person—the student—is crucial. Every teacher, to be credible, has to be alive in the moment. The teacher has to be experiencing what's happening *right now*.)

5 James Ashbrook (1925–1999), Professor of Psychology and Theology at Colgate Rochester Divinity School, shared this story with me. It took place during his Chicago seminar with Martin Buber. Ashbrook—my teacher who became my close friend—authored groundbreaking books on brain science and theology, as well as on human presence. (One such book is included in this chapter's references.)

6 From "Notes from the Director" by Sabell Bender in Oakwood Theater Playbill: "The Hot L Baltimore by Lanford Wilson" (February 1988).

7 Nicola Berlinsky is the educator who has developed this program over the past two decades. These productions have focused on a wide range of social justice causes,

including water resources (*Out with the Old, In with the Aqueduct*); women's suffrage (*Fight for the Right*); climate legislation (*The Greed for Gold*); the Fugitive Slave Act (*The Tale of Archy Lee*); school desegregation (*Tape vs. Hurley*); scapegoating and Mexican immigrants (*Downfall: A Time Drowned in Sorrow*); and, as mentioned in the chapter, *Words Behind Bars* and *The Strong Ones*. I am indebted to her for her pedagogical gifts and her professional generosity.

8 I am deeply grateful to Melanie Jacobson, currently Oakwood School's Director of Studies, who served as a sixth grade teacher for several years. In that capacity, with the active support of her colleagues and administrators, she developed the peace and human rights core curriculum. She also inspired other grades, beginning in the kindergarten, to develop age-appropriate peace and human rights programs. Oxford scholars and peace/human rights educators Cheyney Ryan and Hugo Slim have both visited Melanie's classroom and conversed at some length with her students.

References

Ashbrook, J.B. (1971). *In human presence–hope*. Valley Forge: Judson.

Buber, M. (1965). *Between man and man*. New York: Collier Books.

Buber, M. (1970). *I and thou*. New York: Charles Scribner's Sons.

Carter, C. C. (2015). *Social education for peace. Foundations, curriculum, and instruction for visionary learning*. New York: Palgrave Macmillan. doi:10.1057/9781137534057

Coles, R. (1989). *The call of stories: Teaching and the moral imagination*. Boston: Houghton Mifflin Company.

Dawson, K. et al. (2011). Drama for schools: Teacher change in an applied theatre professional development model. *Research in Drama Education: The Journal of Applied Theatre and Performance*, 16(3), 313–335. doi:10.1080/13569783.2011.589993

Dewey, J. (1966). *Democracy and education*. New York: The Free Press (MacMillan Publishing Co.).

Dewey, J. (1973). *Experience and education*. New York: Collier Books.

Dupuy, K. (2008). Education in peace agreements, 1989–2005. In J. Wedge (Ed.), *Where peace begins: Education's role in conflict prevention and peacebuilding* (pp. 27–37). London: International Save the Children Alliance, Cambridge House.

Eisner, E. (2002). *The arts and the creation of mind*. New Haven: Yale University Press.

Freire, P. (1974). *Pedagogy of the oppressed*. New York: The Seabury Press.

Freire, P. (1985). *The politics of education: Culture, power, and liberation*. Westport: The Greenwood Publishing Group.

Freire, P. (2001). *Pedagogy of freedom: Ethics, democracy, and civic courage*. Lanham, MD: Rowman& Littlefield.

Friedman, E. (1985). *Generation to generation: Family process in church and synagogue*. New York: The Guilford Press.

Gallagher, K., Rhoades, R., Bie, S., & Cardwell, N. (2017). *Drama in education and applied theater, from morality and socialization to play and postcolonialism*. Oxford Research Encyclopedias. Retrieved at doi:10.1093/acrefore/9780190264093.013.34

Galtung, J. (1985). Twenty-five years of peace research: Ten challenges and some responses. *Journal of Peace Research*, 22, 141–158.

Garcia-Mateus, S. (2021). "Yeah, things are rough in Mexico. Remember we talked about hard times?" Process drama and a teachers role in critically engaging students to dialogue about social inequities in a dual language classroom. *The Urban Review*, 53, 107–126. doi: 10.1007/s11256-020-00555-1

Grumet, M. (1988). *Bitter milk: Women and teaching*. Amherst, MA: The University of Massachusetts.

Harris, M. (1991). *Teaching and religious imagination*. New York: Harper & Row.

hooks, B. (1994). *Teaching to transgress: Education as the practice of freedom*. New York: Routledge.

Jackson, A. (1994). Translator's introduction. In A. Boal, *The rainbow of desire: The Boal method of theatre and therapy* (A. Jackson, Trans.) (pp. xviii–xxvi). New York: Routledge.

Jamison, K. R. (2004). *Exuberance: The passion for life*. New York: Random House.

Jech, C. J. (2013). *Religion as art form*. Eugene, OR: Resource Publications.

Karen, R. (1994). *Becoming attached: First relationships and how they shape our capacity to love*. Oxford: Oxford University.

Kotkin, A. et al. (2013). Speak out: Act up. Move forward. Disobedience-based arts education. *Harvard Educational Review*, 83(1), 190–200. doi: 10.17763/haer.83.1.x2j8070452124k

Kramer, K.P. (2013). *Learning through dialogue: The relevance of Martin Buber's classroom*. Lanham, MD: Roman & Littlefield Education.

Lawrence-Lightfoot, S. (1983). *The good high school*. Cambridge: Perseus Books.

Lawrence-Lightfoot, S. (2000). *Respect*. Cambridge: Perseus Books. See, especially, ch. 2, "Healing," and ch. 6, "Attention."

May, R. (1976). *The courage to create*. New York: Bantam Books.

Mackay, S. (2012). Of lofts, evidence, and mobile times: The school play as a site of memory. *Research in Drama Education: The Journal of Applied Theater and Performance* 17(1), 35–52.

Minuchin, S. (1998). In conversation at Santa Barbara workshop.

Minuchin, S. (1993). *Family healing: Tales of hope and renewal from family therapy*. New York: The Free Press.

Nathan, L.F. (2020). Joyful learning at scale: Immersing students in the arts. *Kappan*, 101(8), 8–14.

Noddings, N. (1984). *Caring: A feminine approach to ethics & moral education*. Berkeley: University of California Press.

Noddings, N. (2012). *Peace education: How we come to love and hate war*. New York: Cambridge University Press.

Palmer, P. (1993). *To know as we are known: Education as a spiritual journal*. New York: Harper Collins.

Palmer, P. J. (1998). *The courage to teach*. San Francisco: Jossey-Bass, Inc.

Paterson, D. (1995). *Theater of the oppressed workshops*. Retrieved at www.wwcd.org/action/Boal.html

Read, H. (1949). *Education for peace*. New York: Charles Scribner's Sons.

Reardon, B. (1993). Pedagogy as purpose: Peace education in the context of violence. In P. Cremin (Ed.), *Education for peace* (pp. 101–113). Ireland: Educational Studies Association of Ireland and the Irish Peace Institute.

Rhoades, R. (2021). Ethnodrama of projectivity as hopeful pedagogy in envisioning non-dystopic futures with youth. *Research in Drama Education: The Journal of Applied Theatre and Performance*, 26(2), 335–351. doi:10.1080/13569783.2021.1884059

Rosenstock-Huessy, E. (Ed.). (2011). *Judaism against Christianity: The 1916 War correspondence between Eugen Rosentock-Huessy and Franz Rosenzweig*. New York: University of Chicago.

Ruddick, S. (1995.) *Maternal thinking: Toward a politics of peace*. Boston: Beacon Press.

Salomon, G. (2006). Does peace education really make a difference? *Peace and Conflict: Journal of Peace Psychology, 12*(1), 37–48. doi:10.1207/s15327949pac1201_3.

Salomon, G. & Nevo, B. (2021). The dilemmas of peace education in intractable conflicts. *Palestine-Israel Journal*, 8(3). Retrieved at https://pij.org/articles/843

Schore, A. (1994.) *Affect regulation and the origin of self*. New Jersey: Lawrence Erlbaum Associates.

Schore, A. N. (2003). *Affect regulation and the repair of the self*. New York: W.W. Norton & Company.

Shapiro, S. (2002). The commonality of the body: Pedagogy and peace culture. In Salomon, G. and Nevo, B. *Peace education: The concept, principles, and practices around the world* (pp. 143–154). New York: Psychology Press.

Siegel, D. (1999). *The developing mind: Toward a neurobiology of interpersonal experience*. New York: The Guilford Press.

Snauwaert, D. (2012). Betty Reardon's conception of "peace" and its implications for a philosophy of peace education. *Peace Studies Journal*, 5(3), 45–52.

Stern, D. N. (2004). *The present moment in psychotherapy and everyday life*. New York: W. W. Norton & Co.

Stern, D.N. (1985). *The interpersonal life of the infant*. New York: Basic Books.

Yeats, W. B. (1952). Three pieces on the creative process: The thinking of the body. In B. Ghiselin (Ed.), *The creative process* (pp. 106–109). New York: Mentor Books.

5 From a Place of Not Fully Knowing

Devising Theatre with Young Adults in Austria as a Vulnerable Process of Elicitive Peace Education

Hanne Tjersland

> During the next three weeks you will create a theatre performance together that you will show to an invited audience at the end of the final week. I am here to support you, guide you, and to teach you important aspects about the process of making theatre that will help you along the way.[1]

I look into the circle of participants that I have just met and that have just met me. The participants have travelled from around Europe to spend these warm August weeks in Vienna, Austria, as part of this theatre project. I am here as the theatre pedagogue and peace educator guiding the work.

I can sense how curious I am towards these next three weeks that are to come, eager to discover what the different participants might bring into our shared theatre-making process. I can also feel how I am slightly nervous, wondering if the deeply elicitive approach I have chosen to fulfill the task of making theatre together will work. I know I could have made it easier for myself by choosing a more pre-determined frame to base the final performance upon, but alas; I was pulled towards this scarier, yet I anticipate also more rewarding, endeavor of starting with an open canvas indeed. I therefore wonder how the participants will react to my next words:

> A very important aspect is that I know as little as you about how the final performance will look like at this point. You will create it yourself out of a topic you choose, because what I really want out of these three weeks is for you to feel it has been relevant, having learnt and explored something useful for your lives. I am here, as I said, to support and guide you through the journey.

With these words, I have unleashed a vulnerable pedagogical process—a process in which I am essentially teaching out of a place of not fully knowing.

Introduction

In this chapter, I reflect upon a devising theatre project with young adults that, as mentioned, took place in Vienna, Austria, in August 2020. I served as the theatre pedagogue and peace educator facilitating this work. The reason I have chosen to reflect upon this project is because I see it as an interesting example for how a collaborative, relational and vulnerable process of elicitive peace education (Dietrich, 2013; Lederach, 1995; Tjersland & Ditzel Facci, 2019) can manifest through shared theatre-making. I furthermore see it as an interesting example for how the decision to apply a vulnerable pedagogical approach of not fully knowing and of not having full control (Brantmeier, 2013; Brantmeier & McKenna, 2020; Brown, 2012; Koppensteiner, 2020; Palmer, 1993) from the side of the educator can help unfold valuable learning for peace. 'Elicitive' implies that the work focuses upon and tap into students'/participants' strengths, needs, stories, reflections, skills, understandings, and more, rather than leaning mainly and/or only upon the educator's professional skills and knowledge. It is therefore a deeply relational and, I concur, vulnerable endeavor to engage. In this context, I ask: in which ways can relational and elicitive processes of theatre-making taught from a vulnerable place of not fully knowing unfold valuable learning for peace?

Importantly, as the educator that facilitated this theatre-making process, one of my core foci was to help create a space in which learning could unfold through multiple and ongoing relational encounters shared between me—theatre pedagogue and peace educator—and participants, as well as among the participants themselves. I thus invited collaboration, co-learning, and joint creative efforts to stand in the center, highlighting the participants' individual and collective resources, abilities, needs and responsibilities as the main dynamics necessary for creating the final theatre performance together. In this way, I could make the theatre performance function as an official "goal" that provided a necessary and useful frame for the creative work, yet without making it the sole purpose of our time together. As a peace educator by heart, it was rather the relational capacities—both as regards relations to others and as regards relations to oneself—that manifested as relevant and valuable for peace that stood in the center of my teaching intention. This further means that the theatre-devising process shifted its main foci from making good theatre and into making theatre together.

These deeply relational characteristics of the educative process asked from me as a theatre pedagogue and peace educator a willingness to let go of having full control over both the process and the outcome of the work. I was instead invited to embark on a vulnerable endeavor of teaching that unfolded from a place of not fully knowing. I was with this encouraged to honor the infinite creativity of human relationality and the inherent resources, knowledge, and wisdom of the participants in the place of certainty. My role hence became that of a 'space holder' and 'enabler' for learning (Koppensteiner, 2020), whose main responsibility was to guide and facilitate the process without imposing ideas, solutions, expectations and needs from 'above'. It was at times a highly challenging endeavor, which also unleashed several challenges and fears regarding my abilities to bring this project to a fruitful end. Yet, it was nonetheless a deeply rewarding experience especially in those many moments when I allowed myself to be professionally and personally vulnerable—human—to the participants, to the work and to the theatre that slowly manifested through and between us.

In this context—and focusing upon my personal reflections and observations as the theatre pedagogue and peace educator facilitating the above-mentioned theatre-making process—I intend in this chapter to look at some of the key potentials and challenges I encountered as a way to explore how these potentials and challenges can highlight vital dynamics for peace education as a relational and elicitive venture. Through emphasizing the elicitive approach's ability to underline needs, resources, stories, interests, and more of participants rather than mainly and/or only those of the peace educator, I discuss how learning manifests as a relational and vulnerable co-creation of knowledge (Brantmeier & McKenna, 2020). Moreover, I explore how this co-creation of knowledge can unfold powerful and imperfect (Muñoz, 2006) learning for peace.

I offer with this a small and self-reflective vignette as regards to how important learning for peace can evolve within such a relational and vulnerable process of theatre-making that I facilitated, shedding light onto key potentials and resources as well as challenges as it concerns elicitive peace education. I do this, vitally, from a process-oriented approach, using my personal reflections and movements as an educator during the theatre-making process to highlight vital dynamics highly relevant for peace education. My hope is that this reflective endeavor can benefit educators of all kinds that in one way or another are engaged in peace, creativity, theatre, and, ultimately, the thriving and well-being of students/participants (of whom I assume most are), and which are curious towards, willing to and/or pulled towards daring to include vulnerability—imperfect humanness—in their teaching and work. If one, as I do, understands peace as a deeply relational, and hence, *human* fabric (Dietrich, 2013; Koppensteiner, 2020; Lederach & Lederach, 2010; Muñoz, 2006), including vulnerability in this manner is not only a valuable approach but also a vitally necessary ingredient within the complex, multifaceted and ongoing endeavor called peace education—the process of unfolding human and relational learning and potentials for peace.

I begin the chapter by placing my work within the wider frame of applied theatre, placing with this my reflective account within the larger topic of this book. I discuss in this regard applied theatre in relation to peace education especially as it concerns potentials for engaging human diversity and intercultural learning. This is because the theatre project that I facilitated had explicit goals related to intercultural learning and diversity embedded. From here, I move into discussing the more particular applied process of devising theatre that I applied, arguing how this devising process is a fundamentally elicitive endeavor of theatre-making and (peace) education. Furthermore,

I engage with key dynamics concerned while daring to be present with vulnerability as an educator, identifying a core tension involved. This tension relates to the aspect of needing to be, as the educator, at the same time a professional role with professional responsibilities, expertise, knowledge, and more, and an imperfect and relational human being that humbly shares in the work and co-learns together with the participants. From here, I describe and discuss the theatre project I facilitated in more detail, reflecting upon important challenges and potentials that I encountered. In particular, I reflect upon how I moved with the core tension identified above, being at the same time a facilitator that "holds and enables the space" and an imperfect human being that continuously unfolds and learns together with the participants in a co-creative manner.

Applied Theatre as a Process of Peace Education

Applied theatre is a rather broad term that encompasses a variety of theatrical and dramatic expressions. It can, however, be said to refer to those dramatic and theatrical forms that "primarily exist outside conventional mainstream theatre institutions, and which are *specifically intended to benefit individuals, communities and societies*" (Nicholson 2005, p. 2, emphasis added). This latter aspect of intentionality is key. It points towards how applied theatre involves theatrical forms that are not only focused upon the artistic expression itself, but which expand the foci to include, for example, socio-political, community-building, and/or psychosocial intentions. Peace education, as a process that attempts to sustain diverse ways of knowing, understanding, interacting, relating, and creating together, can in this regard benefit from such a theatrical approach (see for example Mitchell et al., 2020; Premaratna, 2018). It is among others true in relation to how peace education seeks to integrate and engage different aspects of human diversity along with the development of intercultural skills, which are processes that applied theatre undeniably includes in many contexts.

Candice Carter (2021) explains in this respect how comprehensive citizenship, which peace education among others aims to foster, includes the involvement of diversity and intercultural learning within and across a variety of civic domains and geographic regions. She affirms how the domains of comprehensive citizenship are wide, including social, environmental, ethical, geographic, economic, and political, and how the domain of social citizenship in this context involves intercultural collaboration between people with different identities in one region, as well as transnational cooperation. This is particularly true in relation to how the interactions between different individuals and groups can include diverse and different approaches to creative problem solving together (Carter 2015). The learning about intercultural problem-solving capabilities is in this respect one important aspect of comprehensive citizenship, yet another equally important part is the praxis and application of these same capabilities. Applied theatre here carries particularly interesting potentials for peace education, as it can help foster these applied processes of diversity knowledge, intercultural skills, and problem-solving in and through the forms of theatrical expressions that it encompasses.

Intercultural knowledge and interaction skills are in this sense a part of, for example, applied processes of multicultural theatre performances (Lim, 2016; Pao, 2014) where cultural adaptation of a foreign story in an intercultural performance has been shown to be useful for addressing systemic conflict while enacting performance diplomacy (Liu, 2019; Tuan, 2011). Another example of applied theatre processes in relation to social citizenship can be found in intercultural redress theatre, such as the Stevenston Noh Project, where the creation of collaborative performances by members of the victimized and victimizing populations were included (Waisvisz & Vellino, 2013). In this regard, when related to explicit intercultural goals, applied theatre can unfold valuable potentials for diversity knowledge through the multiple creativity processes that it involves.

Miguel Oltra Albiach (2015) moreover asserts how forming intercultural skills are a vital component of citizenship development. He points out in this regard how diversity and creativity can be developed through, among others, intercultural theatre education in schools, including the use of puppetry. Furthermore, while creation and performance of puppets can counter exclusion and misrepresentation of identity groups in this manner other applications of theatre can also advance the goals of diversity skills. For example, peacebuilding through enhancement of self-concept has occurred through use of narrative identity in applied theatre. A harmonic intercultural identity associates in this respect with less depression, anxiety, and loneliness than a person who feels culturally divided and conflicted (Huynh et al., 2012). This work of narrative identity involves the participant exploring, re-constructing and meta-reflecting while the facilitator of the process does "(a) symbolic staging, (b) development of the 'actor's' skills, (c) creating ontological security (d) development of narrative continuity and (e) challenging the culture's influence on the narratives" (Haraldsen & Ingul, 2017, p. 81). This preparation of a performer to think and embody different cultures has in turn involved reconceptualizing time and space on stage, which enables embodiment and expression of different cultural notions (Tsolaki, 2016). In this way, the making of space and time in the rehearsal process as well as the *mis en scène* can work as a counter-hegemonic act that breaks away from the predominately Western and northern cultures represented in theatre performances (Leupin, 2018). In addition to these post-colonial creations of intercultural performance, disability arts include formerly excluded or under-represented performers (Johnston, 2009). It involves the descriptor 'superdiversity', which expresses the expanding boundaries for inclusive identities within a context (Labadi, 2020). Said slightly differently, applied processes of theatre can help convey a shared space for authentically being and creating together in multiple and diverse—both familiar and unfamiliar—manners. For the endeavor of peace education, it is unquestionable an interesting field of diversity potentials that ought to be further explored.

Devising Theatre as an Elicitive Process of Peace Education

Moving from this broader meta-discussion of applied theatre in relation to intercultural learning and diversity knowledge and into the more specific process of devising that I applied in the project I facilitated, I highlight how the term "devising theatre" refers to a collaborative process of theatre-making where the work emerges from a creative, shared, and participatory process rather than centering around an "outside" and pre-determined script (Oddey, 1994). Different topics, pieces of music, poems, images and more might serve as the starting impulse for this work. Yet, as Oddey maintains, "anything" can be the beginning point from where the creative exploration starts (p. 1). The beginning impulse is in this regard meant as a means to ignite the creative collaboration trough offering possibilities to explore, discover and create theatre through and with the different group member's individual and collective experiences. It is therefore not the impulse for its own sake, a fixed theatre script, or pre-determined ideas about how a final performance "ought to look like" that becomes the most important, but the unfolding process of creative collaboration and shared theatre-making that manifests (Heddon & Milling, 2016). Deirdre Heddon and Jane Milling describe in this regard devising theatre as a process and/or mode of making and generating performance that is focused on collaboration and creativity, and that is unfolded "from scratch, by the group, without a pre-existing script" (p. 3). Within this broader definition several expressions and examples of devising theatre exist (Heddon & Milling 2016; Oddey, 1994), including with professional theatre companies and in relation to, among others, theatre with young people and theatre-making in schools (see, for example, Bennathan, 2013).

Importantly for this chapter, when applied to the endeavor of peace education, devising theatre is a process that easily lends itself to an elicitive approach. It is among others due to the key focus on tapping into and making use of students/participants experiences, interests, topics, resources, and more, rather than focusing mainly and/or only upon what is prescribed from "above" and/or the "outside" through the theatre pedagogue's expertise and/or the authority of a text. The term "elicitive" is coined by Lederach (1995) in relation to conflict transformation, yet it has been applied to processes of peace education (see for example Tjersland & Ditzel Facci, 2019). They are approaches through which facilitators/educators/peace workers seek to build upon and "tap into" the already existing experiences, skills, and knowledge of a group/students/conflicting parties as the very resources that unfold learning and transformation within each context (Lederach, 1995). It furthermore turns facilitators and educators into space holders, process guides and enablers of learning rather than "experts," which in relational manners help unfold inherent resources of the group instead of "imposing" their own solutions from "outside" (Dietrich, 2013; Koppensteiner, 2020).

Seen specifically in relation to peace education, elicitive approaches point towards processes in which students/participants themselves manifest, create and unfold the competencies, learning, explorations, and qualities for peace that are relevant, necessary and life-affirming within their lived contexts. It is hence not the peace educator that stands in the center, but the students and participants with their individual and collective strengths, needs, stories, hopes, ideas, interests, and more. In this sense, and as an inherently creative, participatory, and process-oriented practice, devising theatre serves as a fruitful frame in which this elicitive intention of peace education can manifest. It concerns itself with the process of unfolding theatre out of and through the resources, creativity and knowledge already existing within the theatre-making group. It is further an approach that shifts the role of the theatre pedagogue into the before-mentioned enabler and guide that shares in the work together with the participants. This in difference from being a more hierarchically defined creative expert and sole provider of knowledge.

The elicitive endeavor discussed above can indeed be a vulnerable way to engage both theatre-making and peace education as seen from the educators' side. It importantly involves the relational experience of not having full control and of not fully knowing (Brantmeier, 2013; Brantmeier & McKenna, 2020; Brown, 2012; Koppensteiner, 2020), which, although challenging, is undeniably also vital and, I concur, necessary and rewarding. As mentioned, if peace is seen as a deeply relational fabric (Dietrich, 2013; Koppensteiner, 2020; Lederach & Lederach 2010; Muñoz, 2006; Tjersland, 2019), daring to included vulnerability as an educator can be a powerful way in which to tap into and unfold relational potentials and capacities for peace. In this context, the dynamics of vulnerability become key to explore.

Vulnerability as a Peace Educator

Edward Brantmeier (2013) defines a pedagogy of vulnerability as being about " taking risks – risks of self-disclosure, risks of change, risks of not knowing, risks of failing – to deepen learning" (p. 96). Brené Brown (2012) highlights the aspect of fully engaging as the core of vulnerability; of being all in for both the ups and the downs, for the comfortable and uncomfortable dynamics of life (p. 2). Norbert Koppensteiner, not all too differently, bases his argument upon the clinical and transpersonal psychologist John Welwood to emphasize vulnerability as a process of being in direct contact with the basic recognition that "human beings in the final instance do not have control over their lives" (Koppensteiner, 2020, p. 226). Grounded in these three different yet similar perspectives as regards vulnerability, I, in the context of this chapter, relate to the notion of vulnerability as such: vulnerability is a process and quality that centers around the courageous daring to—as "simple" as it sounds yet with the multiple imperfections it involves—showing up as, nothing more and nothing less, *human*. As an educator, it means, among others, daring to let go of the—perhaps both professional and personal(?)—need to have (full) control over and to (fully) know both the outcome and the course of a process, its impact, and its learning.

To shed light onto how this deeply human aspect of vulnerability relates to and is important for peace and peace education, I bring in Muñoz's (2006) notion of imperfect peace. Francisco Muñoz does not understand "imperfect" as something negative or unwanted but embraces it as a vital "unfinished and procedural" (p. 241) quality of the fabric of peace and of human life itself. With this he acknowledges peace as an integrated part of the everyday, relational, and imperfect human processes and highlights how, within these processes, peace and conflict are but two interconnected and necessary dynamics of the integrated relational flow. Conflicts are therefore not the opposite of peace, but naturally unfolding and life-affirming possibilities for relational transformation and change. This furthermore implies that humans—as imperfect beings—carry a key and vital capacity to be both "conflictive and peaceful" at the very same time (Koppensteiner, 2018a).

Francisco Munõz is in this regard a crucial inspiration behind the transrational approach to peaces—in plural—developed and taught by the Unit for Peace and Conflict Studies at the University of Innsbruck, Austria. Within this approach, peace is understood as a continuously unfolding fabric that oscillates in and out of new dynamic equilibriums—peaces—as different relational dynamics and conflicts are engaged and transformed (Dietrich, 2012, 2013; Koppensteiner, 2020; Tjersland, 2019; Tjersland & Ditzel Facci, 2019). It makes any effort to unfold peace, first, always a relational effort, and, second, an effort that includes conflicts. Imperfect humanness and its vital relational vulnerability thus become key dynamics to involve within processes of peace education. It is this transrational and imperfect understanding that greatly guides the discussion of this chapter as well as my engagement with vulnerability as a peace educator and theatre pedagogue. It is among others out of this this approach that I have come to see vulnerability—the courageous daring to show up as human—as a key ingredient in the relational, dynamic, lived, embodied, imperfect and ever-unfolding learning that is necessary for peace to manifest.

Edward Brantmeier (2013) argues how daring to apply a pedagogy of vulnerability is a rewarding yet also challenging approach to teaching, which carries human potentials to create spaces in which deep learning can manifest. Deep learning is learning that is integrated and flexible, and which students can adapt and transform in relation to different and ever-changing contexts and needs (p. 96). In terms of peace education, it implies a form of learning that can creatively respond to different relational conflicts and dynamics in ways that are, hopefully, life-affirming. It is importantly invited through relational encounters of co-learning (Brantmeier, 2013; Brantmeier & McKenna, 2020), in which multiple faculties of both educators and students/participants are engaged. This involves an invitation for students and educators to show up not only with their rational and intellectual selves, but with their full human—vulnerable and imperfect—wholes. It includes dynamics such as emotionality, embodiment, relationality, creativity, soulfulness, and more. In this respect, the key value of holistic-oriented practices such as, for example, theatre-making, becomes visible.

Edward Brantmeier (2013) furthermore argues how "vulnerability invites vulnerability. By opening our frames of knowing, feeling, and doing to co-learners (…) we invite others to do the same" (p. 101). This statement rests upon the assumption that as a peace educator it is hard to create spaces in which students feel safe-enough and invited to show up with their full and imperfect humanness if one as a peace educator is not willing to the same. In the context of peace research Koppensteiner (2018b) maintains: "at the limit point I content that we can only know [and teach] our topics within Peace Studies and we can only know [and teach] each other to the extent to which we are prepared to know [and show up] ourselves" (p. 77). As an educator, vulnerability thus implies a vital practice in daring to show up with our own imperfect humanness—professionally as well as personally—as a way to authentically invite students/participants to potentially–on their own terms and in their own life-affirming manners—dare do the same. This latter aspect lies as a core potential as well as challenge in terms of including vulnerability as an educator within peace education processes. Daring to include one's imperfect humanness is in this sense a venture that involves not only life-affirming and powerful potentials but also challenges and difficulties that deserve acknowledgement and respect.

Brantmeier and McKenna (2020) and Brantmeier (2013) discuss, for example, the dynamics of privilege and power in relation to vulnerability (for whom and in which context is it safe-enough to be vulnerable?), while Koppensteiner (2020) emphasizes the balance between the educator as vulnerable and the educator as stabile-enough and safe-enough to securely 'hold the space' for learning to manifest. Personally, I am respectful towards students' and participants', as well as my own, needs to not always be visibly vulnerable everywhere and with everyone but to evaluate when and in which ways vulnerability is safe-enough, life-affirming, and fruitful (see also Brown, 2012). I therefore affirm how a pedagogy of vulnerability is best approached with respect, awareness, and humility, as well as with profound curiosity and interest towards the human and relational potentials that it carries.

For the educator, an imperfect process of vulnerability requires with this a dynamic balance between engaging one's professional roles, skills, expertise, awareness responsibilities, and knowledge, and engaging one's complex, imperfect and comprehensive human self (Koppensteiner, 2020). This is because it is vital to show up both as an imperfect, relational human being that engages far beyond intellect and rationality only, yet without losing touch with one's key responsibilities to guide the process and to be an educator that holds a safe enough space for learning to unfold. Norbert Koppensteiner (2020) asserts in this regard, in the context of teaching peace and conflict studies, how elicitive processes need to be at the same time open and bounded. This two-fold process requires from the educator a relational capacity to both hold a safe-enough and bounded-enough space while staying open to and moving with the relational spontaneity and unpredictability unfolding. It means that educators need to constantly move with a dynamic tension centered around when and in which ways it is fruitful to provide content-input, structure, and guidance, and when and in which ways it is fruitful to take a step back, allowing the process to unfold through and between the participants themselves while "merely" standing there—with all the presence and skills it requires—to hold the space. This tension between openness and boundedness is vital both as regards how learning and creativity manifest, and as regards how vulnerability can be included as safe-enough within the learning process. In terms of the latter, Koppensteiner (2020) affirms:

> an unlimited space is not safe. Acceptance, relational warmth, and non-judgment provide the basic climate of openness. Yet by themselves they are also often insufficient. It is the task of the facilitator to also provide the boundaries and delimitations that allow a space to become safe.
> (p. 112)

Chris Johnston (2005) furthermore argues how creativity needs boundaries to flourish: "creative adults need structures to funnel their creativity. The structural elements we [facilitators] can introduce (…) anchors participants' energy" (p. 25). Creativity, therefore, paradoxically flows more freely if fruitful frames are introduced. This does not mean to block the creativity energy through rigid and over-controlling rules but to open it up and expand it through helpful "hurdles" along the way. It can among others be seen in relation to key insights from neuroscience regarding how humans learn through having to adapt to new and chancing circumstances, which instigates them to think and relate in novel and different ways (Doidge, 2007). With this, challenges and difficulties involved in a pedagogy of vulnerability prominently center around this core tension: how, when and in which ways can one include and not include one's professional and personal vulnerability within the process of teaching with care, intention, and awareness? In the following, I reflect upon how I moved with this tension in the theatre-making project I facilitated, tapping into both potentials and challenges I encountered that are involved in this manner of elicitive, relational, and vulnerable endeavor. First however, I dedicate some words to describing the theatre-making project I facilitated in more details.

The Theatre-Making Project

The project I reflect upon in this chapter took as mentioned place in Vienna, Austria. during the three first weeks of August 2020. It was organized by the Austrian non-governmental organization *Grenzenlos*, which is a non-profit as well as political and religious independent organization that has worked with intercultural exchange and volunteering programs especially for youth and young adults for more than 70 years. They additionally have a special focus on inclusivity in their projects, promoting volunteer work and international exchange for diverse individuals with different needs and abilities:

The German word *grenzenlos* means "no boundaries" and also "no limits". The word explains the basic mission of *Grenzenlos*: to promote the personal development of individuals (no limits) and intercultural understanding through international encounters, trainings, intercultural living and work experience (no boundaries).

(*Grenzenlos* n.d.: "About *Grenzenlos*")

The theatre project that I facilitated was with this framed as a volunteer summer camp where young adults could experience three weeks of international exchange and shared community work in Vienna through creating a theatre performance together. It gathered 11 international participants (volunteers), four international group leaders (also volunteers), as well an international theatre pedagogue (me) for three weeks of shared theatre-making as well as intercultural, diverse, and inclusive learning about oneself and each other. The four group leaders were mostly involved in the organizational frame surrounding the project and were therefore not actively participating in the theatre-making process. The exception was one group leader that chose to join the participating group halfway through and who was included in the theatre-making work for the remaining time. One participant left the group during the second week after having missed several sessions from the beginning.

Due to the special circumstances regarding Covid-19 that year, participants, leaders, and theatre pedagogue were limited to travel from within Europe only, which made the original "international call" of the project turn into a more "inter-European" one. Cultural diversity beyond European borders was, however, present through participants and group leaders already based in Vienna at the time. Furthermore, everyone involved, including the theatre pedagogue, was aged between 18 and 31, and the group was made up of prominently female participants (2 male, 9 female), male group leaders (3 male, 1 female), as well as a female theatre pedagogue. The project further had, as all projects of *Grenzenlos* do, a specific inclusive approach and involved participants with physical and/or cognitive special needs.

At the end of the final project week, a theatre performance devised collectively by the group out of a topic the group members had themselves selected with support from the theatre pedagogue—"diversity and prejudices"—was shown for an external audience. Due to Covid-19, the audience was asked to register and sign up beforehand yet otherwise the performance was open for anyone interested within the number of people that the Austrian infection regulations would allow. Obviously, the special regulations in place surrounding physical distance and wearing of masks for the audience did influence the way the stage was set up, as well as the ways the theatre-making group could allow themselves to play with the theatre space and how the audience could and could not be included in the performance. Although it did not pose any significant challenge to the theatre-making process, it is an important aspect to acknowledge as a prominent dynamic that influenced the overall work. Furthermore, as a working group we were ourselves allowed to work in proximity to each other during the three weeks, yet as the facilitator I had to, among others, creatively adapt several exercises that in circumstances without Covid-19 would involve, for example, touching each other's hands or being close to each other while singing and/or making sounds. I mention this because I consider it an important dynamic to be aware of as regards how this specific peace education and theatre-making process could—and could not—manifest during this very special time.

With this, the visible aim of the theatre-making project was to produce a final theatre product to be shown for an external audience. However, the process of learning relational competencies and qualities for peace were equally important and driving forces behind the pedagogical approach. This is among others due to how I as the theatre pedagogue was given full professional freedom from *Grenzenlos* to focus, organize, and facilitate the theatre project in manners I saw beneficial for learning. I did, however, need to keep the goal of making theatre and of learning through international exchange and shared community work central in mind. As a passionate elicitive peace educator, I was with this pulled towards daring to let relational and vulnerable co-learning, as well as deeply shared theatre-making, take center stage.

Eliciting Peaces through Making Theatre Together

As I now reflect upon the specific theatre-making process I facilitated as regards the learning, potentials and challenges involved in this manner of elicitive, relational and vulnerable process of peace education, I center my discussion around the core tension previously discussed regarding the peace educator and theatre pedagogue needing to be at the same time a professional role with professional responsibilities, expertise, knowledge, and more, and an imperfect and relational human being that shares in the work and co-learns with the participants. Importantly, these two aspects of the educator are not to be understood as separate and disconnected dynamics, but as integrated qualities and foci that move into the foreground and background of the work in dynamic and intertwined manners. Through shedding light onto how I reflected upon and moved with this tension during the course of the theatre-making project, I seek to highlight key potentials and learning as well as challenges involved in this manner of elicitive and vulnerable peace education process. I ask: how did I as an educator include the dynamic balance between providing structure and guidance, and stepping back to let the group process unfold through the participants' inherent resources? How further, did the ways I involved this balance highlight, engage, and contribute to relational learning for peace?

A key aspect to be aware of in this regard is how the group that I worked with were almost all fresh to theatre. Two central questions for me as an educator therefore became: how much guidance and structure do I *need* to provide (considering how the group are almost all beginners)? And: how much freedom *can* I (and dare I) give while still maintaining a fruitful, held, and safe-enough space? The answers I gave to these questions will, as a side note, obviously change if and when I work with a different group in a different context. This is both the reward and the challenge of elicitive approaches to peace education: the teaching dynamically and relationally changes together with the group, the context, and with a variety of internal and external circumstances that color the process.

During the whole first week of the three-week theatre project, I a conscious choice to focus the group and the work not directly on the theatre performance itself but on different basic theatre skills and techniques I saw as key for the participants, especially as beginners, to practice. This was because I, first, saw it as vital for both the group and I that we had some time to get to know each other and feel safe-enough together before we collectively immersed into the devising work. Second, it was crucial that the participants could practice a basic ground of knowledge and experience regarding theatre before I invited them to create a performance together from scratch. Anything else would be to thrust them into an unsafe and unhelpful process in which little to no learning would unfold. It is in this respect vital to remember how elicitive approaches to peace education do not free the educator from performing professional roles and responsibilities—such as for example teaching students about the subject, skill, or topic in question. Rather, elicitive approaches invites educators to include professional skills and knowledge as *one* important, yet not exclusive, means within holistic and relational learning processes (Koppensteiner, 2020).

I made in this regard an effort to include a variety of theatre exercises, games, as well small—structured and guided—processes of theatre-making together during the first week of the project. I started from a prominently guided and held space, beginning from basic theatre games that could help us get to know each other better. Gradually however, I increased the level of difficulty by, among others, allowing the participants to work more and more independently in smaller groups that created short theatre performances together. In this context, I often started the day with introducing a specific topic or skill that are important for theatre-making—such as the basics of how to tell a story on stage with a beginning, middle, and end—through exploring different theatre exercises. Afterwards, I invited the participants to create short performances in relation to this topic in smaller groups. While the groups worked, I moved around to provide my inputs into what the groups were creating especially as regards the theatre-making topic/skill in question. In this way, I could use these small theatre-making processes as important areas for learning. Furthermore, at the end of the days I would ask the groups to show their short performances to each other, inviting them to reflect upon each other's performance afterwards. I here invited them to highlight especially what worked within each performance in relation to the topic that we were practicing. Importantly, as a peace educator this became a way for me to not only invite learning as regards the skills of theatre-making but also to invite relational learning for peace as regards the giving and receiving of feedback in manners that were empathic, helpful, and supportive. It is in this context important to notice how I towards the participants explicitly emphasized theatre-making as a fundamentally process-oriented endeavor, and how the aim of our short performances was thus not to create good theatre. Rather, it was to co-unfold learning through offering our imperfect processes of creativity into the group.

The most prominent challenge I experienced as a peace educator and theatre pedagogue related to this first week of the project was finding helpful ways in which to acknowledge and integrate the participants', as well as my own, subtle and more explicit concerns, fears, and expectations regarding if and how we could manage to create a performance together in only the two weeks to follow. I knew for myself that creating a theatre performance together from scratch, especially with a beginner group, would, although rewarding, also be a challenging endeavor requiring amounts of dedication and focus especially during the two last more explicit theatre-making weeks. I therefore had to continuously integrate my own insecurities and the small, but important, questions regarding if I could manage to guide the group to a fruitful and meaningful end. I further noticed how I had to recognize and integrate the small, but present, tendencies of impatience and worry—along, of course, with vital curiosity—from the participants' side, which were eager to start creating a performance together already from day one. This made me realize how a key task for me as an educator would be to provide a calm-enough and balancing-enough presence, so as to not allow these subtle yet potentially growing tendencies of fear and impatience take too much focus in the work. I rather wanted the key learning and exploration of the shared theatre-making process to stand in the center.

I decided with this, as an educator, to make an intentional effort to visibly embody trust—both for the participants and for myself—as regards how I authentically believed that it was worth it and necessary to spend the first week exploring theatre more generally and how it was possible to create a theatre performance together during the two following weeks. I could in this way help the participants explore and engage the deeply relational quality of trust together with me, using my own visible expression of it as a perceptible and safe-enough container that could allow it to be dared. Norbert Koppensteiner (2020) asserts in this regard how the facilitator's embodied and grounded presence is a core resource for teaching and facilitation. It allows one to, as a facilitator, show up and inspire students/participants as a full human being who can then relationally resonate with other full human beings—students/participants (pp. 221–225). Importantly for the discussion of this chapter, the embodied and grounded practice of trust did with this not only stay with me throughout the first project week alone but manifested as a crucial way in which I could on an ongoing basis, throughout the course of the project, help create relational spaces in which both my own and the participants insecurities and worries could be integrated and allowed in empathic and helpful ways. It thus became a vital part of the peace education process, manifesting as a core practice through which we could together explore and engage qualities like patience, grit, compassion for ourselves and each other, empathy, as well as mutual support and care, as we individually and collectively struggled and enjoyed through the creative theatre-making process we were unfolding.

It was further through this vulnerable challenge of having to embody trust that I started seeing the key and vital learning for peace that would manifest in this specific theatre-making process. By, among others, choosing to practice a 'slow' start and to patiently trust that a performance would unfold even if it did not appear as such from the beginning, I realized I was going against a prominent societal narrative that was present with both the participants and I. Within this narrative, aspects like efficiency, success, productivity, perfection, and final goals are continuously highlighted as more valuable than, for example, stillness, patience, good-enough, well-being, quality of relationships, processes, imperfection, and joy (see, for example, Ehrenreich, 2007; Midgley, 2001). In the before-discussed context of imperfect peace (Muñoz, 2006), I began with this to see the elicitive process that the participants and I were unfolding as a crucial and life-affirming "procedural and unfinished" (p. 241) alternative to these dominant goal-oriented and perfection-demanding ways of relating and being. My focus as a peace educator and theatre pedagogue hence became—even more prominently than before—a key endeavor in inviting participants and myself to practice exactly imperfection, not as a "negative" dynamic but as a vitally necessary resource for life and for peace, and even, I maintain, as peace itself. Vulnerability thus entered as an even more noticeable aspect in the work, becoming a crucial way through which the participants and I could practice being imperfect humans together—with ourselves, with each other and through the work that we co-created.

As the two last weeks of the project and the more explicit performance-creating part of the process commenced, it was in this sense crucial for me as a peace educator to find supportive ways in which I could balance the teaching approach between the before-mentioned responsibility to guide and provide input for the theatre-making process, and this relational and imperfect intention to "just be there," allowing the participants to explore and engage their own imperfect human capacities, needs, interests, fears, hopes, resources, and more, in a variety of imperfect manners. I focused with this on finding ways through which to support the participants to sufficiently arrive at a meaningful and "good-enough" performance in the end, which they could importantly feel proud about having created, while crucially maintaining the vital learning of the process as the core and main focus of the work. It was furthermore important that the process could include relational learning for peace through, among others, involving dynamics such as cooperation, respect for different experiences, the responsibility to show up and contribute to the group, self-care and care for others, the ability to receive and give feedback, as well as helping and supporting each other through the ups and the downs of the creative process.

After having supported the participants to collectively decide upon a topic for the work and performance—"diversity and prejudices"—I entered in this manner the second week of the project with one intention in mind. I needed to design a helpful and inspiring theatre-making structure that could unfold creativity and learning, and through which the participants could be both supported and guided yet also prominently invited to tap into their own imperfect resources and interests as regards the topic at hand. I therefore started the more explicit "performance-making" part of the project by inviting the participants to engage their own lived experiences—either as an active participant or as a witness of a scene in which 'diversity and prejudices' was central—which would from then onwards serve as the core content and frame for the devising work. In this manner, I could create a structure that was inclusive (everyone both needed to and were given the space to contribute), elicitive (the content of the work and exploration came from the participants themselves), creative (it provided sufficient boundaries while remaining open), as well vulnerable, relational, and human, while still, vitally, staying safe-enough.

The latter aspect of safe-enough was importantly supported from my side through several intentional foci. I did among others carefully instruct the participants to engage and share only lived experiences that they felt comfortable to give into the group and to use as collective working material for the performance and theatre-making process. In this way, I could balance the challenging dynamic between, at the one hand, allowing the theatre-making process to unfold as personal, relevant, and meaningful, and, at the other hand, as safe enough for vulnerability to be life-affirming and helpful for the participants. It was in this regard crucial for me to, first, not put direct or indirect pressure on anyone to share what they did not want to share. Second, I needed to be explicit, transparent, and visible in my communication with the participants regarding how, as with all theatre-making processes, the stories, and experiences they brought into the group would not become only their personal stories anymore. Rather, they would be given to the collective as a gift that would from then onwards be creatively transformed, played with, understood differently and re-invented in numerous ways (Diamond, 2007). This key focus and intention vitally helped guide this process of engaging the participants' lived experience in life-affirming rather than potentially harmful ways. It was furthermore a way in which we could practice leaning upon the collective and symbolic work of theatre to at same time protect us from too much and threatening individual self-exposure as well as into helpful and relational vulnerability through highlighting a safe-enough, playful, shared and seemingly "fictional" space that was both "very real" and "not real" simultaneously (see Tjersland, 2016). As a further note, being able to let go of rigid attachment to one's experiences as "they are and ought to be," allowing them—and even yourself—to relationally change through multiple and diverse encounters is in my understanding a practice for peace in and by itself.

Through using the participants' lived experiences as the base and ground for the collective theatre-making work in this manner, I could anchor the creative process in dynamics that were, I assume, meaningful, relevant, and important to the participants. The potentials of the lived curriculum —"the content of our lives, the past lived experiences, that become the foundation of learning new concepts, skills, and values" (Brantmeier, 2013, p. 97)—entered with this as a core resource in our work. It became a way through which the participants and I could practice, explore, and unfold imperfect learning for peace together through engaging our human and imperfect experiences in relation to the topic. The lived curriculum is in this respect a vital part of a pedagogy of vulnerability, helping one to manifest the deep learning previously discussed by supporting an expansion of the learning to include not only the topic or skill in question, but also vital learning about life itself (Brantmeier, 2013). What, in this respect, is the vital learning about life that was included in this specific theatre-making process that I facilitated and that I discuss in this chapter?

As I see it, and as I continuously seek to work with it as a peace educator, this learning centered around the subtle and explicit exploration of life and of peace as an essentially imperfect and relational journey. This journey is continuously unfolded differently anew as one moves through and with the many contexts, people, feelings, thoughts, hopes, surroundings, needs, understandings, and more, that one encounters. Through creating a space in which the participants and I could tune into and resonate with our human and imperfect experiences through collective theatre-making in this manner, the participants and I were given the chance to practice and experience how our deeply relational and imperfect human qualities, both as individuals and as a group, are indeed a core of what this human life and what these human peaces are about. Getting to know, practice, explore and engage these qualities was therefore, I contend, not only a valuable experience but a crucial and essential exploration of and for peace that is unfortunately not widely encouraged and invited in more traditional institutions and contexts of education. In this regard, the creative, relational, and holistic-oriented process of elicitive peace education that was unfolded through this theatre-making project, could, I content, unfold a vital and life-affirming process through which the participants and I could practice and explore alternative and more *human* ways to be and relate together.

To sum up my discussion of this chapter, I dare to make a personal statement regarding what I see as the key potential and challenge as regards these forms of relational, vulnerable and elicitive processes of peace education that I applied. It revolves around the crucial and life-affirming practice in accepting, acknowledging, and creatively embracing the imperfection of oneself, of others and of life as a vital resource for peace. In my experience, this is a particularly important and balancing practice to engage within surroundings where imperfection and vulnerability is often not encouraged and nourished. Among others, it implies daring to make myself vulnerable as an educator in this text, showing a human and professional me that is deeply process-oriented and that at times also carries insecurities and fears as she seeks to embody the art of teaching (and researching) from a place of not fully knowing. This is, I argue, unfortunately an approach that is not always encouraged within many professional settings. As an elicitive peace educator by heart, it is nevertheless this vulnerable and imperfect intention of being *human* together with students and participants—even as this approach can involve several challenges—that deeply fuels my peace education and theatre-facilitating work.

Conclusion

I have in this chapter explored how a vulnerable, relational, and elicitive process of peace education can manifest through shared theatre-making and how this process can unfold valuable human, imperfect, and relational learning for peace. I have, in particular, reflected upon my experiences as the theatre pedagogue and peace educator facilitating a devising theatre project with young adults in Vienna, Austria, during the three first weeks of August 2020. I have used this project as one example for how daring to apply a pedagogical approach of not fully knowing as an educator can unfold key and life-affirming potentials for peace through engaging learning and teaching as imperfect and relational endeavors. In this regard, I have focused upon how I as the theatre pedagogue and peace educator needed to continuously move with a dynamic balance regarding when and in which ways it was fruitful to provide content–input, structure, and guidance to the participants and the process, and when and in which ways it was more fruitful to take a step back, allowing the process to unfold through and between the participants while "merely" standing there to hold the space. Through this, I have come to highlight and understand the participants' capacities and possibilities to explore, practice, engage, and get to know both their individual and collective human imperfection as the core potential and learning for peace that was unfolded through this theatre-making process. In a similar line, I have attempted to embody this same imperfect and process-oriented focus while writing this chapter.

As a theatre pedagogue, I am further aware that there are many other aspects of this creative theatre-making process that I could have focused upon in this chapter, and which are valuable for peace education. It includes, for example, a deeper discussion of aspects such as embodied and holistic knowing, the empowerment and deep learning involved expressing oneself through a theatre performance, as well as the potentials involved in creativity itself. However, as not just a peace educator but importantly also a deeply committed human and elicitive peace educator, I see the effort to (re)engage, (re) acknowledge, and (re)celebrate human imperfection as a, if not *the*, core and vital life-affirming resource for peace that I can help unfold through my peace education and theatre teaching work. It is therefore also this imperfect human potential of the theatre-making process that I have chosen to focus my reflections upon in this chapter.

Note

1 The words in this paragraph are not an exact quotation of my opening statement while teaching this theatre project, yet they are a creative re-writing meant to capture the essence of the opening session.

References

Bennathan, J. (2013). *Making theatre: The frazzled drama teacher's guide to devising.* London: Nick Hern Books.

Brantmeier, E. J. (2013). Pedagogy of vulnerability: Definitions, assumptions, and applications. In J. Lin, Oxford, R. L., & Brantmeier, E. J. (Eds.), *Re-envisioning higher education. Embodied pathways to wisdom and social transformation* (pp. 95–106). Charlotte, NC: Information Age.

Brantmeier, E. J., & McKenna, M. K. (Eds.). (2020). *Pedagogy of vulnerability.* Charlotte, NC: Information Age.

Brown, B. (2012). *Daring greatly. How the courage to be vulnerable transforms the way we live, love, parent and lead.* London: Penguin Random House.

Carter, C. C. (2015). *Social education for peace. Foundations, curriculum, and instruction for visionary learning.* New York: Palgrave Macmillan.

Carter, C. C. (Ed.). (2021). *Teaching and learning for comprehensive citizenship: Global perspectives on peace education.* Milton: Taylor & Francis Group.

Diamond, D. (2007). *Theatre for living: The art and science of community-based dialogue.* Bloomington: Trafford.

Dietrich, W. (2012). *Interpretations of peace in history and culture.* London: Palgrave Macmillan.

Dietrich, W. (2013). *Elicitive conflict transformation and the transrational shift in peace politics.* Basingstoke: Palgrave MacMillan.

Doidge, N. (2007). *The brain that changes itself. Stories of personal triumph from the frontiers of brain science.* London: Penguin Books.

Ehrenreich, B. (2007). *Dancing in the streets. A history of collective joy.* London: Granta.

Grenzenlos. n.d. *Grenzenlos [homepage].* Vienna: Grenzenlos. Retrieved at www.grenzenlos.or.at

Haraldsen, H. M. Ingul, S. (2017). Negotiating narrative identity in intercultural contexts: The role of applied theatre. *Journal for Research in Arts and Sports Education, 1,* 69–82.

Heddon, D. Milling, J. (2016). *Devising performance. A critical history.* Basingstoke: Palgrave MacMillan.

Huynh, Q.-L., Nguyen, A.-M. D., & Benet-Martínez, V. (2012). Bicultural identity integration. In S. J. L. Schwartz, Luyckx, K., & Vignoles, V. L. (Eds.), *Handbook of identity theory and research* (pp. 827–842). Heidelberg: Springer.

Johnston, C. (2005). *House of games: Making theatre from everyday life.* Revised edition. London: Nick Hern Books.

Johnston, K. (2009). Building a Canadian disability arts network: An intercultural approach. *Theatre Research in Canada, 30*(1–2), 152.

Koppensteiner, N. (2018a). Kulturen der frieden: Eine transrationale perspektive [Cultures of peace: A transrational perspective]. In S. Jalka (Ed.), *Denken. Kunst. Frieden. Annäherungen an das menschsein* [*Think. art: Peace. approaches to being human*] (pp. 23–43). Berlin: De Gruyter.

Koppensteiner, N. (2018b). Transrational methods of peace research: The researcher as (re)source. In J. Echavarría Alvarez, Ingruber, D., & Koppensteiner, N. (Eds.), *Transrational resonances: Echoes to the many peaces* (pp. 59–81). Cham: Palgrave Macmillan.

Koppensteiner, N. (2020). *Transrational peace research and elicitive facilitation. The self as (re)source.* Cham: Palgrave Macmillan.

Labadi, S. (2020). Afterward. Superdiversity and new approaches to heritage and identities in Europe: The way forward. In L. Colomer & Catalani, A. (Eds.), *Heritage discources in Europe: Responding to migration, mobility, and cultural identities in the Twenty-First Century*. York: Arc Humanities Press. doi:10.2307/j.ctv14161jz. pp. 111–115.

Lederach, J. P. (1995). *Preparing for peace: Conflict transformation across cultures*. Syracuse: Syracuse University.

Lederach, J. P., & Lederach, A. J. (2010). *When blood and bones cry out: Journeys through the soundscape of reconciliation*. New York: Oxford University.

Leupin, R. (2018). Making the intercultural: The rehearsal process of Gintersdorfer/Klassen. *Contemporary Theatre Review, 28*(4), 504–521. doi: 10.1080/10486801.2018.1490730

Lim, A. E. H. (2016). Actor training and intercultural jam in a multilingual context. *Theatre, Dance and Performance Training, 7*(1), 74–88.

Liu, S. (2019). Performing intercultural trauma: State, land, and women in Troy,Troy… Taiwan. *Asian Theatre Journal. 36*(2), 453–471.

Midgley, M. 2001. *Science and poetry*. London: Routledge.

Mitchell, J. Vincett, G. Hawksley, T., & Culbertson, H. (Eds.) (2020). *Peacebuilding and the arts*. Cham: Palgrave MacMillan.

Muñoz, F. A. (2006). Imperfect peace. In W. Dietrich, Echavarría, J. A., & Koppensteiner, N. (Eds.), *Schlüsseltexte der Friedensforschung/Key Texts of Peace Studies/Textos claves de la Investigacíon para la Paz* (pp. 241–281). Vienna: LIT.

Nicholson, H. (2005). *Applied drama: The gift of theatre*. Houndmills: Palgrave MacMillan.

Oddey, A. (1994). *Devising theatre. A practical and theoretical handbook*. London: Routledge.

Oltra Albiach, M. A. (2015). Educación intercultural, diversidad y creatividad en el aula a través del teatro: Los títeres [Intercultural education, diversity and creativity in the classroom through the theater] *Madrid: Didáctica, 27*, 167–182.

Palmer, P. J. (1993). *To know as we are known. Education as a spiritual journey. A master teacher offers a new model for authentic teaching and learning*. San Francisco: Harper One.

Pao, A. (2014). The red and the purple: Reflections on the intercultural imagination and multicultural casting. *Contemporary Theatre Review, 24*(4), 467–474.

Premaratna, N. (2018). *Theatre for peace building. The role of arts in conflict transformation in South Asia*. Cham: Palgrave MacMillan.

Tjersland, H. (2016). *Healing spaces between fictions and realities. Drama/theatre as a way to integrate and re-tell one's stories. A transrational approach to peaces*. [master thesis]. Innsbruck: University of Innsbruck.

Tjersland, H. (2019). The dancing body in peace education. *Journal of Peace Education, 16*(3), 296–315. doi: 10.1080/17400201.2019.1697066

Tjersland, H., & Ditzel Facci, P. (2019). Introduction: Unfolding transrational potential. *Journal of Peace Education, 16*(3), 247–251. doi: 10.1080/17400201.2019.1697070. Pp:

Tsolaki, G. C. (2016) Actor training at the Intercultural Theatre Institute of Singapore. *Theatre, Dance and Performance Training, 7*(3), 340–361. doi: 10.1080/ 19443927.2016.1217267

Tuan, H-C. (2011). Zhang Yimou's Turandot in Taiwan: Intercultural spectacle, aesthetic of excess, and cross-strait sensibility. *Theatre Topics, 21*(2), 175–183.

Waisvisz, S., & Vellino, B. C. (2013). The Steveston Noh Project The Gull as intercultural redress theatre. *Canadian Literature, 216*(216), 118–137.

6 Teaching for Gender Equality as Peace Education through Theatrical Performance in Mexican Schools

Lucía E. Rodríguez McKeon and Náyade Soledad Monter Arizmendi

Introduction

This chapter shares some features of two educational intervention experiences involving young students from two public secondary education schools with high rates of violence, located in low-income areas to the west and east of Mexico City. Both projects aimed at problematizing the assumptions that validate gender violence replication, in order to establish more equitable relationships between genders, from a culture of peace and gender equality perspective, through the art of performance and theatre to be developed with students.

Sharing experiences arising from both gender-oriented projects is highly relevant today, both globally and in Mexico in particular, because of the prevalence in this country of a gender ideology that legitimizes the use of violence against women in multiple forms. Therefore, promoting the implementation of educational actions to ensure visibility and awareness of its implications is urgent, in order to enable the development of spaces for coexistence in the relationship between genders that make it possible to fully acknowledge women and their dignity as subjects of rights, capable of building their own life project.

Since these projects take place within the educational context, gender inequalities are addressed in their articulation with school coexistence, understanding that these tend to emerge through sexist practices and discourses usually intrinsic to the formal and hidden curriculum. This is so because school is one of the primary instances of socialization for children and teenagers, which instills values, attitudes, meanings, habits, norms, codes, roles, and gender stereotypes.

Under this analytic perspective, which acknowledges that gender violence is a symptom of the way the culture of violence is replicated in general terms, being mediated by structural and cultural factors that explain it (Galtung, 1998), the need to tackle it creating a culture of peace is emphasized. As gender ideology demonstrates the way society annihilates, destroys and annuls compassion, empathy, bonds, and local and community entrenchment, the

DOI: 10.4324/9781003227380-6

culture of peace perspective in the educational field becomes a radical strategy for the delegitimization of a pedagogy of cruelty, which leaves human beings defenseless because of their exposure to the culture of violence and their lack of socioemotional tools to resist it and build other possible life horizons (Segato, 2017).

We will share the itinerary followed by devices in their different phases, as well as some of the significant findings regarding their pedagogical potential for students' skills development, obtained in the experiences' monitoring and evaluation process, through the use of several instruments, especially observation, interviews, and evidence gathering.

This analysis highlights the value of performance and theatre to stimulate artistic, emotional and body expressiveness in people and to influence students to develop a critical spirit regarding their individual and collective context (Gómez, 2005). Likewise, emphasis is placed on some findings related to its capacity to generate educational processes that allow building creative responses to imagine new forms of relationship between genders, based on what Gergen and Gergen (2012), cited in Ospina (2017, p. 181), state:

> [...] if creative responses are to be obtained, a new paradigm of doing must be articulated, moving from words to actions, acknowledging other forms of expression such as movements, gestures, actions, paintings, photographs and all sorts of expressions that allow us to communicate new ideas through strategies alternative to those we are familiar with.

Applied Theatre as Peace Education

Both experiences were developed with the support of Applied Theatre (AT). This theatrical modality includes a set of creative practices and processes that can be used in different contexts, such as educational or community contexts, and whose purpose is to foster social change (Sedano-Solís, 2019). As to the education area, AT became popular in England in the 1990s, although it originated before the twentieth century. In particular, the use of AT in education aims to improve teaching-learning processes, either as a cross-cutting part of the curriculum, as an interdisciplinary subject, or as a pedagogical method (Sedano-Solís, 2019).

In terms of its pedagogical potential, AT facilitates a holistic learning experience, beyond the official curriculum; however, it is worth mentioning that in order for these interventions to generate changes in people's practices, attitudes, values, and ideas, they must be accompanied by an interdisciplinary approach, and integrate interactive factors that actively and repeatedly engage stakeholders (McElwee & Fox, 2020).

On the one hand, this type of projects put together experiential learning experiences, which contribute to establish more horizontal relationships among those involved through role-playing, by promoting identification processes between those who play the characters and spectators that favor an intellectual and emotional connection between participants with the situated realities of stakeholders (McElwee & Fox, 2020).

In this regard, research studies such as Pradena and Anguita (2020) have found that mainstreaming embodied theatrical art not only connects rational issues with emotional and body issues, but also arouses horizontal, dialogical, and reflexive relationships (Pradena & Anguita, 2020).

On the other hand, AT breaks with traditional and rigid teaching-learning processes' structures by fostering cross-cutting and flexible experiences that enable students to monitor and reflect on the problems they face; this helps them develop a critical perspective of their individual and collective contexts, and encourages their artistic, emotional, and body expressiveness (Gómez, 2005).

Because of these two characteristics AT has become a core pedagogical method for building meaningful peace in the educational field. Being part of this type of project as a strategy towards peace education, students engage in a transformation cycle that helps them become aware of the existence of violence and its implications for subjects' lives, through processes that enable them to cognitively understand the nature of this social phenomenon, as well as to feel the emotional effects that making gender violence look "natural" has on people's distress, by developing empathy.

On the other hand, with the use of AT as a strategy for peace education students can be the actors of their own transformation process and increase their self-awareness, by consciously getting in touch with the values and beliefs that steer their practices and implicitly legitimize the culture of violence. By fostering students' participation in dramatization processes, AT provides a unique opportunity to enhance moral deliberation processes based on analyzing different scenarios among which, although somehow counterintuitive, troublesome, or conflicting, they have to choose the best alternative. For example, by staging violent practices such as the use of foul verbal language, bullying, mockery, exclusion, discrimination, aggression or self-aggression, students not only create different meanings and reflections on these situations, but also learn more about some attributes of them and their peers, such as having the sense of listening, valuing differences, showing empathy, and exploring several states of mind, feelings, and points of view (Posso et al., 2017).

In other words, as a method of peace education, AT positions students in a scenario in which they must face a conflict and solve it; thus, in parallel, it drives them to reflect on their actions and on the responsibility they individually and collectively imply. But that is not all; in addition to creating educational processes that prevent violence from being considered "natural" as a constitutive element, regarding gender relations in this case, AT allows students to develop moral imagination processes (Lederach, 2007) that are essential to build other ways of transforming conflicts that arise in daily life, by building creative responses to imagine new ways of gender relations based on what Gergen and Gergen (2012) cited in Ospina (2017, p. 181) state:

in order to have creative responses, it is necessary to embed a new paradigm of doing, moving from words to actions, acknowledging all forms of expression such as movements, gestures, actions, paintings, photographs, etc., that facilitate the communication of new ideas through strategies alternative to those known.

In this respect, we conclude by stating AT's effectiveness as a pedagogical method for questioning and building new viable realities for peace education, analyzing the contributions of both devices in terms of the problematization of beliefs about the culture of violence based on deliberation and critical understanding, fostering students' empathy and participation in collaborative processes that build social cohesion and helping raise awareness for bringing about social transformation, all of which are essential characteristics of peace education.

Gender Equality for a Culture of Peace

Gender inequalities usually come up in daily school life. School, as one of the first instances of socialization, instills values, attitudes, meanings, norms, gender roles, stereotypes, and codes that model an ideal masculinity and femininity type among students. In this regard, Valdez-Medina, Díaz and Pérez (2005, p. 46) mention that "gender systems are deemed [...] as binary systems that oppose men and women, masculine and feminine, and this [...] in a hierarchical order [...]."

In Mexico, gender perspective -acknowledged in the General Law on Equality between Women and Men, among other instruments, refers to those "mechanisms that make it possible to identify, challenge and evaluate discrimination, inequality and [the] exclusion of women [...], as well as those actions that must be undertaken to [...] create conditions [...] that enable progress in gender equality construction" (LGIMH, 2006, p. 2).

Thus, gender perspective refers to a conceptual tool that uncovers culturally constructed differences between women and men, and it can be used to build symmetrical socialization among people. In line with this, Marcela Lagarde (1996, pp. 25–26) points out that gender perspective "is a political commitment to transform gender order… [which] implies not only acknowledging the existence of a social order that divides us as men and women… [but also constructing] non-oppressive gender alternatives."

The sex/gender system notion was suggested by Gayle Rubin (1996), who defined it as the host of provisions through which a society translates biological sexuality into human activity (Rubin, 1996 in Serret, 2008, p. 43). In other words, as Martínez and Bonilla (2000, p. 10) state:

> every individual is subject to the value system associated with the sexual difference constructed by the culture in [which] he/she is immersed; gender, as a behavioral component, will have a differential impact not only among all subjects involved but also throughout their life cycle.

However, according to Butler (2007), gender is not a direct consequence of sex; the sex–gender system is not automatic, far less fixed, universal, and unable to be modified.

That said, economic and political revolutions have created certain changes in women and men's roles and stereotypes, entailing other ways of coexistence.

Clearly, traditional models still persist, "that represent a constellation of attributes and behaviors sanctioned as appropriate for men and women respectively" (Valdez & González, 1999, cited in Aguilar et al., 2013, p. 46).

Within this framework, the culture of peace becomes a useful instrument to address cultural gender mandates and overcome the violence with which they are articulated, replicated, and justified. In a school setting, peace is related to developing coexistence skills in all stakeholders, aimed at understanding, acknowledging, and strengthening girls, boys, and adolescents' potential, and ensuring that, once they have identified themselves as change and transformation agents, they can choose paths different than those of violence and inequality (Ospina and Ospina, 2017).

The construction of peace in the classroom should enable students to learn how to coexist with their differences in a democratic and fair manner that, far from standardizing thoughts, bodies, voices, identities and practices, values heterogeneity (Muñoz, 2001). Therefore, peace is established within systematic mediation processes in continuous and daily reconstruction that at the same time enable the development of more peaceful and fair settings, which, even if they imply a continued challenge to learn and adopt new behaviors, also contribute to the denaturalization of gendered stereotypes and promote a new way of seeing, understanding, and living the world (Fisas, 1998).

Thus, taking a hard look at gender relationships in the classroom allows people to create new ways of being and of being in school, by generating new consensus to reach a supportive and egalitarian coexistence. However, this requires an analytic lens that explains the existence, persistence, and perpetuation of inequalities between men and women, with the following as the gender perspective:

> Given [...] the urgency of establishing equal treatment conditions between men and women [...] [and] promoting egalitarian education [...] with a gender perspective capable of differentiating [...] the cultural origin of [power relations between men and women] [...] and proposing social alternatives (such as education) for their resolution.
> (Lamas, n.d., p. 1)

Description of the Proposals

The two proposals were submitted as professional dissertation works by graduates of the Master's degree in School Coexistence Management in the Violence, Human Rights and Culture of Peace program delivered by the National Pedagogical University since 2015.

Created as intervention devices over a period of approximately two years, both proposals were developed within school contexts by classroom teachers at the secondary school level.

With the support of Action Research (AR), defined as a type of research performed by teachers themselves, in school and from school, aiming at "providing a specific response to problematic situations that arise in the classroom" (Latorre, 2005, p. 21), this perspective facilitates the improvement of teaching, when teachers reflect on the need to change and innovate their own educational practice (Elliott, 1993).

The process of building both devices took place in several stages leading to the articulation of different action and reflection cycles that made it possible to develop strategies linked to the situated problems of classroom and school practices. Below we share some of their features.

First Proposal: The "Storytelling" Intervention Device

The "Storytelling" intervention device, developed in 2017–2018, was designed to allow students to create a critical storytelling of gender binary schemes. It aimed at helping students play an active role in their development, seeking to reflect on their gender praxis and on how this experience can transform them and transform their socio-cultural context, by participating in the generation of a transformation process for themselves and others.

The project was based on the performance category proposed by Taylor (2012), who defines it as an extremely useful way to stimulate artistic, emotional, and body expression in people. The author states that more than a dramatization, performance is an act of representation with a real personal and social transgression potential. Thus, in the educational field, performance may drive students to adopt an attitude of criticism of their individual and collective background, since it favors the development of awareness of their own body and emotions and enables the expression of feelings, experiences, and ideas. It contributes to develop this critical spirit, to experience another type of socialization and the ability to work as part of a group, delving into interpersonal relationships among students. It also helps value other uncommon forms of expression, stimulating curiosity and creativity in students (Gómez, 2005).

Problem Diagnosis

In order to inquire into their social and coexistence relationships from a gender perspective, the first activity undertaken was a qualitative diagnosis, through open interviews with a third-grade group of 30 students (15 women and 15 men) taking the "Tutoring" subject in a public high school located in the south of Mexico City. The results obtained from such diagnosis highlighted the continued manifestation of tension and conflict situations among students related to the existence of relational dynamics based on gender inequality identified as the main problems.

These results triggered the design and implementation of an educational strategy aimed at promoting gender equality and a culture of peace in secondary school students, through a dynamic conceived to problematize gender roles and stereotypes among them, based on planning and dramatizing several performance proposals that at the same helped promote classroom and school coexistence dynamics, based on collaboration, inclusion, empathy, and respect for the different personalities of men and women.

The Intervention Strategy

The experience planning and implementation process included multiple educational activities and strategies aimed at training students, who played an active role in their development, using two means of expression: body and language; these in turn became the main spaces for intervention, while the teacher played the role of "companion" of the students. Below we share a description of some of the activities undertaken.

Invitation to a New Project

During the first working session, the teacher invited students to participate in the project, sharing the proposal to create stories that would be represented in a performance intended to problematize gender, thus demonstrating that activities such as this would allow them to recognize and reflect on inequality circumstances that women and men face in everyday life.

Subsequently, the work focused on understanding the performance features, emphasizing their similarities to the theatre, although some of their differences were also highlighted since performance involved planning moments in a story (beginning, development, climax, and end), with no totally defined dialogues, since its main feature is improvisation.

In the final activity students worked in four- to five-people mixed teams with the purpose of identifying a story, a conflict in the story, and possible alternatives to solve it within a specific time period and in a specific place.

Then, the groups discussed the creation of characters (to be personified by students) and exchanged ideas about scenography, costume selection and cardboard, paper or cloth items used to set the scene. At the end of this process, each team had created a draft with the performance title, story, and characters.

Performance Planning

The second moment marked the beginning of the process of planning the stories they wanted to represent. The plot focused on the problematization of traditional gender roles and stereotypes, sexism, the division of labor at home and at the workplace, school coexistence from a gender perspective, hegemonic masculinity, and street sexual harassment.

Based on this discussion, students decided that performance should be organized in two moments. First, the story should represent traditional situations according to gender. Second, the story would take a turn, that is, the characters would do the opposite of the initial situation proposed. On the other hand, at this moment the role the students would play in their teams when designing the performance was also defined, distributing different tasks such as: writing the story, the characters acting or building the scenery. When monitoring the activity, the teacher constantly emphasized that designing a performance was a collective creation, in which everyone had to work equally.

We Are Halfway

First, students created the characters—what they do, what they say; they designed the narrative moments in their stories and decided what the title of the performance would. Then they rehearsed, and while doing so, they determined the characters' attributes (strong, weak, happy, melancholic, aggressive, or obstinate), their age (children, teenagers, young or old people), their tones of voice (soft, sharp, shrill, or loud), their body movements—fast, slow, agile, heavy, in motion or static. In addition, students created the scenery using paper, cardboard, or other materials, made the costumes (with paper, fabric, or other reusable materials) and gathered the objects to be used (saucepans, balls, kitchen utensils, makeup, etc.).

We Are Ready!

In the latter process, collaborative work among students was essential to make decisions and set up agreements to achieve the desired product; they made adjustments and adaptations they deemed pertinent. The teacher attended each team at all times, to help solve any situation that may arise, such as the lack of an item or a change in the stories, as well as in the equal engagement of female and male students on the task. Finally, each team conducted a dress rehearsal of the performance.

3, 2, 1, Action

The work was exhibited in a museography entitled "Ethical Stance towards Gender Roles and Stereotypes in Secondary Education, 2017–2018 School Cycle," which included the following performances: *There Are no Kings nor Queens at Home, Who Are the Kings and Queens at Work?, Ceasing to Be Cavemen, Are There Male Winners and Female Winners?, The Street and the Stalking Vampires, Secondary School Warriors* (see Figures 6.1 and 6.2).

Before presenting the performances, the students set up the scenery, adapted the chairs and organized a space as a stage. Some first-grade students attended the presentations as audience. The museography was inaugurated, students were welcomed, and all performances were presented. Upon completion of

Teaching for Gender Equality 99

Figure 6.1 Performance: *The Street and the Stalking Vampires*.

Figure 6.2 Performance: *Secondary School Warriors*.

the presentations, a closing ceremony was held, thanking all students for their engagement. In the following classes, the teacher used a self-evaluation rubric and four unstructured interviews to inquire about the students' experience in developing the intervention process.

Second Proposal: Play *Femicide in Five Acts*

This experience was proposed in order to promote a space for the denaturalization of gender violence, a phenomenon that is assumed as normal in our Mexican culture, with strong macho characteristics. The term femicide implies a denunciation of the macho violence exercised by men against women, because of the anger felt regarding the status of woman as the main motive for a deliberate attack resulting in death by gender.

Considering the national relevance of murders of women, which have significantly increased in recent years, developing this project was essential to break the silence and to incorporate into public debate, issues that, although deeply embedded in our culture, are barely mentioned in everyday life scenarios and much less in school.

Through a methodology that privileged students' leading role, as well as through playful work focused on creativity development, in 2017 we promoted the creation and staging of a play with third-grade students in a public secondary school located in the western area of Mexico City. The purpose was to openly debate and question such practices, demystifying the natural way with which they are perceived and even considered as normal in our society.

Through a thoughtful-sentient training strategy, emphasis was placed on building a process that would allow students to deeply question their beliefs about gender, as well as to raise their awareness of the circumstances under which women experiencing violence live and of the need to reach commitments to fight for its eradication at all social life levels.

Here we share the development of core activities that, organized in different phases, gave meaning to the work done.

The Visit to the Museum as an Awareness-raising Strategy

The process began when students visited the Museum of Memory and Tolerance in Mexico City to see the exhibition on Femicide in Mexico. This museum, specialized in treatment and denunciation of discriminatory processes, organized this exhibition to pay homage to the victims, as well as to create a forum to inform on the high levels of violence and impunity involved in these phenomena, and to reflect on misogyny and machismo as mechanisms to prevent the replication of these acts among young people. (See general data on the exhibition at https://artsandculture.google.com/exhibit/eQLS6cF5Dj33Kw?hl=es-419).

The elegantly assembled exhibition thoroughly narrated the cases of many women who suffered femicidal violence. Drawing nearer to these women's stories and faces was a first exercise of awareness of the problem, without which it would have been difficult to involve students as a whole in the project.

Reflection on the Denaturalization of Gender Violence and the Importance of Saying "Stop It!"

The first activity involved recovering the students' experiences during the visit to the exhibition. The teacher encouraged them to reflect on the factors that contribute to the cultural replication of gender violence, highlighting gender violence cycle analysis and the diversity of ways in which it is legitimized.

On the other hand, emphasis was made on another activity related to the diagnostic identification of the way in which such invisible types of violence arose in their daily lives and their effect on the possibility of building gender relations that would help their full development as human beings.

The Theatre: A Strategy to Raise Awareness of Femicide and Denaturalize Gender Violence

Following the teacher's suggestion, the possibility of staging a play based on this issue was analyzed. The decision was made to consider the testimonies on some femicides as the basis to develop a script that would narrate the stories that resulted in the murder of some women.

Students, along with the teacher, undertook the task of researching testimonies about some of these events and chose five stories to be dramatized. Taking them into consideration, the script was written and enhanced by students in several working sessions.

Staging the Play and Organizing the Work

This was the phase when roles were defined and those who would represent them were chosen. In these sessions, the group concentrated on collective rehearsals, on analyzing what would be the best way to personify each character, modulate the voice, and express the experiences lived by the main characters of each story.

Other tasks required to stage the play were also distributed among the group. Some students worked on the scenery, other students engaged in selecting and collecting the costumes to be used, and others engaged in a recyclable plastic collection campaign, seeking to obtain economic resources to pay some expenses.

Performing the Play

The play was performed in the center of the school courtyard, in the presence of the students' families, who were invited to share this moment with them. Subsequently, the play was performed in an auditorium at the *Universidad Iberoamericana* in Mexico City and in the Human Rights Commission facilities. Both experiences were highly formative for students and proved that it is possible to learn in a meaningful way by problematizing what we live and becoming aware of it.

Reflection on the Formative Potential of the Experiences

Based on the analysis of the information gathered in the focus groups and interviews with students, as well as other evidence collected when monitoring both experiences, we were able to identify their contributions to promoting significant training processes at various levels, in order to increase gender equity from a culture of peace perspective.

A first element that is worth mentioning is the potential of students to speak and problematize reality, as expressed in several testimonies of students who reflect on what the experience taught them:

- "Enacting the play (was useful to) helped us reflect on what was going on" (E1, 2).
- "You are learning to coexist, to grasp other people's knowledge, to look around, to see what is happening in your country […] it was very cool any way you think about it" (E2, 9).
- "We become aware of a problem that our country has been experiencing in recent years" (E2, 4).
- "I pay attention to a problem I didn't know of" (E2, 3).
- "It helped me a lot to open my eyes" (E2, 4).

Students appreciate having participated in these experiences because they allow them to foster a transformative dialogue by connecting with the situations that concern them. According to González (2012), this type of strategy has an advantage: they facilitate the connection between historical, social, political, psychological, and literary notions and life itself. This coincides with Trozzo and Sampedro (2004), who highlight the importance of using reflection to promote a more comprehensive and meaningful learning process at school and thus bridge a gap that traditional school cannot close if it continues to focus its task on mere knowledge of things in themselves and not on understanding reality and oneself, through the knowledge of things.

When we connect with what is lived, experiences are valuable because they allow us to understand how all problems occurring on a large scale are reflected on micro situations where gender violence is replicated in the daily life dimension.

In relation to the above, another factor highlighted in the students' testimonies is how significant they think experiences are to develop their capacity to understand reality from a critical perspective. This is emphasized when they describe that experiences allowed them to talk about issues that are rarely mentioned, breaking the silence about unspeakable realities, as can be detected in the following fragments:

- "The country has the red spotlight quite lit because there is a lot of violence here, that sincerely is not normal, we should not see it as a normal event because it happens every day, we should not allow more girls go through this ordeal" (E2, 3).
- "This allowed us to problematize the macho relationships within the group" (E1, 6).
- "This made us be aware that it is not normal, problematize what it means to be a woman, realize that women and men can do different things" (E2, 4).

- "This made us reconsider it… we women must take care of ourselves, we must not let others hurt us, we must promote respect for us" (E1, 1).
- "It also helped us want/wish that people who see us and listen to us are able to open their eyes" (E2, 4).

Based on students' comments, which are shared as an example, we clearly see their potential for the denaturation of gender violence as a specific contribution of the experiences analyzed, since they no longer see the practices that they and many other women go through, as *normal* because of their gender status.

Another factor to be highlighted in the analysis is its potential to generate a collective urge to imagine other possible realities by questioning beliefs that hold that reality is immutable and impossible to transform, thus going well beyond the mere critical attitude towards situations no longer desired, as two students said: "This made us want/wish to promote this situation to change" (E2, 4); "Contribute even a little for this to stop happening" (E2, 3).

In this regard, it is worth emphasizing, in accordance with Doat (1961), that this potential benefits from this type of pedagogical resources features, which put at the center the use of other languages that boost the overflow of vital forces, such as collective arts, by allowing the demonstration of the immediate, direct and fleeting aspects of experiences, a synthesis of all means of expression in time and space, thus avoiding the imposition of a dominant rationality.

Another factor implies undertaking and striving to achieve the construction of a collective project, which is extensively valued by students because it strengthens their interdependence with each other in order to achieve common goals, as appreciated in the following comments:

- "Building the project was in itself very formative… it was like putting a puzzle together" (E5, 2).
- "The experience of getting organized helped us come closer and pull together" (E10, 2).
- "We learned to support each other" (E1, 1).
- "This allowed us to connect as a group and we are very close now" (E4, 2).
- "The experience promoted bonding; groups used to be very divided and some of us didn't even know each other" (E3, 1).

Students depend, trust, and contribute to each other when building a project from rehearsals to staging and concluding with representation; this encourages all to enjoy the acknowledgment of the work done and the satisfaction of shared success.

By undertaking the experiences, we learn to work collectively and to participate; also, links within the group are intensified, supportive, and collaborative attitudes are strengthened, and the diversity of skills in others is acknowledged, respected, and appreciated; all this contributes to an approach beyond pre-existing differences in the group, which allows the social fabric to be rebuilt as a learning community.

In this respect, through the implementation of the intervention devices students promote the know-how to be and know-how to live together dimensions (Delors, 1996), as the axis of a training process in the culture of peace. All of this framed in the development of agency skills towards active citizenship training, by raising awareness of themselves, their environment, and their social role in their capacity to act in relation to transforming the conditions that hinder the construction of new gender relationships (Yurén, 2005), as discussed in some testimonies:

- "We learned that we can feel we can act as a group" (E5, 1).
- "I learned that the femicide situation can change" (E3, 2).
- "It is possible to do what you want [...]. We can change this [...] we can make changes" (E6, 2).

Finally, another important factor to be highlighted concerns the experiences' potential to promote the capacity to express emotions and feelings as an essential component in the elaboration of what is lived and thus foster the implementation of holistic formative processes in the field of education for peace.

Students highlighted that theatre and performance work enabled expressiveness and creativity. On the one hand, the experience improved their ability to communicate and now they are able to talk about their moods, their affections, and also their sadness. By knowing their own voice and using words as their means of expression and finding in their bodies (hands, voice, gestures, look, movements) communicative resources and enjoying them.

Thus, as above-mentioned authors Trozzo and Sampedro (2004) said, developing expressivity and creativity, on the one hand, promotes more spontaneous, free, and uninhibited subjectivities and, on the other hand, strengthens the capacity to identify one's own needs and draw up demands, by living a process of self-building as a person that acknowledges oneself as a subject with dignity and rights.

Conclusion and Recommendations

Theatre and performance are pedagogical methods with a rich potential for advancement of learning about and for increased gender equity from a culture of peace perspective.

The analysis of the contributions drawn from documented experiences show how such experiences helped develop critical thinking targeting the denaturalization of gender-based violence. Also, they fostered the construction of agency skills, as well as engagement and collaboration in common projects, which enabled shaping educational processes to strengthen the construction of a culture of peace in the classroom and the school as a whole, and the possibility of developing capacities to express young people's needs and demands.

In both projects, gender perspective was a useful lens to promote education for peace and human rights. This perspective helps reveal different invisible discriminatory practices (related to gender, sex, social class, health condition, physical appearance, ethnic origin, sexual preferences, age, etc.) exerted towards people in different spaces of socialization such as: family, school, community, among others. It was important to work with this perspective since it made it possible to build new consensus around students' empathic and egalitarian coexistence.

Also, the intervention allowed students to express themselves "from another location", basically using their own body instead of complex instruments. This implied a practical experience where students had an active and creative role through their participation in the performance, in which, on the one hand, they problematized their hierarchical gender relationships and, on the other hand, they made visible elements that helped them develop new coexistence relationships with their peers, based on seeking mutual well-being and care.

Therefore, we recommend that the attributes towards a new educational practice with a gender perspective in (formal and non-formal) teaching-learning processes may consider the following issues: (1) renewing curricular contents (with no gender stereotypes); (2) using inclusive (oral and written) language; (3) exchanging gender roles (assigning activities other than traditional ones); (4) using similar materials and spaces for both men and women; (5) introducing feminine references (in history, art, science, etc.); (6) avoiding the use of sexist popular phrases, sayings and proverbs; (7) fostering mixed-teams work; (8) introducing gender equality-related topics and activities; (9) ceasing the use of gender binary tags (such as quiet–naughty or princess–champion [girls–boys]); (10) remembering that students are diverse (avoiding homogenization and generalization) (see Figure 6.1). Further, we recommend that AT productions include opportunities for revision of gender relations towards a culture of peace. The cases of revision in this paper offer models of performance revision for that purpose (Figures 6.3).

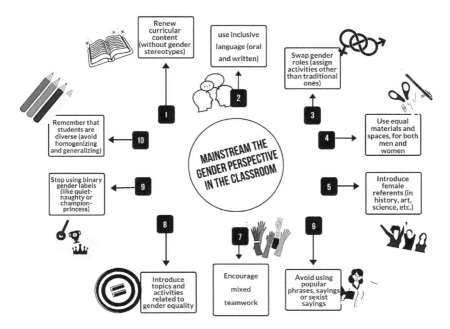

Figure 6.3 Gender mainstreaming in the classroom.

References

Aguilar, Y. et al. (2013). Los roles de género de los hombres y las mujeres en el México contemporáneo. [Gender roles of men and women in today's Mexico]. *Enseñanza e Investigación en Psicología [Teaching and Research on Psychology]*, 18 (2), 207–225. ISSN: 0185-1594. Retrieved at www.redalyc.org/articulo.oa?id=29228336001

Butler, J. (2007). *El género en disputa: el feminismo y la subversión de la identidad.* [*Gender in dispute: Feminism and identity subversion*]. Barcelona, Spain: Ediciones Paidós Ibérica, S.A.

Delors, J. (1996) *La educación encierra un tesoro.* [Education is a treasure]. Informe a la UNESCO de la Comisión Internacional sobre la Educación para el Siglo XXI. [Report to UNESCO delivered by the International Commission on Education for the 21st Century]. Madrid, Spain: Santillana/UNESCO.

Doat, J. (1961) *Teatro y público. Teoría y práctica del teatro.* [*Theatre and public: Theatre's theory and practice*]. Buenos Aires, Argentina: Compañía General Fabril Editora.

Elliott, J. (1993). *El cambio educativo desde la Investigación Acción* [*Educational Change from a Research Action Perspective*]. Madrid, Spain: Editorial Morata.

Fisas, V. (1998). Cultura de paz y gestión de conflictos. [Culture of peace and conflict management]. In *Una cultura de paz* [*A culture of peace*]. Barcelona, Spain: Icaria/UNESCO. ISBN: 9233034992. Retrieved at http://cort.as/-Rw3I

Galtung, J. (1998) *Tras la violencia, 3R: Reconstrucción, reconciliación, resolución.* [*After violence, 3 Rs: Reconstruction, reconciliation, resolution*]. Bilbao, Spain: Ed. Gorgoratuz.

Gómez, J. (2005). Posibilidades educativas de la performance en la enseñanza secundaria. [Educational opportunities of performance in secondary school]. *Arte, Individuo y Sociedad [Art, Individual and Society]*, 17, 115–132. Retrieved at https://revistas.ucm.es/index.php/ARIS/article/view/ARIS0505110117A/5810

González, M. (2012). "El teatro como estrategia didáctica". [*Theatre as an educational strategy*]. Actas del III Simposio internacional de didáctica de español para extranjeros del Instituto Cervantes de Argel 2012. [*Proceedings of the Third International Symposium on Spanish Education for Foreigners of the Algeria Cervantes Institute 2012*]. Khelifa Boukhalfa, Algeria: Instituto Cervantes de Argel. Retrieved at https://cvc.cervantes.es/ensenanza/biblioteca_ele/publicaciones_centros/PDF/argel_2012/04_gonzalez.pdf

Lagarde, M. (1996). *Género y feminismo. Desarrollo humano y democracia.* [*Gender and feminism: Human development and democracy*]. Madrid, Spain: Ed. horas y HORAS.

Lamas, M. (n.d.) La perspectiva de género. [The gender perspective]. *Revista de Educación y Cultura [Education and Culture Journal]*, Vol. 8 (January–March). Retrieved at www.ses.unam.mx/curso2007/pdf/genero_perspectiva.pdf

Latorre, A. (2005). *La investigación-acción.* [*Research-action*]. Barcelona, Spain: Editorial Graó.

Lederach, J.P. (2007) *La imaginación moral. El arte y el alma de la construcción de paz.* [*Moral imagination. The art and soul of peace construction*]. Bilbao, Spain: Editorial Gernika Gorgoratuz

LGIMH (2006). *Ley general para la igualdad entre mujeres y hombres.* [*General law for equality between women and men*]. Retrieved at http://www.diputados.gob.mx/LeyesBiblio/pdf/LGIMH_140618.pdf

Martínez, I., & Bonilla, A. (2000). *Sistema sexo/género, identidades y construcción de la subjetividad.* [*Sex/Gender System, Identities and Subjectivity Construction*]. Valencia, Spain: Universidad de Valencia.

McElwee, J., & Fox, C. L. (2020). Young people's perceptions of the 'Love Hurts' programme: Is theatre an effective means of addressing teenage relationship abuse? *British Educational Research Journal*, 46(5), 1026–1043. doi: 10.1002/berj.3611

Muñoz, F. (2001) La paz imperfecta ante el universo en conflicto. [Imperfect peace in the face of the universe in conflict]. In F. Muñoz (Ed.), *La paz imperfecta* [*Imperfect peace*] (pp. 1–36). Granada, Spain: Instituto de la Paz y los Conflictos [Institute of Peace and Conflict].

Ospina, D., & Ospina, C. (2017). Futuros posibles, el potencial creativo de niñas y niños para la construcción de paz [Possible futures, creative potential of girls and boys for the construction of peace]. *Revista Latinoamericana de Ciencias Sociales, Niñez y Juventud* [*Latin American Journal on Social Sciences, Childhood and Youth*], 15, 175–192. ISSN: 1692-715X. Retrieved at https://www.redalyc.org/articulo.oa?id=77349627011

Posso, P. et al. (2017). El teatro, una alternativa pedagógica para fomentar la cultura de paz en la IERD Andes. [Theatre: A pedagogic alternative to promote a culture of peace in the IERD Andes]. *Revista Ciudad Paz-ando* [*Peace-ing City Journal*], 10 (1), 68–81. Retrieved at doi:10.14483/2422278X.11695

Pradena, Y., & Anguita, N. (2020). Promoción de la igualdad de género a través del teatro en F.P. un estudio de casos. [Fostering gender equality through theatre in F.P. a case study]. In E. J. Díez, & Rodríguez J. R. (Eds.), *Educación para el Bien Común: Hacia una práctica crítica, inclusiva y comprometida socialmente* [*Education for the common good: Towards a critical, inclusive and socially committed practice*] (pp. 781–790). Barcelona, Spain: Ediciones OCTAEDRO, S.L.

Sedano-Solís, A. (2019). El teatro aplicado como campo interdisciplinario de investigación en los Estudios Teatrales. [Applied theatre as an interdisciplinary research field in theatrical studies]. *Artnodes*, 23, 104–113. UOC. Retrieved at doi:10.7238/a.v0i23.3260

Segato, R. L. (2017). *La guerra contra la mujer.* [*The war against women*]. Madrid, Spain: Traficantes de Sueños.

Serret, E. (2008). Qué es la perspectiva de género.? Qué es y para qué es la perspectiva de género? [What is gender perspective? What is gender perspective and what is it for?]. In I. J. Sierra & L. B. Ibarra (Eds.), *Perspectiva de género en educación superior* [*Gender perspective in higher education*] (pp. 15–59). Oaxaca, Mexico: Colección Instituto de la Mujer Oaxaqueña Ediciones. Retrieved at https://repository.icesi.edu.co/biblioteca_digital/bitstream/10906/87025/1/buchely_perspectivas_genero_2020.pdf

Taylor, D. (2012). *Performance.* Buenos Aires, Argentina: Asunto Impreso.

Trozzo E., & Sampedro, L. (2004). *Didáctica del Teatro I. Una didáctica para la enseñanza del Teatro.* [*Theatre didactics I: Didactics for theatre teaching*]. Mendoza, Argentina: Instituto Nacional del Teatro y Facultad de Artes y Diseño de UNCUYO.

Valdez-Medina, J. et al. (2005). Capítulo 3. Los roles sexuales en el México contemporáneo. [Chapter 3: Sexual roles in today's Mexico]. In J. L. Valdez-Medina, R. R. Díaz-Loving, & M. Pérez, *Los hombres y las mujeres en México: Dos mundos distantes y complementarios* [Men and women in Mexico: Two distant and complementary worlds] (pp. 45–59). Toluca, Mexico: Universidad Autónoma del Estado de México.

Yurén, T. (2005). Ethos y autoformación en los dispositivos de formación de docents [Ethos and self-education in teachers' training devices]. In T. Yurén, C. Navia, & C. Saenger, (Eds.), *Ethos y autoformación del docente. Análisis de dispositivos de formación de profesores* [Ethos and teacher self-education. An analysis of teachers' training devices] (pp. 19–45). Barcelona, Spain: Ediciones Pomares.

7 Theatre Arts in Peace Education

The Praxis at the Mindanao Peacebuilding Institute in the Philippines

Kyoko Okumoto, Babu Ayindo, and Dessa Quesada Palm

Introduction: The Genesis of Arts and Peacebuilding at the Mindanao Peacebuilding Institute

In reflecting on the praxis of theatre arts and peacebuilding, we trace the evolution and promise of the praxis of the Mindanao Peacebuilding Institute (MPI), based in Davao city, southern Philippines. The violent cycles of conflict in Mindanao, the second largest island in the Philippines, can be traced to colonial history. The Spaniards, the Americans, and the Japanese sought to establish settler colonialism in the archipelago through military means, land dispossession, and violent suppression of resistance. Unfortunately, the post-independence governments of the Philippines largely borrowed from the colonial handbook to quell the quest for self-determination by the Bangsamoro people and the Indigenous communities, which continues to date. Right from its inception in 2000, MPI recognized the central role of culture and theatre arts in peacebuilding. Reflections on this praxis over the last two decades illuminates how MPI functions as a crucible of diverse art forms, from multiple world regions, in enhancing a culture of peace and justice. This explorative chapter traces and reflects on the evolution and promise of this Mindanawan experience. The term, citizen, is used as Howard Zinn (2003) emphasizes in his discussion of the role of the artists in the war times that regardless of our discipline or professionalism, we are first and foremost, citizens. In our Mindanawan experience, citizen artists not only re-assert the fundamental and inalienable political rights for all humans but, more importantly, all humans must also reclaim their innate individual and collective creativity to re-imagine, transform and—to use Zinn's phraseology—"transcend" the chaos in their society (p. 7).

Myla Leguro and Deng Giguiento, who were part of the co-founding team of MPI, firmly believed that to break the cycles of decades of violent conflict and militarization in Mindanao and other parts of the world, peace training and education undertaken at MPI needed to be anchored and built on Indigenous cultures of peace. For the founders, it was "natural and organic" for the arts to be an integral part of the peacebuilding efforts in Mindanao. Therefore, peace education had to be an inclusive process undertaken through arts-based learning in formal and informal spaces of the institute. So, for the founders of MPI, the arts were

> not just as expression, but also a way of touching the heart of the people and using arts processes to engage people in very sensitive and heavy issues […] *we had learned that you can always gain entry into people's lives through arts.*
>
> (Ayindo, 2017, pp. 146–147)

Therefore, right from the inaugural MPI in 2000, the annual three-week training program offered various five-day courses that addressed needs and themes most relevant to the ongoing violent conflict and militarism in Mindanao. In all courses, the facilitators and trainers adopted an artful methodology in their teaching in the spirit, to use Leguro and Giguiento's words, "not just as expression, but also a way of touching the heart of the people and using arts processes to engage people in very sensitive and heavy issues […]" (Ayindo, 2017, p. 147).

In addition to adopting an artful pedagogy, MPI in its second year offered a course that intentionally explored theatre and other arts in peace education and peacebuilding. Borrowing from Marian Liebmann's 1996 book, *Arts Approaches to Conflict*, the inaugural arts-based course was entitled "Arts Approaches to Conflict" to reflect the conflictual nature of the Mindanao context at the time. In subsequent years, the course title was changed to "Arts Approaches to Peacebuilding" drawing from the mood and momentum for peacemaking and peacebuilding. After a few years, the title was revised to "Arts Approaches to Community-based Peacebuilding" to reflect the resurgence of grassroots peacebuilding in Mindanao and beyond. As we write, due to the COVID-19 pandemic, the course is now offered through a digital platform and is entitled "Arts Building Peace: Creative Approaches to Conflict Transformation." The changes in the title of the course, therefore, reflected the needs, challenges, opportunities and promise for peace in Mindanao, in South East Asia and, indeed, other parts of the world.

In 2002, Babu Ayindo, an artist and educator from Kenya, was tasked to lead the designing and facilitating of the first arts-based course. Working with two Filipino artists, Bert Monterona, a leading visual artist and Tony Apat, a veteran of Indigenous theatre arts in Mindanao, the facilitation team explored and experimented with diverse arts forms.[1] In subsequent years, Babu co-facilitated the course with Dessa Quesada Palm, a leading theatre educator from the Philippines and Kyoko Okumoto, a writer, educator, and citizen artist from Japan. In this chapter, these three artists and educators—Babu, Dessa, and Kyoko—trace their journeys and convergence at MPI and reflect on the praxis of theatre arts, peace education and peacebuilding over the last two decades. Four key questions guide our exploration and reflections:

1. How do we (re)define art and theatrical performance in light of the praxis of the Mindanao Peacebuilding Institute?
2. What are the key milestones over the two decades of offering the course and co-learning with diverse participants from all over the world?
3. Why do we use theatre arts in peace education?
4. From a Mindanawan perspective, what is the status of praxis in arts and peacebuilding?

In discussing these questions, we offer examples and case studies from our personal journeys and experiences as facilitators of the MPI course, and how our convergence shaped and reshaped the praxis. We shall also draw from the co-learning and co-creating processes and cultural products with a variety of participants from Philippines, South East Asia, and beyond.

We begin by (re)defining the key terms of art, theatre arts, applied theatre, peace education and peacebuilding from the context of our experiences, cognizant that other reflective practitioners have defined the terms in different ways.

Recasting Art, Theatre Arts, Applied Theatre, Peace Education, and Peacebuilding from the Mindanawan Experience

Since 2000, the fields of peacebuilding and arts-based peacebuilding have evolved significantly. Of note is that in the last decade numerous peacebuilding training courses, such as nonviolent direct action, conflict transformation, trauma healing, and restorative justice, now "use" the arts-based approaches at a variety of learning or simulated settings. On the other hand, even though artist-peacebuilders have been learning from much of the accumulated experiences in the fields of theatre, psychology, expressive and creative arts that improve citizens' quality of life—from individual to professional, and to relational—the theatre arts approaches to peacebuilding trainings remain heavily under-theorized. Therefore, the terms and definitions we propose in this chapter are the result of our own experiences and theorizing as trainers, facilitators, educators, and artists for more than 20 to 40 years at different settings, including universities, schools, other institutions, and communities.

The series of the arts courses at MPI defined "arts" in the manner Indigenous people do; that is, art as integral part of everyday life. In fact, in many Indigenous languages, there is no equivalent for the English word "art." Indigenous people encounter each other and nature through visual, performance and other arts. As Rama Mani (2011) notes, "art is a fundamental component of culture and a primary vehicle of cultural expression and transmission, including of religious belief and ritual practices" (p. 549). Therefore, for Indigenous peoples, the value of the arts in building a more peaceful and just world is encoded in their paintings, their handiwork, songs, dances, rituals, and performances, to mention a few (Ngũgĩ wa Thiong'o, 1981, 2003).

In the context of Mindanao, it was quite clear from the beginning of the course that "theatre" or "performance" is not restricted to what happens in a proscenium stage where the division between the performers and audience (or spectators) is clear or enforced. To build a culture of peace, and to "gain entry into people's lives through arts" as Leguro and Giguiento put it, the creative process of theatre—an amalgam of many other arts—had to be inclusive, participatory and anchored on the Boalian dictum that all humans are artists and, therefore, all humans have to "act" in the creative process as a preparation of "acting" to constructively transform society in real life (Ayindo, 2017, pp. 146–147; Boal, 1979, 1995).

It is in this spirit that we associate ourselves with Kirsten Broekman (2014) that "Applied theatre is a relatively recent label for a much older practice" (p. 19). In general, at the heart of applied theatre is the intentional effort to engage in creative processes that: (a) defy or exist outside the conventional modes of performance; (b) amplify democratic and participatory modes of cultural production; and (c) seek solutions to the fundamental problems of the human condition. In a sense, therefore, applied theatre shares key elements with arts-based peacebuilding work in Mindanao. However, as we shall show, the term, applied theatre, is not a sufficient conceptual vehicle for the diverse praxis of arts and peacebuilding at MPI.

The evidence of our experiences at MPI demonstrates that "peace education" and "peacebuilding" need to be defined in ways that are responsive to the local contexts and amplify local agency. In a context of violent conflict and a culture of militarism that permeates the entire society, peacebuilding is a process of affirming humans as makers of a culture of peace and justice. Peace education and peacebuilding then become processes of healing broken relationships, rebuilding social bonds, reclaiming agency and creativity, and reimagining a just world with thriving institutions and where violence is not the *modus operandi* of resolving conflicts. Peace education contributes to this process through formal and informal spaces and encounters where citizens reclaim their role as artists of their lives and their worlds.

We now trace the evolution of our praxis through the key milestones over the last two decades.

Milestones in the Praxis of Arts, Theatre Arts, and Peacebuilding: An Outline of the Four Phases at MPI

As mentioned in the introduction, the leadership of MPI at its inception was crystal clear on the need for a grassroots approach in building a culture of peace through creative processes that engage people in highly sensitive and emotionally heavy issues. The challenge was how we make that change happen within a five-day-course that brings artists, educators, cultural workers, and community animators, among others, from the Philippines and other parts of the world. In looking back, one can trace four contiguous phases in our praxis. We shall outline these phases in this section and then elaborate with examples and case studies in subsequent sections. The four phases are: (1) What works at the convergence of visual arts, theatre arts, and peacebuilding?;

(2) The "Peace Education Factor" and the influence of the Philippine community theatre; (3) Of dynamic peace and dynamic art; and (4) Reconnection, convergence, and the promise.

Phase One: What Works at the Convergence of Visual Arts, Theatre Arts, and Peacebuilding?

The first phase lasted between 2002 and approximately 2004. This was the phase of exploration, of experimenting, and of taking risks. The leadership of MPI created an environment where the facilitators had the space and freedom to explore "what works" within a context of conflict vulnerability and militarism. Facilitators, Bert Monterona, Tony Apat, and Babu Ayindo, drew from Indigenous arts, Augusto Boal's *Theatre of the Oppressed*, Paulo Freire's *Pedagogy of the Oppressed*, and Indigenous African storytelling performance to create a poetics of conflict and a poetics of peace. This pedagogical encounter included exploring key questions through visual and performance arts: (1) How would reconciliation look like for the diverse people of Mindanao? (2) In the context of Mindanao, are peace and justice complimentary or are they incompatible? (3) How does the artist–peacebuilder contribute to peacemaking and peacebuilding?

Three significant lessons emerged from this first phase, namely: the five days allocated for the course were not sufficient to undertake a creative and emotionally charged learning experience; to build peace through theatre arts or applied theatre required a combination of techniques of expression that sought to validate Indigenous traditions, cultures, and experiences; and intercultural learning and solidarity were essential in intentionally building peace through the arts and culture.

In seeking to answer these questions the trainers and participants developed two significant art pieces through a combination of visual arts and theatre arts. One was the logo currently being used by MPI and the other was a collaborative arts process that was built on John Paul Lederach's conceptual framework of reconciliation outlined in *Reconcile: Conflict Transformation for Ordinary Christians* (2014).

In producing the logo, the class of 2002, led by Bert Monterona, had to be sensitive to the conflict dynamics in Mindanao that involved fault lines amongst the Moro, the Indigenous Lumad and the Christian "settlers." This logo was a product of long hours of conversations and creative process that went beyond class hours to build consensus on what needs to be captured in imagination, in color and in words hence Kalinaw, Salam and Peace and the symbols of peace represented in the stars and colors of the dove (see Figure 7.1).

Like the MPI logo, the mural was developed first from performance. The participants worked in four groups to discuss what each element meant for them. In other words, from their perspectives and experiences, how were peace, justice, mercy, and truth supposed to look like? Thereafter, the

Figure 7.1 The logo of the Mindanao Peacebuilding Institute Foundation Incorporated.

participants "translated" their reflections into a character fully costumed. The creative process was symbolic of the conflict in Mindanao at the time. Subsequently, each of the four characters was required to interact with other characters through Image Theatre. Finally, Bert Monterona made a sketch of the drama and tasked the participants to work collaboratively to produce a mural of reconciliation.

Phase Two: The "Peace Education Factor" and the Influence of the Philippine Community Theatre

Dessa Quesada Palm joined the facilitation team at MPI in 2004 bringing rich experience from her work with the Philippine Educational Theatre Association (PETA). PETA had worked on issues of conflict and violence in Mindanao well before MPI. From 2004 onwards, the course at MPI was revised to provide a more structured content and facilitation plan while retaining the flexibility of drawing from diverse experiences of the participants who came from different parts of the world, including Zimbabwe, Kenya, the USA, and Canada.

Four significant lessons emerged during this phase: (1) the need to go beyond the "arts are powerful" mantra and clearly articulate how the arts in general and theatre arts in particular, contribute to social change; (2) the need for a theorization on what creative processes are possible in conflict settings and in peace settings (for example, could one do Forum Theatre in a situation of ongoing violent conflict?); (3) the need to ensure that aesthetics are never compromised in arts processes in the community; and (4) the need to build South–South solidarity in theatre arts and peacebuilding.

To strengthen South–South solidarity, Dessa also led a similar Arts Approaches to Peacebuilding course at the African Peacebuilding Institute (API) in Kitwe, Zambia, in 2005. During that same trip, she also conducted a series of workshops with Ubuntu Arts in Nairobi (Kenya), which confirmed the need for greater research and learning exchange in theatre arts and peacebuilding.

Phase Three: Of dynamic Peace and Dynamic Art

After a pause of several years, this phase occurred between 2012 and 2019. Kyoko Okumoto joined the facilitation team in 2012. Kyoko, one of the founders of the Northeast Asia Regional Peacebuilding Institute (NARPI) and its facilitator, already started exploring the arts-based approaches in Northeast Asian settings from 2011. This was a historically inevitable coincidence because then it became possible for NARPI to follow the path of MPI, with its organizing methods and facilitation know-hows.

At that time, MPI was also undergoing major restructuring in its leadership and formalizing itself as a credible peace resource organization in the Philippines and the world. Within the arts course, two challenges emerged. One was the drastic increase in the number of participants registering for the course. While the facilitation team found it easier to work with a class of about 15 participants, the numbers sometimes increased to nearly 30. Second, whereas MPI courses lasted three weeks, the arts course was usually offered in the second or third week. Over the years, most of the participants who registered for the arts course had already taken one or two foundational courses in peace education. So, the facilitators could safely assume that everyone had some background in peace education and peacebuilding and that the five days could focus on tackling and exploring creative approaches. However, it became apparent that more participants, even from outside Philippines, were only registering for the arts course in the second or third week without having completed the foundational courses.

Therefore, the framework on "Dynamic Peace and Dynamic Art" became an important reference point to level off (Okumoto, 2017). More crucially, the framework has an important theoretical platform in subsequent years to distil experiences from diverse settings. Table 7.1 is the outline of the framework and theorization of violence and peace as first used in 2013.

To examine the effectiveness of the arts-based approach in peacebuilding work and education/training, some forms of art are investigated utilizing peace studies concepts such as direct violence, structural violence, and cultural

Table 7.1 Direct/structural/cultural violence and peace and negative/positive peace

Violence		*Direct Violence (DV)*	*Structural Violence (SV)*	*Cultural Violence (CV)*
Peace		Direct Peace (DP)	Structural Peace (SP)	Cultural Peace (CP)
	Negative Peace (NP)	Absence of DV (ceasefire/a desert/cemetery)	Absence of SV (no exploitation/ no structure)	Absence of CV (no justification/ no culture)
	Positive Peace (PP)	Presence and building of DP (cooperation)	Presence and building of SP (equity/equality)	Presence and building of CP (culture of peace/ dialogue)
Peace		NP+PP	NP+PP	NP+PP

Galtung, J. Table 2.3. Peace: negative and positive, direct, structural, cultural (p. 31) in "Introduction: Peace by Peaceful Conflict Transformation—the Transcend Approach," *Handbook of Peace and Conflict Studies*. Eds. Charles P. Webel and Johan Galtung (Abington: Routledge, 2007, pp. 14–32), revised by Okumoto.

violence on the one hand and direct peace, structural peace, and cultural peace on the other. In fact, the art forms in relation to peace and violence can be classified into two groups: "art that promotes violence" and "art that creates peace." One art form developing from the latter group is labelled as "art that reveals and highlights conflict" or "dynamic art." Later in this chapter, we shall elaborate how the framework has been shaped and reshaped.

Phase Four: Reconnection, Convergence, and the Promise

This phase is still fresh. It began with the COVID-19 pandemic in 2020 and 2021. MPI tasked the facilitation team to develop an online version of the course. What began with doubts and skepticism has led to an important reunion and convergence of the three authors. Dessa re-joined the teaching team after several years. Entitled "Arts Building Peace: Creative Approaches to Transformation," the course has been restructured and offered twice in the autumn of 2020 and the spring of 2021. Participants meet for three hours a week over a period of 10 weeks.

Three lessons have emerged thus far: (1) the online course confirms the adage that the innate artist in all humans is best experienced during crisis (like the pandemic); (2) the digital space provides opportunities and promise in continuing creative work in peacebuilding; and (3) as Arudhati Roy (2020) says, the pandemic is a portal and humans must "break with their past and imagine their world anew." The learning and the cultural products of the online class show that humans have no option but to reimagine their world anew. This comes with challenges but there is promise.

In the following paragraphs we engage in-depth with our praxis through the questions: Why theatre arts in peace education? What are the elements in the theatre arts practice that contributed to peace education and peacebuilding in a context of violence and militarism? In engaging with these questions, we offer examples, anecdotes, and case studies from our course and from select alumni.

The Tapestry of Theatre Arts in Peace Education and Peacebuilding

In our view, the goal of peacebuilding work is to have peace workers as citizen artists/actors practice their creation of the value of peace. The process itself is the most essential, and peace work carries with it peaceful value. To teach this important concept, using a variety of arts methods in the peacebuilding facilitation and training is immensely helpful. Of all the art forms, theatre is most akin to real life. At its core is mimesis, a mirroring of realities that are lived by people in specific personal and social contexts. But it is also more than just a direct reflection of reality as an integral part of theatre is distilling experiences and making sense of life.

In dissecting, for instance, a play script, we are tasked to unravel the back stories and driving motivations and goals of characters. We are required to take stock of and draw from our own personal experiences and memories but also encouraged to step out of our shoes and to assume other characters without judgment but with an attitude of openness and understanding. These levels of reflection and spirit of openness are likewise valuable elements in creating peace.

Peacebuilding is hinged on opening spaces for deep conversation and courageous reflections that rekindle or enhance empathy. And theatre, by its nature and through intentional interventions, provides a dynamic platform for peacebuilders.

At the MPI arts courses, theatre arts praxis unfolds in the following ways:

1. As a form of awakening senses and intuitive capacities,
2. As a pedagogical tool for interrogating our performative acts,
3. As a dialogical process, and
4. As a celebration of our diverse cultures through storytelling,

How are the five-day in-person course and, most recently, the 10-week online course structured and delivered to attain these pedagogical goals? First, the theory component on work at the intersection of arts (including theatre arts) is explored through experiential learning, heavily borrowing from Freire (1997) and Boal (1979). Second, Johan Galtung's (1996) proposition that to transcend violent conflict, we need three elements, namely, creativity, empathy and nonviolence is also explored experimentally integrating Boal's techniques and Indigenous arts from Mindanao and African storytelling. Third, the participants spend a day working with reflective practitioners from Mindanao to critically appreciate the Mindanawan approach to creative conflict transformation. In the past decade, the course has worked with the Kaliwat

Theatre Collective led by Sheila Labos and Richard Vilar and Mindanao's leading visual artist Kublai Milan. The fourth and last part of the class is spent in developing individual and collective initiatives that are relevant in the participants' contexts.

The general pedagogical approach is described hereunder.

As a Form of Awakening Senses and Intuitive Capacities

Our senses are our immediate conduits that allow us to experience the world. One of the tragedies brought about by societies steeped in violent conflict and its accompanying cultures of violence is the infringement on personal and collective freedom to experience life with vigor and zest, and the denial of the right to be ensured of safety as people exercise their creative will and critical thinking. As a result of conditioned habits reined in by structures of social control, of trauma and fear, or of inadequate opportunities and spaces that nurture and value dialogue, independence and diversity, more people in militarized contexts are increasingly being denied of a chance to tap fully into their creative potential and to realize their human agency. Our bodies and voices are both receptors and expressive devices that manifest our conditions, values, and dispositions. That is why most of our participants come into class believing they are not artists. Our experience shows that work on transforming society will therefore have to integrate the agenda of freeing and rehearsing people's bodies, voices, and minds towards an alternative sense of themselves and vision of the world.

Warming up to individual and collective creativity is done as a ritual practice at the arts course, in a similar way to warm-up exercises during a theatre arts rehearsal. With face-to-face classes, sessions start with physical and voice warm-ups, and then some group games and improvisation to encourage spontaneity and develop collaboration. Interspersed with the various activities and discussions are response-style chants that any member can initiate to energize the group when the energy begins to wane.

Even as the course pivoted to an online platform, Zoom in particular, the warm-up exercises continued as well as improvisation. Zoom has largely constricted its users in a shoulder-to-face frame, and so there is a deliberate breaking of that frame by introducing exercises that allowed them to come closer for a tight shot of their faces, or to take several steps away so that they can see their half or full body, establishing variant distances in relation to the device's camera. Typically, physical classes are in large rooms where each one sits in a circle, often on the floor, allowing for all to better see everyone, and jump into various activities that are done individually, in pairs or in various-sized groups. This has become trickier in Zoom. As a way of creating a sense of connection especially during the first few classes, the "imagined circle" is established by passing a ball of peace, each one creating their unique gesture for the ball of peace and passing it to another member of the learning group who has not been called, until all names are called, and the circle is completed.

As a Pedagogical Tool for Interrogating Our Performative Acts

Theatre arts in this specific discussion pertains to the performative acts in a structured learning experience. The nature of the exercise has undergone changes through the years.

In its earlier versions, groups of five or six are formed. Instructions are given to participants of the class to write free-verse poetry with each group member contributing one line per round. Any member who feels inspired may initiate the starting line but will only get a second chance when everyone else has had their turn.

The finished written pieces are then passed on to another group for a creative interpretation. Everyone has a kick watching while the other group brings a refreshing twist to their works. The next round, each group is handed a paper with instructions by the facilitators to vandalize or shred into pieces the poems they received from the other group, and to return the poem in its tarnished or mutilated form.

Interestingly with this exercise, very few have come forward to ask why they had to comply. Even a lot less refused to join in executing the instructions. More often, groups would unquestioningly agree to the task and would even relish gleefully while smearing or tearing the other group's work. It is only in a few instances where a group refused to obey the instructions of the facilitators or used cunning ways to hide their artwork.

When the torn and vandalized pieces are returned to the original group that authored them, cold silence often follows. And then participants slowly recover and speak up. Receiving their original works beyond recognition evokes sadness and anger, since the act of destruction is regarded as a betrayal of a fundamental social contract hinged on trust.

It also leads to a discussion of the role of the instigator of this act of violence. In this case it is the facilitator, a symbolic representation of an authority figure. What did that mean for those who followed what was written in the instruction without any questions? Who are these figures in our own lives? In addition, what was the effect on certain individuals of peers who started, sometimes even cheerfully, to vandalize and tear up the pieces in encouraging others? Did complicity to the destructive act become more acceptable because others had initiated it, even if they had initially hesitated to take part in it?

The group is taken further into a reflection of their own narratives. What were their stories and narratives that have been vandalized, silenced, shredded into pieces, and rendered insignificant? A long list emanates, of historical injustices that do not enter history books, of Indigenous beliefs and cultural practices used pompously as tourist attractions, of struggles treated with complicity for silence. This leads to participants' realization of the importance of collective remembering, of documenting experiences, of continuing age-old traditions of telling and re-telling stories. And how the arts can contribute to this project of reclaiming people's stories, especially those that had been rendered unimportant or even invisible.

Another version of this exercise is "playing with colors," which requires participants to paint freely individually and eventually go through a process of collaboration in groups. Also, another example would be a collaboration activity called "Lukasa" with some craftwork using hands to create an artificial "community" on a large sheet of paper. According to the Metropolitan Museum of Art (n.d.), "Lukasa" is a concept from Luba culture in Democratic Republic of Congo. It means memory boards, which are hand-held wooden objects that present a conceptual map of fundamental aspects of Luba culture. Each board is designed and carved uniquely with shells and beads affixed to their surfaces. The wooden boards illustrate stories such as the political system, history, and territorial diagrams of local chiefdoms. The people of Luba use Lukasa as a tool for transmitting collective memory. The authors learned that there are inspiring experiments globally to apply this into the learning tool to creatively let workshop participants explore storytelling in a fictional form incorporating actual experiences of their own contexts. Some of them who happen to be shy in group discussions tend to be more talkative during the exercise by being immersed into the activity, which lets them use their creativity expressed through their hands. Then, artwork that is done by the participants goes through vandalism by the outer powers—practiced by the facilitator—and this inevitably leads the participants to experience emotional moments, just like what happens with "playing with colors." Also, at the final stage of the activity, some restorative activities are conducted in groups, such as putting the pieces together again, and re-creating a new artwork that includes new ideas of transformation and sense of togetherness.

Guide questions for the participants include:

1. How did it feel (at a personal level and group level) to see your artwork destroyed?
2. What lessons can we draw from this exercise on the role of the art/artist in building peace?

This destruction of the collective written piece or the artwork is a metaphor for lives and narratives affected by conflict. Events marred by violence brought by conflicts often radically disrupt people's sense of the familiar, replacing it with damaged worlds filled with discordance and chaos. The telling of stories, or constructing narratives, plays an important role in this circumstance. Lesley Fordred (1999) writes:

> Narrative is an essential cultural and social process for making sense of events, for reassuring us that our worlds are not out of control. By narrating events, we link a series of actions – whether by chronology, conspiracy, or psychological predispositions – into a comprehensible framework. In this way the violent event that has radically disrupted the flow of normality appears to have been predictable, and the moment of chaos that has challenged order is tamed

Nigerian writer Ben Okri (1997, p. 113) puts it more succinctly: "When we have made an experience or a chaos into a story, we have transformed it, made sense of it, transmuted experience, domesticated the chaos."

As a Dialogical Process

Boal applies Freire's "Pedagogy of the Oppressed" into theatre practice and offers an exciting perspective on theatre and political history. He chronicles the development of theatre, from pre-Christian aboriginal aesthetics where theatre is a communal celebration for and by the people, performed out in the open air, and where everyone freely participates. "And then came the aristocracy and established divisions: some persons will go to the stage and only they will be able to act; the rest will remain seated, receptive, passive – these will be the spectators…" (Boal, 1979, Foreword, p. ix). The structure of this new dramaturgy depends on its capacity to invoke empathy and catharsis, and the audience leaves the theatre feeling that they have lived the lives of the protagonists. Boal cautions us about this form, because successfully cutting off any dialectic, it leads to inertia and the withering of people's agency and subjectivity. Moving beyond object–recipient position and towards becoming an actor, Boal develops a theatre form where "the barrier between actors and spectators is destroyed: all must act, all must be protagonists in the necessary transformations of society." (Boal, 1979, Foreword, p. ix). The audience is now transformed into a *spect-actor*.

Forum Theatre (FT) is one of the most important forms that reflect this changed relationship in theatre. Dessa has used Forum Theatre in and out of the MPI course setting. Working with youth in various settings, they have used this participatory form in addressing issues such as bullying in schools, corporal punishment, and sexual harassment.

In one workshop Dessa facilitated with faculty, staff and a handful of high school participants, a short story is performed—a professor is obviously smitten with a student and asks her to stay after class. He discusses her dismal performance in class and her sub-standard required writings. The girl is distraught and asks if she could do anything to improve her grades. The teacher looks at her meaningfully and puts his hand on her lap. She cannot budge, somehow shocked, and can only venture to say, "Sir." The teacher makes his move and takes it further, slipping his hands onto her shoulders and proposes, "Meet me later at 7 p.m. at the parking lot." The student leaves the room disoriented and fidgety. She seeks one of her close friends in school, explains the situation to her and her current dilemma. The friend dissects each of the options. End of performance.

The group of spect-actors is informed that the whole scenario will be repeated. They are then invited to freeze the dramatic action at any point during the repeat performance, and to replace any of the actors onstage and proceed with the scene acting out their proposed action extemporaneously.

During the forum, three women each took turns in stopping the drama. The first was an elderly guidance counsellor who replaced the student.

When the teacher starts physically getting close, she squirms about to dodge the advances of the teacher, but still smiling impishly while sweetly saying, "sir, sir…". The second intervention came from a student of social work, who calmly puts away the teacher's hand and firmly says, "No, sir. Don't do this, sir." But the one who garnered the most robust applause was a high school student whose solution was to punch the teacher smack on his nose while screaming in protest, "SIR!"

And then there is a variation that had been tried out for several years at the MPI arts course, a sort of Forum Theatre with a twist. Instead of playing out the scene in dramatic action, Babu and Dessa enact the scene in sound-drama. The spect-actors assume the role of a bystander, a neighbor who can hear the goings-on from another household. They are asked to close their eyes and imagine that it is late at night, and they are trying to get some sleep.

Babu and Dessa as the neighbors improvise the scene with a basic plot. They play a married couple who have a sick child. It is late at night, Husband arrives drunk and demands food from Wife, who in turn laments that he has not left any money for her to buy food and other supplies. Husband gets more agitated and raises his voice. Wife tries to hush him, explaining about their child who is sick and will be awakened by the ruckus. But he becomes even more incensed, and the argument intensifies until Husband begins to physically (through sound) abuse and disempowers Wife.

Many people can relate to the experience, as someone's neighbor, of hearing but not seeing domestic violence erupting in people's homes. Without seeing, the imagination works even more powerfully. After the sound-drama, a facilitator (hopefully a third one who did not perform in the drama) presents three prototypes of neighbors and what they will do to respond to the abusive situation:

1. Neighbor 1 hears the whole even unfold, expresses concern, and decides to sleep it off and check on what happened the following day;
2. Neighbor 2 calls the barangay (village) captain, reports the incident, and prays that something will be done to remedy the situation;
3. Neighbor 3 goes out of the way to mobilize a few friends and enter the house and stop the husband/father.

Each participant chooses one of the options closest to their likely reaction. Those with shared responses meet in groups, discussing why and how they would have done it. A summary of their reasons is shared to the big group and an enthusiastic discussion or debate about strategies ensues. Alternately, each group performs their scenarios, and the proposed solutions are then tested using Forum Theatre.

As a Celebration of Our Diverse Cultures through Storytelling

"Boomalaka boom!" Babu exclaims.
"Chingalaka ching!" the chorus explodes in response.

In the MPI arts course, Babu is the chief storyteller, and he would begin with memories of his childhood in his grandmother's village where all children gather around the matriarch to listen as she regales them with her stories. And then he begins,

> Long time ago, when the earth was still young, all the animals in the forest of Hope would gather every evening to celebrate who they were and who they were not. And, so it was for many years till one evening, during the season of the red sun when Yordit, the Kind Lion, suddenly changed the tradition. Well, usually the Lion came late—this was his idea of showing his power—but no one really cared. But on this occasion, not only did he come late but also demanded, in a thunderous roar, that one of the animals prepare him breakfast. This had never happened in this history of the forest of Hope. The Lion ordered antelope to prepare him breakfast. But when antelope consulted with the rest of the animals who had now stopped celebrating, they responded in a manner never witnessed in the forest. "Well," they said, "he is the King and we do not know why he chose you."

The story goes on to chronicle the daily demands that Yordit, the Lion in the Dinka language of the people of South Sudan, imposed on the animal community—breakfast consisting of different species every day—the antelope, giraffe and a few more. It also described the pattern of indifference displayed by other animals who have not been called to satisfy the Lion's palate. And then it was Ma'rabbit's turn, with Yordit ordering her to cook all her nine children because they were too small.

Ma-rabbit is smart, and plots to subvert Yordit's intentions by playing on the Lion's vanity. Yordit falls for it, and ends up jumping into the river, unable to swim. He realizes he could drown, and he screams for help as the animals congregate on the riverbank to decide on the Lion's fate.

The storytelling ends with a cliff-hanger, and in a mischievous tone, and Babu reveals that he has nodded off to sleep before he could hear how the story ended. It is at this point when he invites the participants to discuss in small groups how they wish to end the story from the perspective of all the animals who hold in their hands the fate of the tyrannical lion. The groups are urged to perform their endings during face-to-face classes.

Invariably, various themes emerge from the endings, but always the situation presents difficult dilemmas for participants. The four themes that intersect in the model of reconciliation that Lederach postulates—truth, justice, peace, and mercy—begin to take various forms of expression and value for each group and even individually. The additional layer of applying the story to specific contexts where despotic leaders rule or where militarized states control the country accounts for difficult questions to emerge and to be grappled with.

Interestingly, when this story is (re)told often participants would remember similar stories in their own cultures. Indigenous cultures are filled with folk tales and allegories that allude to human characters and relationships.

When peacebuilders can harness these stories and allow communities to make their own interpretations and create their narratives out of an existing story, it also reveals their own intrinsic values and biases that become important in self-awareness and collective dialogues.

Most traditional cultures will have some form of storytelling. It is one form of drama that had existed way before the proscenium theatre was invented. Telling stories has been an integral expression of community life. It is where collective memories reside and are preserved, where lessons are taught, where values are upheld, and where hopes are spun and held together.

Boomalaka boom!

Revisiting Dynamic Peace and Dynamic Art: The Status of Praxis from a Mindanawan Perspective[2]

Having looked at these examples, anecdotes and case studies, we now return to the status of our theory about arts, theatre arts, and peacebuilding. In so doing we shall reflect on how the dynamic peace and dynamic art framework has been shaped and reshaped over the years.

Conflict and Conflict Transformation

In addition to definitions of peace and violence mentioned earlier (see Table 7.1), a definition of conflict is also crucial in peace education and peacebuilding work. Conflict occurs when each actor/party possesses its goal(s) and acts on it (them), but there is incompatibility or contradiction between/among those goals. Conflict is a natural phenomenon, and can be an opportunity to transform the society that actors/parties live in. Conflict can be at the micro (individual) level, mezzo (societal) level, macro (national/international) level and mega (regional/ideological, etc.) level (Table 7.2).

Table 7.2 Art, direct/structural/cultural violence and peace and negative/positive peace

Art that promotes violence	Direct Violence (DV)	Structural Violence (SV)	Cultural Violence (CV)
Art that creates peace	Direct Peace (DP)	Structural Peace (SP)	Cultural Peace (CP)
Negative Peace (NP)	Absence of DV	Absence of SV	Absence of CV
Positive Peace (PP)	Presence and building of DP	Presence and building of SP	Presence and building of CP
Peace	NP+PP	NP+PP	NP+PP

A rearranged version of Table 7.1 (D/S/C Violence and Peace and N/P Peace), revised by Okumoto.

The reason why looking closely at conflict is essential here is that the category, "art that creates peace," as referred above, embraces "art that reveals and highlights conflict" as explained now. Conflict is dynamic and organic because it always changes, and its change processes can affect society and its people either positively or negatively. When conflict impacts on people positively, they learn how to create something constructive and start transforming society for the better. When it negatively affects society, people may victimize each other in various ways.

Therefore, the key is to learn how to use conflict wisely—by peaceful means. Conflict transformation is such an important tool for people to learn to live peacefully together. In this way, society would be able to reduce violence and increase peaceful elements. Art can be used in the change processes of conflict transformation. This chapter frames this kind of art as "art that reveals and highlights conflict." Its purposes are:

1. To reveal and highlight the essence of conflict,
2. To make covert conflict overt,
3. To play a role in making people realize its existence, and
4. To create within the audience the attitude and behavior for conflict transformation, when a peaceful spirit works along with a critical mind, and when creativity and dialogue emerge freely.

Art has an impact on society and human beings in mainly two ways: one is direct, and the other is indirect. Direct influence is practiced by direct/structural components of art. Art that is a cultural phenomenon as direct/structural peace/violence directly affect people. Indirect impact is achieved through the cultural aspects of art. Art that is a cultural phenomenon as cultural violence/peace justifies direct/structural violence/peace, that affects people indirectly.

Dynamism of Conflict and Peace

In relation to what is explained above, the concept of "dynamic peace" is crucial. Conflict is dynamic. Traditionally, peace has been regarded as static. Static peace was the image people kept in their mind and society presumed it as an expected form. However, in reality, peace does not always maintain such a form, and it appears as dynamic as well because peace embraces conflict transformation, in other words, change processes of conflict/peace work.

To understand the concept of peace within the context of action (peace work), the authors propose a new definition, "dynamic peace," as opposed to "static peace." With this definition, people can grasp the meaning of peace in a more realistic way.

Dynamic peace is based on two concepts: process and direction. Dynamic peace embraces the process ("where" and "when") and direction ("who" and "what") of peace/conflict work. Dynamic peace involves the process and requires a "place," and it corresponds to both time and space. Process is essential in conflict transformation and peace work because both need to be dynamic in their movement. The concept of direction highlights society's questioning of the value of peace. It also needs actors and their actions for conflict transformation. These concepts broaden the concept of peace and encourage society and its citizens to seriously question what is required for their lives—conflict transformation. Therefore, as a result, the concept of conflict makes us realize that peace is dynamic in its nature rather than simply static.

In this way, peace that includes the process and direction of conflict transformation becomes regarded as naturally dynamic. This study is based on the importance of a "peaceful spirit" that is accompanied by a "critical mind," in addition to the "actors" who play the role of dynamic peace workers. This new perspective transforms traditionally defined peace (static peace) into the new concept of dynamic peace.

Dynamism of Art

Art is dynamic as well (otherwise, art may not be art in its essential form and becomes "dead"). Therefore, dynamic peace can be achieved by the arts-based approach in peace work, especially by "dynamic art." This is one of the approaches on "how" to transform conflict after all. With this new definition, this chapter proposes a practical approach to peace work using the arts. Process liberates peace, and direction demands that we question our values continuously. Within this approach, dynamic art can also be defined as "art that reveals and highlights conflict."

Additionally, "why" do we need the arts-based approach in peace work? It is simply because society desperately needs conflict transformation. What is important is not theoretical categories themselves but the process of categorization where people get together and critically examine which category the particular artwork belongs to.

Also, people can work together to figure out how to change the world they live in. They might be able to figure out how to apply the arts-based approach. Some might use it in such a way that they heal the trauma of the past war/direct violence. Some might use it as a powerful tool of resistance by performing to highlight the problem. Some might build bridges between/among the international community and the oppressed and voiceless.

Citizen Artists and Citizen Actors

The arts-based approach is enriched by creative dialogue, and its actors become peace workers who are in essence "citizen artists." Essential elements used for peace are: (1) peaceful spirit and critical mind, (2) expressiveness of art and communicativeness of art, and (3) creativity and dialogue in peace work. When all these elements work together organically, the arts-based approach reveals and highlights conflict, functioning fully and successfully as peace work. The actors, "peace workers," then become citizen artists, or one can call them "citizen actors" as Jonathan Fox (1986) did.

A citizen who lives as an artist maintains freedom, a window for dialogue, when a peaceful spirit resides in a critical mind. This artist becomes a citizen artist/actor by getting involved in art that reveals/highlights conflict, and lives with the spirit/mentality. Then, the citizen artist becomes the subject of peace work, and transforms the society.

The goal of peace work is to have peace workers as citizen artists/actors practice their creation of the value of peace. This is always an unfinished process. Furthermore, it should be emphasized again that the process itself is the most essential. In this process, peace work carries with it peaceful value. In other words, peace work is not only a means to achieve peace, but also *is* peace.

Over the years, we have retained a dense network with our alumni and our continuing conversations indicate that majority continue to function as citizen artists. For example, In Sierra Leone, Charlie Haffner who attended MPI in 2014, serves as Founder Director General at Freetong Players International and works with a variety of artists in training and community work in engaging with the urgent needs and challenges of a post-conflict society. Hazy Aspera from Mindanao, another 2014 participant, is a medical student who combines her visual arts and writing in creative communication on issues of health and peacebuilding. In 2015, Julius Nzang from Cameroon, a radio journalist, and radio drama writer and director attended MPI. He values empathy embedded in poetry-writing, reflecting personal, collective, and community lives to bridge people. Saw Phoe Kwar, a musician from Myanmar, attended MPI in 2016. For him MPI was an affirmation of his mission as a citizen artist in Myanmar. Even during the turbulent times, he continued mobilizing young people for peace through his reggae music. Anas Younes from Syria participated with MPI in 2019. He uses puppetry in theatre arts for youth empowerment in Syria, Lebanon, and other parts of the world. Adriana Anjani from a 2021 online course works in a civil society organization based in Indonesia that produces and uses board games, videos, and podcasts that promote peacebuilding through social media by mobilizing the young generation in a creative way. Therefore, at all levels of transformation, the work of majority of our alumni indicates the yearning for freedom, an amplification of dialogue, and a praxis that retains peace as a value orientation. Again, this is always an unfinished process.

One of our alumni in 2020, Diptarup (Dipto) Chowdhury, a clinical psychologist and a narrative therapist from India best captures this spirit of a citizen artist:

> Resisting single hegemonizing stories and creating newer possibilities of more preferred future was something I was already familiar …. However, my mostly one-to-one client work within the four walls of clinic always left a gap in me in fully understanding how resistance gets played out in larger canvas of community/society in creating a more peaceful and

harmonious and humane world. The course... introduced to me multiple creative sites where resistance is planned and creatively played out using various media of arts.

However, resisting to power could often be tiring and a lonely process.... I had started working more and more with groups of like-minded people, youth and have always been on the look-out for a community of solidarity. The course introduced me to the 'co-creative power' of arts practiced by citizen artists. Not only was use of arts transformative by breaking walls of injustice and dehumanization, but also its ability to foster community of solidarity showed me its healing power by building bridges. Thus, during one of the most tumultuous phases of my life (and our lives) during pandemic, the course acted as a lighthouse to me, a ray of hope amidst all the hopelessness around! MPI-ABP provided me a new language and made my and my team's voice louder.[3]

For Dipto, realizing the organism between resistance and connection was critical. This realization also points to the possibilities for the years to come in the praxis of arts-based peacebuilding.

In Lieu of a Conclusion

In a sense, this chapter is a recharging pit stop in the long journey of arts-based peacebuilding. This journey is a convergence of not only three writers but also many other people with whom we have interacted within and outside MPI. The question remains: what are the possibilities for arts-based peacebuilding in the years to come, as well as now while humanity struggles with the effects of the COVID-19 pandemic?

Research and practice have brought us to an important point. Very few would doubt why the arts are critical in the building of peaceful and just communities. As we have shown, it is primarily through the arts that individuals and communities reclaim their agency and creativity as makers of culture and rebuild social bonds necessary to confront the challenges of our time.

In terms of theory and practice, MPI has functioned as an important crucible, creating space and opportunity for citizen artists from all over the world, to reclaim their agency, affirm the innate artists, test ideas, and engage in the aesthetics of peace. Again, this is an unfinished process. Nothing is finally settled, there can be no conclusion. The praxis has to continue. At this juncture, we recall the words of Fr. Rudolfo 'Dong' Galenzoga who was a peacebuilder, interfaith dialogue icon, and Mindanao theatre pioneer:

> All peacebuilders are artists because they are dreaming and working for a new world [...] I do not mean the elitist artist, but artists grounded on the actual realities [...] all peacebuilders can call themselves artists and all artists can call themselves peacebuilders.[4]

Notes

1 Melindi Banas-Malang from the Philippines met Babu at the Summer Peacebuilding Institute (SPI) at Eastern Mennonite University in the USA in 2001. Melindi was Babu's student in an Arts-Based Peacebuilding course at SPI. It is Melindi who proposed to MPI that Babu lead the MPI course.
2 This section is a revision of the theoretical framework used in Okumoto (2017).
3 Chowdhury, D. email communication. July 12, 2021.
4 Cited in Ayindo (2017, p. 126).

References

Ayindo, B. (2017). *Arts, peacebuilding and decolonization: A comparative study of Parihaka, Mindanao and Nairobi*. Unpublished doctoral dissertation. New Zealand: University of Otago.
Boal, A. (1979). *Theatre of the oppressed*. London: Pluto.
Boal, A. (1995). *The rainbow of desire: The Boal method of theatre and therapy*. London: Routledge.
Broekman, K. (2014) *The meaning of aesthetics within the field of applied theatre in development settings*. Unpublished doctoral dissertation. United Kingdom: University of Manchester.
Fordred, L. (1999). Taming chaos: The dynamics of narrative and conflict. *Track Two*, 8(1). Retrieved at https://journals.co.za/doi/pdf/10.10520/EJC111761
Fox, J. (1986). *Acts of service: Spontaneity, commitment, tradition in the nonscripted theatre*, New Palz, NY: Tusitala.
Freire, P. (1997) *Pedagogy of the oppressed*. London: Continuum.
Galtung, J. (1996). *Peace by peaceful means: Peace and conflict, development and civilization*. Oslo: Sage
Lederach, J. P. (2014). *Reconcile: Conflict transformation for ordinary Christians*. Harrisonburg, VA: Herald Press.
Mani, R. (2011). Women, art and post-conflict justice. *International Criminal Law Review*, 11, 543–560. Retrieved at doi:10.1163/157181211X576410
Okri, B. (1997). *A way of being free*. London: Phoenix.
Okumoto, K. (2017, May 8). *The arts-based approach in peace work: Dynamic peace and dynamic art*. TRANSCEND Media Service. Retrieved at www.transcend.org/tms/2017/05/the-arts-based-approach-in-peace-work-dynamic-peace-and-dynamic-art-2016/
Roy, A. (2020, April 4). The pandemic is a portal. *Financial Times*. Retrieved at www.ft.com/content/10d8f5e8-74eb-11ea-95fe-fcd274e920ca
The Metropolitan Museum of Art. (n.d.). *Memory Board (Lukasa) 19th–20th century*. The Met. Retrieved at www.metmuseum.org/art/collection/search/690570
Thiong'o, Ngũgĩ wa. (1981). *Decolonizing the mind: The politics of language in African Literature*. Nairobi: East African Educational Publishers.
Thiong'o, Ngũgĩ wa (2003). *Penpoints, gunpoints and dreams: Towards a critical theory of arts and the state in Africa*. Oxford: Oxford University.
Zinn, H. (2003). *Artists in times of war*. New York: Seven Stories Press.

8 Storytelling in Burundi

Traditional and Theatrical Education to Support Peacebuilding

William M. Timpson, Fulgence Twizerimana, and Godelieve Nisengwe

In this chapter we look at the potential for an innovative Peace English Club to utilize aspects of storytelling to help Burundi, a nation intent on recovering from the racism ("tribalism") imposed by colonial powers, entrenched poverty, 40 years of civil war, and past threats to democratic rule. We include a personal account of danger, violence, survival, resilience, and more as a young Burundian teacher shares his own story and then connects it to his current passion for peacebuilding education. Real "drama" is often at the heart of serious entertainment and applied theatre. We believe that the skills of dramatic storytelling and theatrical performance can help engage learners of all ages to understand more about sustainable peacebuilding in the context of the cases of conflict about which they learn. We recognize that this is uncommon in formal school curricula but so very promising for the future of learners who have experienced violence, like many Burundians.

Fulgence's Story

The story of Peace English Clubs in the City of Ngozi is a personal story; it is a reflection of his childhood experiences and motivation for peacebuilding instruction. Fulgence writes: *My life is subdivided in three important chapters, three contradictory chapters. I was born in 1986 in a cool, modest and peaceful upcountry area called Nkanda in Burundi. My father was a soldier and my mother a peasant. People were poor but could satisfy their basic needs for food, clothing, and basic health care. They could attend their lands, grow different crops that they sold, and get the money they needed. In general, they lived a very cooperative lifestyle, helping each other with their farming and often sharing their crops, what they referred to as 'Ukugemura or 'carrying a gift to' to someone else."*

I remember our family receiving much from neighbors and people I didn't even know who lived on our hill; bunches of ripe bananas, baskets of tomatoes, and more. In turn, they went back home with baskets of potatoes, beans, peas or nuts from my mother. My father was often absent because of his military service. On other days, my mother visited different families with these kinds of 'gifts'.

DOI: 10.4324/9781003227380-8

When we held large group parties, people mobilized themselves and contributed food, beer and more. A household's party became the whole hill party. Everybody participated and contributed. When my father came back home for his days off every six months, he carried packages of bread and children's clothes that he distributed to neighbors. On the weekends, he passed most of his time training a local church choir with new gospel songs that he had learned as he was himself a fervent Catholic.

In 1992, one year before the 1993 election and the assassination of the newly elected president of Burundi, things started changing. I no longer saw people visiting our family. For the first time I heard about the 'Hutu" and 'Tutsi' ethnic groups. During the subsequent political campaigns, the situation worsened. Two political parties were vying to win the election. We were told that there was one party for Hutu and another party for Tutsi. This period was the start of the second chapter of my life.

In November 1993, the elected president was assassinated launching the beginning of bloodshed throughout the whole country. It was said that the president was killed by a group of soldiers and that made the soldiers' families targets for murder. Many soldiers' families perished. The wives, children, and relatives as well as other Tutsis died. My family was also targeted. But some neighbors, including Hutus protected us and helped us to escape.

I remember one evening when a woman secretly came to alert my mother about a group of men who were planning to pay us a "friendly" visit that night. She told my mother not to open the door. She had heard her husband and other men planning our murder. Later that night the group did come by, telling my mother through the window that they were patrolling. They then asked her some water to drink. My mother said there was not any water in the house. They insisted but finally left.

Eventually our neighbors helped us join a nearby refugee camp before we were able to join a military camp in the city of Bujumbura where my father worked. It was there that we met other families who had also escaped threats to their lives. However, life in the military camp was not easy at all. Although we were safe and protected, there was a negative climate and everyone could feel it. Many soldiers had their families killed and we heard that they were eager to get revenge by killing local populations. In the camp we also had orphans whose mothers or brothers and sisters had been killed, as well as mothers whose children had been killed. Everyone was heartbroken. Sorrow was everywhere and everybody could feel their pain.

As the conflict and violence went on, many soldiers perished leaving their families alone in the camp. I remember our mums gathering in different homes to comfort one mother who had just heard that her husband had died on the battlefield. I remember the children we used to play with coming together and crying. I remember military trucks coming back into camp with much blood inside because they had been ambushed by rebels while taking soldiers to battle, carrying the wounded to safety or transporting the dead.

Many soldiers also committed suicide. I remember once when it was announced that an entire family had been killed in a rebel attack. This soldier's family lived in the countryside. He was working in a military office where there were many guns. He took one and started to shoot through the window. Other soldiers asked him to stop shooting. He said he only wanted to see his wife and children. Eventually, he shot himself.

But my biggest memory in the military camp is Michel, one of my best friends. We always used to play together. One day his father came back from the battlefield. Michel's mother told her husband all the problems that her son had committed. The father punished his child so severely, beating him with a long stick before tying his hands behind his back with a cord. But this father made a big mistake. He left his Kalashnikov in the bedroom where Michel was attached. My friend took that gun, removed the safety, put his throat on the barrel and pressed the trigger. There was a huge explosion and we were told later that his skull had been exploded. The whole camp was terribly shocked.

The third chapter of my life started in 1998 when my father decided that we should leave that military camp to join an internal camp for refugees in my native area. These camps existed in many places in Burundi and they were protected by military personnel. Everything had changed, however, and we had trouble integrating ourselves. Makeshift houses were scattered all over the hills which before had been dominated by the bush with large eucalyptus trees. All this vegetation had been cleared for the small houses where families now lived.

Although the war continued in most corners of the country, my province was relatively calm and that allowed refugees to reach and cultivate their lands. Some felt lucky because their lands were close to the refugee camp. My family did not have that good fortune. We had to walk two hours to reach our fields and another two hours to come back home. My mother made this journey four times a week. In addition, my father spent six or seven hours working with a hoe in the fields and then had to carry a basket of food or a pile of firewood when he came back home. This was also the life of many other refugees including kids, adults, the young and the elderly. In those years my life was made up with this farming, other housework as well as my studies. However, in 2004 I went off to a boarding school and then to the University in 2008, a chance that many of my friends did not have.

In general, my life resembled the lives of many other Burundians who experienced much conflict and trauma during childhood. In truth, they spent most of their lives fearing for themselves and their families. I now realize that when you have experienced this kind of life, you had two alternatives: you could try to heal the wounds of the past and move forward as an individual or heal those wounds, move forward but then contribute to ensure that what happened does not happen again. I chose the second path.

Storytelling Literacy

Because this story has so many references to trauma, we believe that the performing arts, with skills and principles of storytelling, in particular, provides crucial communication in getting others to engage, learn and tell their stories as a means of restoration. We also expect that in teaching the fundamentals of peacebuilding, those who can engage through storytelling will be able to advance harm-free ways forward through global as well as local challenges.

Whenever people face the big issues of war and peace, violence, and reconciliation, they may need to step outside of what's conventional to get noticed and be heard. The theatre has long been a source of inspiration for engaging audiences and telling stories in compelling ways. In *Teaching and Performing*, Timpson and Burgoyne (2002) describe the many ways that instructors in every discipline and every level can use "lessons from the stage" to energize their teaching and stimulate a deeper learning. Over the past 30 years, trends in higher education point toward the use of approaches that actively engage students and challenge them to think more critically and creatively, including the use of case studies as is common in professional schools of law and business (see Davis, 1993; Eble, 1988; Johnson, Johnson and Smith, 1991; Johnson and Johnson, 1998; Lowman, 1994; McKeachie, 2002; Ramsden, 1992; Timpson & Doe, 2008; Timpson & Holman, 2011; Timpson & Holman, 2014).

The model for this work is Paulo Freire's (1970) national literacy campaigns that had such profound success in Brazil, Cuba, and Nicaragua when the curriculum was refocused from simple innocuous stories targeted at different reading levels to materials that spoke directly to improving the lives of those wanting to learn to read and write. These highly relevant materials proved deeply motivating and defied the logic of needing to start with the simplest of words.

What was also common to these successful literacy campaigns was their use of small groups and peer interactions, not the hierarchical classroom model that had been the norm with the teacher in front directing instruction. Defying conventional thinking and the prevailing paradigms of educational researchers, Freire was going for something deep, a motivation to improve the lives of the illiterate once they understand how to read about their own realities. In nations ruled by autocrats and dictators, this approach proved so successful that it threatened the ruling elite with newly aroused populations of poor people wanting to change the entire system and make it more fair for everyone.

Although Freire was exiled from his native Brazil when the powerful heard the tremors of the disaffected from below, revolutionaries in Cuba and Nicaragua saw in this model a valuable tool in their efforts to unseat those in power. Instead of vacuous, simplistic primers for learning language, Freire's model put meaningful material into the hands of small groups. Anyone who could reads could become a "teacher" and help others use these materials to better understand why they were poor and what they could do to improve their lives. Again, performance skills could do more to prepare these small group leaders than a formal teacher training curriculum could accomplish. In Burundi, our focus on the understanding of the peace process—i.e., peacekeeping, peacemaking, and peacebuilding—will serve to strengthen the nation with new ideas and skills for improved communication and cooperation, negotiation and mediation, critical and creative thinking.

Teaching Peace with a Common Language

Burundi is a landlocked country that mainly depends on its neighboring countries' cooperation: Tanzania, Uganda, Rwanda, Kenya, Democratic Republic of Congo, and South Sudan. Those countries are linked by the same destiny as they share the same regional (Great Lakes) and historical background.

Benefiting from each other will be much more possible if these countries can communicate by means of the same language. Four of these countries now linked in the East African Federation use English as a second language. The only exception is the Democratic Republic of the Congo, which was colonized by Belgium and teaches French in its schools.

The native language of Burundi is Kirundi but the language taught in schools is French, an imposed requirement from the German and Belgian colonizers. Yet in East Africa, colonized by Britain, the language that is taught in schools is English. Burundi is a charter member of the East African Federation, which was founded in 2000 at the time of the Arusha Peace Agreement that ended some 40 years of civil war. After years of colonization, violence, disruptions, and poverty, Burundi also has much to teach others about resilience and peacebuilding.

In his 2018 thesis, *The Effect of Conversational Practice on the Development of Speaking Skills in Basic School*, Twizerimana Fulgence (2018) states some of the reasons that motivated him to focus on the need to learn and teach English in Burundi:

> (1) Burundi is a member of the East African community and other international organizations such as the UN, COMESA, AU, etc. (2) Most countries of the region and most member countries of such organizations which Burundi has close links are English speaking countries. (3) Development in Education, business, technology, communication and sciences require abilities to express oneself and to communicate in English. (4) Many international, regional and national job opportunities require some knowledge of that language.
>
> (p. 4)

Brumfit (1982) further supports these ideas when he argues that possession of any language leads us to communicate with various groups as we all become more interconnected through business, improved communication, sharing medical science or political concerns or cultural exchanges. A common language can enable people to influence their futures and this impact should only increase.

Along with the benefits of a common language, the word "peace" is familiar with Burundians both culturally and historically as it is one of the most used words every day. In fact, the most frequent greeting is "*Gira amahoro!*" or "*Amahoro!*" ("Have peace"; "Peace!"). Unfortunately, this "peace" has been weakened over many years by ethnic, regional, and political conflicts and ideologies as well as by the stresses of poverty, in general. We believe that peace is a subject that should be taught in schools everywhere, but especially considering this past in Burundi. Unfortunately, this small nation does not currently have an institute or center to promote the culture of peace through research and studies.

That said, it is our hope that the University of Ngozi, founded in 1999 at the end of the civil war and just before the signing of the Arusha Peace Accords, could come to play this role. In their book Timpson, Ndura, and Bangayimbaga (2015) posit that with a commitment to peace and reconciliation, this university is uniquely situated to be a laboratory for promoting an education in peacebuilding. And hopefully, this can be extended to every student in every program, an education for a new kind of citizen for challenging times in Burundi and the world. Importantly, without a formal teacher education program, the performing arts become that much more important for embedding aspects of peace studies across the various disciplines and programs.

These histories and realities in Burundi parallel what has been true in many other countries. What can be accomplished in Burundi should help people in other war-torn countries build better relationships among their citizens and with their neighboring countries using traditional communication, a common language, and principles of peacebuilding.

Uniting Communities

In the summer of 2013, Twizerimana Fulgence was hired for two months by an organization called East Africa Community Language Learning (EACLL) as an English trainer in the Kayanza province, which is located in the northern. region of Burundi. His mission was to train local people—the impoverished, businessmen and women, civil servants, taxi-bike drivers, etc. EACLL had decided that anyone who wanted to learn English could attend regardless of their level of proficiency. There was even one class of learners who could neither read nor write. It was surprising how excited they were and how fast they learned. Fulgence reports that after just one month, there were testimonies like this one:

> Do you know, teacher, last weekend I went to Uganda for business affairs. I hired a translator as usual, but now, I was able to get many words between him and my suppliers and sometimes express my needs myself. Thank you.

Classrooms were always full and some were obliged to follow lessons from outside through windows. Links and partnerships were created among these participants since many of them were business and craftsmen. Fulgence could read on their faces their strong interest, their growing friendships, and their commitment to these studies. English became more than a subject to learn; it become a language that united this new community of learners across different ethnic groups, a founding goal of peacebuilding. After the class, some taxi-bike drivers went so far as to transport their classmates for free, never asking for money.

Peace English Clubs

Fulgence observes that communication together in a Peace English Club (PEC) can play a similar role promoting peace and reconciliation through

136 *William M. Timpson et al.*

inclusion of everyone who wants to participate and relevant topics for communication. These can be organized outside the formal school day when students and others come to learn and practice their English through the studies of peace. Importantly, their topics need to be related to their daily lives, including their concerns and conflicts. Sexuality as well as ethnicity, for example, have been "forbidden" topics in Burundi. This fact has proven to be dangerous in the past when various problems and conflicts have arisen. However, it is our hope that when the youth, in particular, advance their communication skills while collectively using their critical and creative thinking capabilities, they can address sensitive issues of the past, present and future. With study and rehearsals, hallmarks of performance preparation, we believe that there is a much better chance for their success (Figure 8.1).

Be a Winner Academy (BWA) is the name of the PEC of the University of Ngozi (UNG). On May 23, 2020 this PEC had a very special day for BWA's members for two reasons: first, the Rector of UNG, Dr. Father Apollinaire, attended the club; and second, the topic of the day was the controversial statement that "it is good to have sex before marriage!" Because sexuality is taboo as a topic, some assumed that this would be disturbing and that everyone would argue against, it. Moreover, the Rector is a Catholic priest and his attendance as the campus leader was significant. However, after he encouraged everyone to feel free to express their opinions, participants with different perspectives

Figure 8.1 Peace English Club meeting with Fulgence Twizerimana.

were able to communicate their thoughts. Each one listened attentively in a calm and peaceful atmosphere and fearlessly asked sensitive questions.

As Timpson (2019) emphasizes in *Learning Life's Lessons*, there is a commitment to sustainability that means asking hard questions and interrogating the responses that are offered, including the systems that govern our economies, society in general, our politics—local, regional, national, and global—and that also underlie our values. In Burundi where the educational system is teacher-directed rather than a student-centered process, case-study analysis through storytelling as well as the use of other aspects of performance will foster students' confidence and commitment to developing their critical and creative thinking abilities.

Discussions on sensitive topics can enhance effective communication among students. While they examine the perspectives of those on all sides of an issue, they can develop their abilities to better understand others who may differ from them as well as the intellectual and emotional skills that can help them through these kinds of inquiries. In their 2009 book on teaching peace and reconciliation, Timpson, Brantmeier, Kees, Cavanagh, McGlynn, and Ndura-Ouédraogo argue that the study of peace and reconciliation can help people know how to communicate more effectively, listen deeply and reflectively, take different perspectives and reserve judgment, demonstrate acceptance and build empathy, mediate, negotiate and manage conflicts, build consensus, and more.

In other places and without this kind of study, divergent opinions have led to violence. For example, in some countries the young have been exploited by ill-intentioned politicians. Students who have developed these skills in classrooms or through experiences like the Peace English clubs could be models for others and help their communities avoid further violence.

One of the PEC's lessons at Hope Elementary School was designed around positive words and expressions related to peace. On that day, students rushed to offer examples and words including: "peacebuilding, reconciliation, independence, hope, rest in peace, friendship, love, peace of mind, and development." Students then formed groups and tried to explain to each other what these words meant to them. One student from each group then stood in front of the class and reported on the group's discussion. It was encouraging. As a follow-up assignment for the next Peace English Club session, students reported cases where they acted as mediators when the topic was "reconciliation." At that next Peace English Club meeting, their reports and the follow-up discussions were impressive.

Indeed, students are very motivated to learn English with a specific topic like peace because they are accustomed to learning English in a teacher-directed format with a defined curriculum. After the study of seemingly irrelevant content and the testing of their memories, they move on. Tapping into the performing arts, however, can produce very different reactions and results.

Moreover, a universal concept like peace can include many related social values that can spark related topics such as love, justice, equity, fidelity, respect, generosity, and sincerity (Carter, 2015). Most students live in families and have also witnessed or experienced hatred, injustice, disrespect, and infidelity between their parents or among their neighbors. Through our work on peacebuilding they have been excited to learn that they can play an important role as mediator among their parents, neighbors, friends, and classmates.

At Sainte Bernadette School, another PEC now gathers very young students. Topics such as "What is peace?" are first discussed in their native language of Kirundi and then translated into English using only key words. This activity has shown how interested these children can be in these kinds of learning activities. They see the lack of peace that too often occurs in their families, at school, and among their friends. We have found that starting with the younger ones appears to be the best way to develop their knowledge and skills for communication and peace.

Learning Life's Lessons (2019), describes a process of communicating for peace that changed the landscape in the Middle East, what many considered a hopeless vortex of anger and violence reflective of deep differences in history, beliefs, culture, and language. This then led to the signing of the Egypt–Israel Peace Treaty in 1979 in Washington, DC following the 1978 Camp David Accords. Responding to an invitation to these talks by US President Jimmy Carter, Egyptian President Anwar Sadat and Israeli Prime Minister Menachem Begin signed their names, inspiring many in the world by the promise of accomplishing what had seemed impossible. Israel returned land it had seized during the Six-Day War while Egypt agreed to allow Israel free passage of ships through the Suez Canal. It is notable that with this act Egypt became the first Arab state to recognize Israel officially. We believe that these experiences on neutral ground in the US and mediated by a US President Carter who motivated their agreement with hope for a peaceful future contributed to the success of these talks on peacebuilding (Carter, 2005). Far from the glare of their own nations, Sadat and Begin could feel free to "walk in each other's shoes" and compromise for the sake of the younger generation living in peace.

Clearly, motivating adversaries to embrace peacebuilding process' open the way for transformative actions that can benefit many. We believe that telling stories like this Egypt–Israel Peace Treaty from 1979 can challenge audiences in Burundi to persist in their studies of peace and inspire them to explore further what is possible both locally, nationally, and in the region to address the suffering of the past as well as forge new and more peaceful ways forward.

We see our work as rethinking this traditional teacher–student relationship, shifting from a role as 'expert' to learning 'facilitator' of student learning through inclusion of their stories and those about peacebuilding, to enable their thinking about their lives as individuals and as members of communities. A performing perspective can help move teachers and others away from a sole focus on expertise or telling, and, instead, do more to help students and other audiences discover insights that will help improve their lives. Much of this succeeds when students are first 'hooked' by the challenges put in front of them, like the engagement of an audience member to a gripping scene on stage.

In the *Pedagogy of the Oppressed*, Paulo Freire wrote:

> Revolutionary leaders commit many errors and miscalculations by not taking into account something so real as the people's view of the world: a view which explicitly and implicitly contains their concerns, their doubts, their hopes, their way of seeing the leaders, their perceptions of themselves and of the oppressors, their religious beliefs (almost always syncretic), their fatalism, their rebellious reactions. None of these elements can be seen separately, for in interaction all of them compose a totality.
>
> (2018, p. 182)

Using the performing arts to help engage learners more deeply in their studies is too often overlooked by teachers who are preoccupied by the knowledge on which students will be tested. Our project focuses on first engaging students in stories and helping them develop some of the knowledge and skills of peacebuilding (communication, cooperation, conflict management) for improving their lives.

We can say the same about the study of peacebuilding. This is another story that is part of our work in Burundi, encouraging students to persist in their studies while addressing the violence in their lives, a challenge that puts them outside the formal school and university curricula. This is also what can be said about the performing arts, i.e., success and impact typically require study, rehearsal, and experience. Integrating peacebuilding education with the performing arts can move communities in new directions.

The Power of Storytelling

Godelieve Nisengwe is a Ngozi Rotary Club member and a committed peacebuilder. She is a coordinator of Society for Women against Aids in Africa (SWAA-Burundi). She has graduated from the University of Burundi, its Institute for the Applied Pedagogy, and the English Department. She also has a master's degree in Public Health. Since 2008, she has been teaching adults in evening classes. In her first year of teaching, she was intent on finishing what she had planned for the curriculum. A term later, she realized that her students had forgotten most of those lessons. She decided to change her strategy, giving students time to tell related "stories" at the end of every lesson, cases and examples of the "applied curriculum," and where and how their studies played out in real life. Dramatically, her students began to understand everything from class, not at a surface and memorized level but at a deeper and application level, and all in a very short period of time.

She used the same strategies when she was teaching the concept of the "peace fence" in her community. She identified couples who were living in conflict and some who were experiencing violence. She planned a course of 10 lessons to teach them how they could live in peace and confront the gender violence in their homes and communities. For example, some of them put two beds in the same room, one for a husband and another for a wife. There was a cupboard which separated the two beds, acting like the "peace fence" that divided East and West Germany after the Second World War.

Like a skilled performer, Godelieve used engaging stories to make these lessons work. At the end of each chapter, she assigned topics on peace as homework. At the beginning of the next class, she would introduce the lesson with a short story that related to what they studied and experienced the previous day. She then allowed 15 minutes for students to present their homework. As a result of telling these stories, student conflicts actually decreased; they had learned to change their attitudes and behavior. They became more caring for each other. They started to share all that they had. At their homes wives as well as husbands became more involved in the management of the family possessions. At the end of this program they seemed very happy, doing all the activities together. They were also teaching others in their communities how to make and maintain peace.

When people come together and share stories about peace and reconciliation, conflict, and violence, they can learn from others and improve their abilities to resolve conflicts using nonviolence techniques. From these stories they get different ideas that can help them to face their own challenges. Skilled story telling can make listeners feel as though they are living through real situations of violence and conflict. This can help them explore ways to avoid violence and resolve problems in their own lives. The whole community then can benefit from this reduction of conflict as more become committed to avoiding problems and promoting peace. Since everyone uses stories, these ideas can connect all of us committed to sustainable peacebuilding with the broader community.

After people have listened to the stories, they then get an opportunity to offer their insights and express their feelings. Many in Burundi have been living with violence for a long time. Engaged discussions can serve as a kind of therapy. Participants get the chance to express their ideas and begin to relax. While listening, some may feel as if they are reliving a real occurrence of violence. Some may cry if a story reminds them about their own problems. After that release they may feel relief.

From these stories, the students get different ideas about changing behaviors that have been problematic. They learn to avoid violence and resolve conflicts in peace. Stories help students get beyond the confines of traditional classroom instruction with its narrow focus on tested memorization. Stories that are told well are engaging and memorable. Students learn to work hard for themselves instead of just following their teacher's instructions. They are more involved in a relevant and applied process of learning. Telling stories can help see them alternative responses to conflict as well as reflect on their roles in their lives.

When sharing stories about peace and reconciliation or about conflict and violence, feedback allows us to see what might be done differently in the telling or described relations. This process is very similar to what happens in most rehearsal settings when actors and dancers hear about what worked well and what needs improvement. Everyone can see how important peace can be in everyday life. They can realize how reconciliation can occur after a conflict. Individuals and communities can follow these kinds of models and become better peacebuilders. They can also learn how to resolve problems by avoiding violence. When we make the necessary adjustments, the stories we tell can connect us with all ages and backgrounds.

In her professional activities, for example, Godelieve has to look after those infected with HIV. Among them are children and adolescents. These individuals have to take medicine every day for their entire lives. However, some adolescents do not respect our guidance and may even stop taking their medicine. Some will say that it is difficult for them to swallow the drug every day when they do not feel any pain. It is very tiring for them to have this disease and maintain a daily discipline about their taking their medication.

Accordingly, Godelieve has organized a session for adolescents who are on antiretroviral treatments to share stories about their struggles and successes. They talked about how important it is for them to adhere to the treatments and how dangerous it can be to stop these treatments. One boy told the others that he was repeatedly admitted to the hospital before he decided to take the treatment and respect the doctor's instructions. Today, he is very healthy and plays soccer. He is at the university and is about to finish his studies.

Another girl who also missed many of these treatments said that she is now healthy after she decided to take them every day. She is the only child in her family living with HIV. She suffered for many years and was stigmatized by her sisters and brothers. She had then decided to stop the treatment in order to die and avoid further pain, suffering, and discrimination by her siblings. She said that she was always sad; she could not understand why she had to take the medicine alone. She hated her mother and she used to ask for a "good death" in her prayers. She often quarrelled with her mother, asking why she gave her such a horrible gift of a disease. She was always frustrated and refused any task at home that was assigned to her by her mother. She did not respect her mother.

One day her friend, who is also on antiretroviral treatment, explained to her that parents did not make their children infected on purpose. She told her that a person living with HIV can live as long as someone who is not infected, but only if she respected the doctors' advice. Since then this young woman changed her behavior; she forgave her mother and both became close friends. This is the kind of drama and impact that is available in every community if we probe conflicts and pursue sustainable peacebuilding.

Due to these stories Godelieve reports that the majority of adolescents now adhere to prescribed antiretroviral treatments. They are no longer discouraged by the treatments and they no longer quarrel with their parents and classmates. Storytelling helped her as a teacher and can help others avoid conflict and violence while promoting peace and reconciliation. Godelieve has shown that we can succeed in making peace with ourselves and our families as well as our friends while addressing basic health issues. The marrying of performance skills with peace-oriented education can indeed produce remarkable results. We will briefly review storytelling as peace education and applied theatre.

Applied Theatre as Peace Education

Applied theatre has advanced peace education by enabling performance that results from processes that promote well-being as well as develop knowledge and skills. Peace education is contextually responsive with goals for learning how to individually and collectively thrive without harm as well as create solutions to problems. It incorporates the cultures and interests of the learners while it fosters analytical skills needed for understanding and responding to challenges in their lives, community, and the world (Carter, 2021, Carter & Pickett, 2014). Expression and practices of one's culture that support understanding of occurrences in the past, present, and future are aspects of sustainable living. Continuation and maintenance of cultural practices expressed in the arts has been recognized by the United Nations Educational, Scientific, and Cultural Organization (2005) as components of peacebuilding. Storytelling, remembering, critical thinking, coping with and healing from trauma, along with acquisition of conflict skills are peacebuilding processes, among others, that applied theatre has facilitated. The compilation of examples that Hazel Barnes presents in *Arts Activism, Education, and Therapies Transforming Communities Across Africa* (2014) illustrates many ways applied aesthetics has been occuring across the continent. Each of these processes can contribute to recovery at the individual and community levels in contexts of violence, as well as constitute peace education. Storytelling has been facilitated as one of the main purposes of applied theatre, a means of response to harm, for advancement of community's well-being (Kandil, 2016). Community theatre is a type of applied theatre that addresses the needs of the community.

Storytelling has been featured through applied theatre in multiple ways. As a performance, storytelling sustains a learning tradition in Africa and indigenous communities worldwide while it counters the homogenization of Westernized education, that inconsistently includes culturally relevant pedagogy (Brock-Utne, 2018; Jirata, 2014; Sone, 2018). It conveys theatrical pluralism with incorporation of the performers' cultural norms and worldviews, especially in intercultural performance (Odom, 2021; Peimer, 2016). Storytelling in culturally responsive education is a bridge between traditional learning practices and contemporary curriculum. Digital storytelling, for example, incorporates these learning modes while featuring the cultures and voices of artists, who often choose to tell stories about their personal and community traumas (Altruz, 2015; Stewart & Ivala, 2017).

Storytelling in education is transdisciplinary as well as multidisciplinary, anti-oppressive, and therapeuatic. While it expresses the truth of the storyteller, it creates new knowledge drawing on epistemological and cosmological practices in the culture of the story (DeGloma, 2015; Velthuizen, 2014). The inclusion of counter-stories, that present the experiences of the marginalized and dominated, is an important contribution to community memory as well as the voices of the oppressed (Quayle, Sonn & Kasat, 2016). Peace development occurs through listening to the experiences and needs of everyone in a conflict while peacebuilding involves continuation of those processes for advancement of well-being (Bird, 2007). According to Oluwaseun Bamidele, (2017), Constructive "stories can acknowledge trauma, attain healing, build resilience, and counter the violent narrative of the [dominant] group" (p. 69). She explains how constructive storytelling exercises can help survivors of violence heal and she proposes a program for that purpose. In their description of prison theatre, Fesette and Levitt (2017) explain that the collaborative performance is a way for the performers to cope with trauma, self-humanize, and heal. For these effects and resolution of intergroup conflict, it is important that the stories performed avoid denigration of the 'other' and the self (Folami & Olaiya, 2016). Cultivation of imagination about a peaceful reality involves:

> letting go of old stories and creating an openness to the possibility of new ones is an emotional and affective labour that requires attention to processes of grief and loss, as well as hope and fear. Work such as this engages with hope not as a form of magical thinking that enables us to run away from contemporary and historic realities but as state that is achieved precisely through acknowledging fear, failure, loss and grief.
> (Facer, 2019, p. 8)

Conclusion

Our personal experiences with use of storytelling as peacebuilding education and the findings of research on storytelling as well as the performing arts are rationale for our pedagogical suggestions in this chapter. The inclusion of storytelling in communities supports the well-being of its members and maintains its traditional cultural practices, including education and conflict resolution. While storytelling in education is culturally responsive, its use as performance instruction provides space for inclusion and creation of new perspectives, ideas and expressions pertaining to the past, present and future, along with curriculum relevancy. Therefore, storytelling is transformative while it enables established ways of communicating, learning, and problem-solving. It belongs in applied theatre, along with informal and formal education, where storytelling has been used across disciplines and in extra-curricular activities, including celebrations, memorials, and entertainment. It must also continue as traditional education and applied performance, which are important components of peacebuilding and sustainable living together on this planet.

Acknowledgment

We are grateful to the Rotary Foundation for the Global Grants that paved the way for the instruction that we have provided in Burundi.

References

Altruz, M. (2015). *Digital storytelling applied theater and youth: Performing possibility.* London: Routledge.

Bamidele, O. (2017). "There's no thing as a whole story": Storytelling and the healing of sexual violence survivors among women and girls in Acoliland, Northern Uganda. *Sexuality, Gender & Policy, 1*(1), 69–88. doi: 10.18278/sgp.1.1.5

Bird, L. (2007). Learning about war and peace in the Great Lakes Region of Africa. *Research in Comparative and International Education, 2*(3), 176–190.

Brock-Utne, B. (2018). Researching language and culture in Africa using an autoethnographic approach. *International Review of Education, 64*(6), 713–735. doi: 1010.1007/s11159-018-9746-6

Brumfit, C. (1982). *English for international communication.* Oxford: Pergamon.

Carter, C. C. (2015). *Social education for peace. Foundations, curriculum, and instruction for visionary learning.* New York: Palgrave Macmillan. doi:10.1057/9781137534057

Carter, C. C. (Ed.). (2021). *Teaching and learning for comprehensive citizenship: Global perspectives on peace education* (Routledge Research in International and Comparative Education). Milton: Taylor & Francis Group. doi:10.1057/9780367548049

Carter, C. C., & Pickett, L. (2014). *Youth literature for peace education.* New York: Palgrave Macmillan. doi:10.1057/9781137359377

Carter, J. (2005). A peace of pictures. In Canfield, J, Hansen, M. V., Carter, C. C., Palomares, S., Williams, L., & Winch, B. (Eds.), *Chicken soup for the soul: Stories for a better world* (pp. 311–316.) New York: Simon & Schuster.

Davis, B. (1993). *Tools for teaching.* San Francisco: Jossey-Bass.

DeGloma, T. (2015). The strategies of mnemonic battle: On the alignment of autobiographical and collective memories in conflicts over the past. *American Journal of Cultural Sociology, 3*(1), 156–190. doi:10.1057/ajcs.2014.17

Eble, K. (1988). *The craft of teaching.* San Francisco: Jossey-Bass.

Facer, K. (2019). Storytelling in troubled times: What is the role for educators in the deep crises of the 21st century? *Literacy, 53*(1), 3–13. doi:10.1111/lit.12176

Fesette, N., & Levitt, B. (2017). Pedagogies of self-humanization: Collaborating to engage trauma in the Phoenix Players Theatre Group. *Teaching Artist Journal, 15*(3–4), 100–113.

Folami, O. M., & Olaiya, T.A. (2016). Gender, storytelling and peace construction in a divided society: A case study of the Ife/Modakeke conflict, *Cogent Social Sciences 2*(1). doi:10.1080/23311886.2016.1159015

Freire, P. (1970). *Pedagogy of the oppressed.* New York: Seabury.

Freire, P. (2018). *Pedagogy of the oppressed (50th anniversary edition).* New York: Bloomsbury.

Hazel Barnes, H. (2014). *Arts activism, education, and therapies transforming communities across Africa.* Amsterdam: Rodopi.

Jirata, T. J. (2014). Positive parenting: An ethnographic study of storytelling for socialization of children in Ethiopia. *Storytelling, Self, Society, 10*(2), 156–176. doi: 10.13110/storselfsoci.10.2.0156

Johnson, D., & Johnson, R. (1998). *Learning together and alone.* Boston: Allyn and Bacon.

Johnson, D., Johnson, R., & Smith, K. (1991). Cooperative learning: Increasing college faculty instructional productivity. In *ASHE-ERIC Higher Education Report No.*

4. Washington, DC: The George Washington University, School of Education and Human Development.
Kandil, Y. (2016). Personal stories in applied theatre contexts: Redefining the blurred lines. *Research in Drama Education, 21*(2), 201–213. doi:10.1080/13569783.2016.1155408
Lowman, J. (1994). *Mastering the techniques for teaching.* San Francisco: Jossey-Bass.
McKeachie, W. (2002). *Teaching tips.* Boston: Houghton Mifflin.
Odom, G. (2021). Asking the wrong questions: Musings on a conversation with Gakire Katese Odile about "intercultural theatre". *Studies in Theater and Performance, 41*(1), 50–67.
Peimer, D. (2016). Re-considering intercultural actor training in South Africa today: 'Borrowing on our own terms'. *Theatre, Dance and Performance Training, 7*(3), 403–416.
Quayle, A., Sonn, C., & Kasat, P. (2016) Community arts as public pedagogy: Disruptions into public memory through Aboriginal counter-storytelling, *International Journal of Inclusive Education, 20*(3), 261–277. doi:10.1080/13603116.2015.1047662
Ramsden, P. (1992). *Learning to teach in higher education.* New York: Routledge.
Sone, E. M. (2018). The folktale and social values in traditional Africa. *Eastern African Literary and Cultural Studies, 4*(2), 142–159.
Stewart, K. D., & Ivala, E. (2017). Silence, voice, and "other languages": Digital storytelling as a site for resistance and restoration in a South African higher education classroom. *British Journal of Educational Technology, 48*(5), 1164–1175. doi:10.1111/bjet.12540
Timpson, W. (2002) *Teaching and learning peace.* Madison, WI: Atwood.
Timpson, W. (2019). *Learning life's lessons: Inspirational tips for creating peace in troubled times.* Tucson, AZ: Peace Knowledge Press.
Timpson, W., Brantmeier, E., Kees, N., Cavanagh, T., McGlynn, C., & Ndura-Ouédraogo, E. (2009). *147 Practical tips for teaching peace and reconciliation,* Madison, WI: Atwood.
Timpson, W. & Doe, S. (2008) *Concepts and choices for teaching: Meeting the challenges in higher education,* (2nd ed.). Madison, WI: Atwood.
Timpson, W., & D. Holman, (Eds.). (2011). *Classrooms and communication: Integrating diversity, sustainability, peace and reconciliation. A volume of case studies available on the internet.* Madison, WI: Atwood.
Timpson, W. & Holman, D. K. (Eds.). (2014). *Controversial case studies for teaching on sustainability, conflict, and diversity.* Madison, WI: Atwood.
Timpson, W., Ndura, E., & Bangayimbaga, A., (2015). *Conflict, reconciliation, and peace education: Moving Burundi toward a sustainable future.* New York: Routledge.
Twizerimana, F. (2018). *The effect of conversational practice on the development of speaking skills in basic school, fourth cycle level:* Case of from 9 of some public basic schools in Ngozi City. (Unpublished B. A. Thesis). Bujumbura: University of Burundi.
United Nations Educational, Scientific, and Cultural Organization. (2005). *Convention on the protection and promotion of the diversity of cultural expressions.* Paris: Author.
Velthuizen, A. G. (2014). On truth-telling and storytelling: Truth-seeking during research involving communities with an oral culture and a history of violent conflict. *The Journal for Transdisciplinary Research in Southern Africa, 10*(3), 19–35.

9 Desiderata
Dancing Social Cohesion in Cape Town

Gerard M. Samuel and Charlotte Svendler Nielsen

Introduction

Writing about educating for peace at a time when one of your university students attempts suicide, a high school learner reaches out to their teachers to announce "Sir, can I get an extension? I think my water has broken… (on account of her teen pregnancy)," and a child/arts project participant's outburst "people are raping children" seems like a world gone mad for any artist–educator. But this harshness is part of the reality of many of the children with whom we have worked in Cape Town since 2017. Sadly, such crime-ridden and unequal worlds may not be that unusual for readers of this chapter about how an arts project can contribute to create hope and needed peace in the harshly violent and challenged context where these children live. In April 2018 Cape Town was living through one of its toughest periods of water restrictions when discussions of Day Zero was everywhere. In the same period of our project, i.e. 2017–2019, electricity supply was intermittently (and often without warning) interrupted, resulting in widespread disturbance. By March 2020, children and their teachers now faced the new global challenge of the rapidly mutating corona virus. Has the COVID world we live in and its "waves" spreading rapidly across our blue planet, and resultant conflicts, not flung children into a Dickensian "worst of times"? What, if any, are the tiniest hints and successes that are still present in these acrid ashes?

In this chapter we will discuss what is the relevance of arts education and our project in the light of societal and personal disasters. We will unpack this question through three themes emerging from interviews and close participant observations. Our work is mainly based on the method of reflective group dialogues, which we have developed during the project (Svendler Nielsen et al., 2020). This method of inquiry is based on recalling of experiences and indirect questioning using question cards and photographs from our earlier sessions. Here we include quotes from dialogues with the group of Lihle, Michaela, Ovayo, and Fahiem in November 2020 and Paul, Mandla,

DOI: 10.4324/9781003227380-9

and Lutho[1] in February 2019. The first broad theme uncovers the relationship between identity, language, and affirmation (or lack thereof) of culture. Such formation and development of children's identities in school plays a strong role in their lifelong experiences and for us, in the outpourings of self and its expressions. The way children feel and "are" comes from somewhere (family, school, "church," community)—a cultural paradigm. It is apt to review this older debate given the complex palimpsest of multilingualism, post coloniality, and socioeconomic chasms in South Africa. The second theme introduces a further layering from the perspective of the girls about their views of crime in their society illuminating the inner horror of daily experience. What makes life in and out of school worthwhile when children do not have enough food or water, and their lives happen in a society filled with crime? What is the role of the arts in such a milieu? We conclude our hermeneutic–phenomenological analysis (van Manen, 1990) with a view of our creative and nurturing process sharing the eyes and minds of the children and the teachers.

The continued need to develop mutual respect, kindness, and understanding as precursors to peace remains and we have seen many examples of how our project contributes to this goal. Peace may not have been our explicit objective, but the "side effects" (if you will) of our project may contribute to peacebuilding among different racial and ethnic groups. We contend that our actions ungird our advocacy and cautious manifesto—a desiderata for dance in Cape Town.

It is easy to romanticize the power of dance to act as social healer, and there are many studies that reference the critical pedagogy of dance including Shapiro (2008), Antilla (2004), and Stinson (2010). Dance phenomenologist Maxine Sheets-Johnstone's (2010) commentary on the repercussions and agency of dance and meaningful movement applies here too. She wrote,

> We might feel apprehensive in shaking hands with someone, for example, just as we might feel discouraged and weary that there are so many dishes to wash. In effect, whether friendly or antagonistic in a social context, and whether uplifting or dreary in a practical one, individuals involved in synergies of meaningful movement are not simply moving through a form, going through the motions unmoved as it were; on the contrary, the form is moving and moving affectively through them.
> (Sheets-Johnstone, 2010, p. 6)

What this chapter offers is a glimpse of the affect induced by movement and visual art encounters by some of the children who have engaged periodically with a small group of artist–teachers from South Africa and Denmark in an integrated arts experience. This project addresses long-term goals of peacebuilding, arts appreciation, and celebration of cultural difference.

Forging One South African Identity
Exploring Multiple Languages Including Dance

Extract from a reflective group dialogue based on question cards with Lihle, Michaela, Ovayo, and Fahiem, November 2020.

In the short extract from the interviews below we chose to share the exact words as the children have used them to highlight the significance of their voice in our process.

CHARLOTTE: One question in a reflective dialogue session that I asked in relation to how we could dream of the future of schools was what would you keep from school as it is and what would you change? The intention by this question was to indirectly create knowledge about what they like, what they have missed during lockdown, and what would be important to them. (to the group) And if we speak about the different subjects. Which subjects to you think should be in school? If you could…
MICHAELA: *(quickly)* Xhosa!
CHARLOTTE: Yes?
OVAYO: Art!
MICHAELA: Yes, miss and…
OVAYO: Xhosa
LIHLE: isiXhosa!
MICHAELA: Because…
OVAYO: And we should kick out Maths.
FAHIEM: No!
LIHLE: No.
OVAYO: And Afrikaans.
MICHAELA: No. If you want Maths…
OVAYO: Maths must stay, miss. Afrikaans it must go, go, go!
LIHLE: But some people don't know isiXhosa.
MICHAELA: But can I just say something if you want isiXhosa then…
OVAYO: Only those who wants Afrikaans they should do. They should learn Afrikaans miss.
MICHAELA: Yes.
OVAYO: Those who don't want Afrikaans they should not learn Afrikaans.
CHARLOTTE: So, you should have a choice? That would make sense.
ALL WITH ONE VOICE: Yes, miss!
MICHAELA: If you want to study Xhosa 'kan jy Afrikaans'…
OVAYO: For once. Because…
MICHAELA: Because some of us are not good in Afrikaans.
OVAYO: Joh that's me miss.
MICHAELA: We don't understand that at all.
OVAYO: Anything.
MICHAELA: But it keeps getting better as the grades, as we get…
OVAYO: Better. Better? It gets worse.

CHARLOTTE: *Are you learning more?*
MICHAELA: *Yes, miss.*
CHARLOTTE: *Yeah. But your own language is Xhosa?*
LIHLE AND MICHAELA: *Yes miss.*
CHARLOTTE YEAH: *And they don't teach you that at all?*
LIHLE AND MICHAELA: *No, miss.*
CHARLOTTE: *So, do you know to write in Xhosa?*
LIHLE: *Yes, miss.*
MICHAELA: *Miss we can…*
OVAYO: *We can type, we can write, we can talk miss.*
CHARLOTTE: *OK.*
MICHAELA: *Miss because we don't study Xhosa, we study Afrikaans. I study Xhosa and pronouncing some words and the writing in Xhosa. So I've forgotten about Xhosa and I'm focusing on Afrikaans, which is why I say we should have a choice.*

Reading through Charlotte's notes and the quotes from her dialogue with the children Gerard recalls that in preparing for the live sessions with our group in November 2020, he was reminded by what had become a new norm including: mask wearing, carrying extra bottles of sanitizers that were stashed in satchels, backpacks, and cars. The new measures of social distancing, sanitizing, and more recently in South Africa the mandatory call to wear a mask when in public. Was what a new normal pattern for us teachers was also quickly becoming a non-negotiable pattern for the children? We lamented the constant shepherding and lack of choice that most children seem to face in their learning environments. Both Charlotte and Gerard are strong advocates for the constitutional protection of individual rights and champions of the debates in education including free education and the significance of arts in education. Eustace Davie asserts in his book, *Unchain the Child—Abolish Compulsory Schooling Laws* (2005) that the products of such a free and enlightened educational environment will have a different perspective on life. He maintains that they will be philosophically better prepared to create a more peaceful world (2005, p. 38).

In the context of multi-cultural South Africa, we contend that such an argument for greater choice and freedom extends to the whole discourse of language and medium of instruction in schools and the nature of compulsory languages, which can constrain children's development. Children are required to master a first language and select from the 11 official languages, which vary in dominance from province to province. In the case of our specific encounter in Athlone, a former Coloreds only suburb in Cape Town and the facilitatory nature of work (teaching through the arts) with children, all of whom could be defined as Black or Colored, the languages most visible to our group included English, Afrikaans, and isiXhosa. The slippages of Danish would have also been introduced over time as, for example, the names of some games that were hard to translate directly would need to be explained and sometimes we realized that the Danish term was very close to what it would be in Afrikaans. There is also a further dimension to this line of thinking which should mention—"Afrikaaps" is not a separate language *per se* but a dialect unique to the Cape Flats and a Colored community of Athlone in which this school (the key site of our project) is found.

Language as a cultural carrier is further loaded through histories of marginalization but is also currently being celebrated in spaces such as musical theatre. Some vibrant examples of Afrikaaps as a sub-cultural, language world could be tasted in works such as Taliep Pietersen's and David Kramer's *District Six* (1986), *Poison* (1992) and *Kat and the Kings* (1996)—the latter toured in London to great acclaim in the glow of a post-apartheid era. This list extends to a more recent offering by stand-up comic celebratory, Mark Lottering's 2000s brand that has become "Aunty Merle…" produced at the Baxter Theatre in Cape Town. Lottering's alter ego is proudly Cape Colored and in fierce denial of a complex cultural aspirational tug to Whiteness that is useful to unpack here. These musicals can act as windows into multicultural and intercultural worlds and are highly illustrative of amongst many other new South African artistic and aesthetic concerns, a fervent desire and affirmation of Colored identity, and thus embody the "cultural collisions" (Bharucha, 1984) by the rich diversity of contemporary South Africa.

The unfolding discussion by some of the children in our project of their rejection to learn Afrikaans and passionate desire to rather learn isiXhosa (which is a mother tongue), needs careful unpacking and in a far wider context given the contestation of languages in South Africa, the Western Cape region, the city of Cape Town (with its population of over 5 million inhabitants) and Athlone the former "Coloreds only" suburb. Furthermore, entering this soup of multi-lingualism (and inter- and intra-culturalism) are our own beliefs and goals of the ripe possibilities that dance offers in terms of an education for peace and mutual respect. How can we move towards a greater respect for children's choices in a world that remains so limited and brutal? How do we respond to issues of diversity in our classrooms? Doug Risner and Stinson's (2010) call for honest self-reflection of one's positionality and privilege in relation to the children we teach is apt. Writing in the context of dance teaching in the USA they exclaimed

> we must also confront our inability to look at ourselves and those who, on the surface, look like us. The whiteness of academic dance generally and dance education more specifically, creates a number of challenges for understanding the socioeconomic complexity of white experience and the multiple realities of white identity in the USA.
>
> (2010, p. 9)

Such a relational stance can only equip the teacher to better respond to issues of diversity in her teaching and learning space. Furthermore, relational aesthetics (Bourriaud, 2002) highlights the very nature of collaborative work, but to what extent is it possible to be truly collaborative and overcome power issues in an educational setting in which a hierarchy between teachers and learners is the norm and the children have been educated to consider adults/teachers to be those who know the right answers? Perhaps only to some extent can the post-colonial aspect (a tearing down of "White" privilege, Western aesthetics) of the methods that we have used and developed help to overcome inherent power issues of differences of participants' age, gender, culture/race, and educational background/professional position? We accept that for many burnt-out teachers who are otherwise committed to social justice work Risner and Stinson's enquiring—"Why do they need to deal with the individual differences, personal problems, and cultural issues that their students will bring with them?" (2010, p. 2) remains a conundrum. This begs the question, how should a culture of care be developed and nurtured in such a world where teachers themselves feel unsupported and invisible, where their actions are construed as anti-authority and who then face the possibility of permanent expulsion?[2] A grade 9 pupil (from Heathfield High school), Jemima Bokolomba Batanda called on supporters of Neumann noting "He has brought change to our school that nobody else has done. He loves and cares for us and he wants to keep us safe" (Africa, 2021, p. 6).

As researchers we needed to ask multi-layered questions as to the drivers of such assertions. For example, what is our interpretation of the Black Xhosa-speaking girls and their need to foreground their cultural identity in the larger group of children? We observed this both in their break times when they would start to sing songs in their language and as ways of participating in group work where they would be very outspoken and physically engaged, almost dominant in relation to the Colored Afrikaans speaking girls. How is the history of racially separated schools for Black and Colored children (only) made visible in their post-apartheid bodies? The mirrored wall of the "ballet room" at the school might hold some answers. These mirrors are a manifestation of a once privileged colonial and apartheid dance form—ballet. Today, the same school can offer ballet but only as an extracurricular activity. Perhaps ballet remains as an aspirational White and Eurocentric culture or an unattainable artform for the Black girl child.

Crime on Their Minds

Extract from talk between Charlotte, Michaela and Ovayo in a break February 21, 2019.

This talk started by the girls asking Charlotte if Denmark is a nice place. She responded with a firm yes, but that she also liked to be in South Africa. She said "I think it is a beautiful country, lovely people." Michaela then interrupted her by saying—but it's exciting and amazing and nice because you're new and you don't live here…!

OVAYO: *Miss, did you go to Eastern Cape once?*
    Charlotte answered "no" as at the point of time for this talk she had not, but now reflecting back at a point in time when she has also visited there, it becomes clear to her why Ovayo's question in the context of this talk is important—the Eastern Cape has even higher crime rates and generally the people are even poorer than in the Western Cape capital are, but this is where Ovayo's family originally came from and where she probably has childhood memories of a more safe period of her life as she says 'It's very nice, miss.'
MICHAELA: *But miss if you would have to live here you find it quite boring.*
CHARLOTTE: *Do you think so?*
MICHAELA: *Yes, miss.*
CHARLOTTE: *Why?*
MICHAELA: *I can say it's because of the crime here. I bet it's more than in Denmark, more crime here.*
OVAYO: *People are raping children.*
CHARLOTTE: *People are raping children? Wow...*
OVAYO: *Or committing murder miss.*
MICHAELA: *Killing your own family.*
OVAYO: *Yes, miss.*
CHARLOTTE: *That is definitely... (then we are interrupted by the school bell and the talk stops).*
    Extract from interview with Paul, Mandla and Lutho February 2019—we are sitting in the hallway looking at photos from some of our past sessions.
CHARLOTTE: *So what's this?*
PAUL: *We had to make a big circle and we had... sometimes we had to close it and open it.*
CHARLOTTE: *So, what do you prefer, to be outside or inside?*
PAUL: *Inside.*
CHARLOTTE: *Inside?*
PAUL: *Because I feel safer inside.*
CHARLOTTE: *You feel more safe inside?*
PAUL: *Yes, ma'am.*
CHARLOTTE: *So what could happen outside?*
PAUL: *Outside, something could attack you miss.*
CHARLOTTE (FINDS IT HARD TO HEAR AND WANTS TO BE SURE SHE HEARD RIGHT, SO ASKS): *Something could what?*
PAUL: *Attack you.*
CHARLOTTE: *Someone could attack you?*
PAUL: *Yes, miss.*
CHARLOTTE: *But do you think that could happen here in the school?*
PAUL: *No, miss.*
CHARLOTTE: *No. I think you are safe here, but could that happen where you live for example?*
PAUL: *Yes, miss in the community, miss.*

CHARLOTTE: *So have that happened to anybody you know?*
PAUL: *Yes, miss. This boy was...* (The school bell rings again, and we are drowned out by the sudden noises and sounds from all directions. I say thank you to group and they leave to join the rest of their school friends).

When reading through the interview quotes and considering what were some of our questions and reactions in the moments of these brief talks with some of the children, Charlotte acknowledged that she is from a privileged and safe place in the world. She is also the mother of three children (the oldest of whom is a girl the same age as some of the children she was talking to here). What they are telling her therefore goes directly to her own sensuous experiences of being a mother who is constantly thinking about her children's welfare, but in these interview situations her own worries are really put into the perspective of what some mothers in Cape Town may have to worry about daily. Every time she returns to Denmark from her work in Cape Town, she finds herself being somewhat irritated with her own children because they complain over what initially seems to be non-issues. For example, they cannot have this pair of trousers, or they cannot go to the cinema, or simply because they throw a full glass of water into the sink. She becomes annoyed when food on their plate often lands up in the bin! Charlotte commented that it is hard to feel "between two places." While Charlotte knows that her children's perspectives are linked to where they are, and that the problems and issues that they are dealing with also have value, as they are *their* experiences, she still hopes that sharing her experiences from South Africa with her children will in some way also challenge them to acknowledge their privileged realities.

Crime and the consequences of crime are never far away from conversations amongst the children. In another talk, this one held in March 2019 with Ovayo and Michaela the word "juvenile" was bandied about. What did children understand by the term "juvenile" or to be placed in a facility for juveniles (read vulnerable children and youth)? Such correctional service structures and Places of Safety are found throughout the country, and we were curious to learn more of their understandings of these places and what their perspective were about what might be occurring in these centers.

Ovayo shouted out to one of the boys: "You'll end in juvenile!" as a response to him disturbing her and Michaela. Charlotte approached them and asked what a juvenile is, and could they describe what such detention centers for young people are. She was puzzled that they seem to know many details of such places. For example, they seemed to know what the ages are of youngsters who can be sent there and what these young people have done to end up there. Later when we spoke, Gerard wondered how much of their account was true and how much fiction or hearsay? From where does this kind of evidence originate and how does it proliferate? As researchers we struggled to establish concretely how such knowledge is transferred in their homes, schools, and wider communities but it was self-evident that the fear and mythology surrounding juvenile detention centers that was generated was palpable and part of daily life. Significantly, the children asked Charlotte whether such places also existed in Denmark. They wanted to know what happens to children who have done something illegal. Their inquisitiveness about legal issues at such a tender and developing age in relation to their lived experiences and embodied storytelling spoke volumes. South African dance artist and scholar, Lliane Loots reminds us that

> Sometimes we tell our own story, sometimes we tell stories reflected in the imagination of our dreams and nightmares, sometimes we tell the stories of our own personal and shared histories and politics, and sometimes, we tell the stories of the lives of others.
>
> (2018, pp. 58–59)

Loots' discussion of the need and import of narrative offers a welcome insight into the value of dance itself. Throughout our process or part of our desiderata (if you will) has been an openness, acceptance, and active encouragement—an invitation as various role-players to tell our stories. In that spirit, Charlotte responded from her Danish perspective that yes there is such a thing as a juvenile facility but that in many cases of which she is aware, if (Danish) youngsters do something illegal, they would be placed in a new family as their authorities often think that the problem might be that their families do not take well enough care of them. The children remained quiet and seemed puzzled. We were reminded once more to explore actions and responses from their bodies and listen attentively not only to the words from their lips if we are to better understand from a girls' eye view.

Arts Education, Help with Life

Our project is shaped by significant teaching moments and instinctive shifts in pedagogic emphasis. One of the ideas that the children and we had explored, for example, in an earlier creative movement session was the concept of threshold and boundary. We used our bodies to create large stepping-stones and the children were invited to fill in the 'negative' spaces made by the initiating first mover's 'positive' frame. This led to an ever-lengthening group that was able to cover ground and occupy space. Typically for such an experiment, the children were invited to work slowly to see and identify gaps before filling in any empty spaces. This coupling and intimacy of new sculptural formations made with little bodies was also captured, and the ideas reinforced by the visual arts teacher who investigated through cut-out figures the possible negative and positive spaces and shapes the cut-out figures create. This invites further discussion of spaces that were restricted, "no go" areas and the most recent lockdown periods for avoiding the spread of COVID. This specific moment in the exercise did not include Charlotte as the dance teacher. In many of our previous workshops we deliberately chose to work *with* and not *for* the children by exploring tasks with them. This shift in hierarchies and power relationships underpinned the philosophy of our educational work as it highlighted ideas of respect for one another in spite of our roles as teachers and children, young and old and male and female.

During our final visit in November 2020, which culminated at the Zeitz Museum of Contemporary Art Africa in Cape Town, we wandered around this colossal concrete space and I observed the children's amazement at the scale and vibrancy of the many and varied works of art. The museum was once an eight stories-high chamber/ silo for grain, now skillfully, re-imagined as a central hall with its concrete sides spliced as if it was melted butter with swift bubble elevators that glide to various floors. The children stood wide-eyed marveling at the elaborate wall hangings that could easily be 15 meters across and 26 meters long! Dwarfed in comparison to such splendor, Gerard instinctively responded to a more life-sized sculpture when he noticed that the children had formed their own semi-circle around the object and other multimedia artworks. He did an impromptu, butoh-esque performance, which we observed changed an excitable mood to a quieter reflection without words or instruction in a sea of experiences for the children and some of the general public who were also witnessing postmodern, contemporary African art.

We returned to the children to find out more about their experiences over the past few days of our last workshop week. They have the last word. It is their desiderata now…

CHARLOTTE: *So, if you were to make an interview with some of the other children, which questions would you ask? Have you had time to think of that?*
MICHAELA: *Miss, how have the activities help you with your day-to-day life and…*
CHARLOTTE: *Let's start with that. So would anybody like to answer that? Have the activities helped you in your day-to-day life in some way, do you think?*
OVAYO: *It made you more flexible, used more effort to lose weight miss.*
CHARLOTTE: *So flexible like being able to stretch longer?*
MICHAELA: *Yes, miss. And being able to dance.*
CHARLOTTE: *So it has also helped the other dance.*
LIHLE: *Yes, miss.*
CHARLOTTE: *Anything else?*
OVAYO: *To feel more comfortable miss…*
CHARLOTTE: *To feel more comfortable?*
OVAYO: *in your own body miss. When you're dancing must you feel comfortable, must in anything miss because dancing is very much easy miss. And hard at the same time miss.*
MICHAELA: *But miss if you struggle with dancing you don't get comfortable. So that's why, that's, the dance activities help. Have helped us.*
CHARLOTTE: *So, was there another question?*
MICHAELA: *How do you feel about the activities?*
CHARLOTTE: *How do you feel about the activities we have done?*
OVAYO: *Happy, miss.*

CHARLOTTE: *We've done a lot of things these years. What have you felt about the exercises?*
LIHLE: *I felt so calm and so happy to be outside for once. Because at school you're always writing, studying and like learning. And we're outside playing, ja so.*
CHARLOTTE: *Did you write any questions, Fahiem?*
FAHIEM: *No, miss. I didn't get that far.*
CHARLOTTE: *But if you think of a question which... would you like to ask a question? If you were to ask a question about this project what could that be?*
FAHIEM: *In the future would you like to work in the Peter Clarke art center?*
CHARLOTTE: *Would you like to work in the Peter Clarke art center in the future?*
ALL WITH ONE VOICE: *Yes, miss.*
CHARLOTTE: *Yes. And what would you like to do there?*
MICHAELA: *Miss, probably give art lessons to help others with their drawing and their creative side.*
CHARLOTTE: *Are there any other questions?*
LIHLE: *If you were to choose between art center and school, which one would you choose?*
OVAYO: *Art center!*
MICHAELA: *Art center.*
OVAYO: *Straightforward!*
LIHLE: *And why?*
OVAYO: *Why? Because miss, art miss gives you that, makes you more confident miss. More you know miss it boosts your self-esteem more miss. And makes you do more things, want to achieve more things in life. Modern art and, you know miss.*
LIHLE: *Education ja.*
CHARLOTTE: *So what do you think makes that happen?*
OVAYO: *Encouragement. Believing in someone miss and people telling them you can do better than this. You can do that, that, that. That is what encouragement is.*
CHARLOTTE: *And you think that is something that happens in the arts project?*
THE GIRLS WITH ONE VOICE: *Yes, miss.*

Michaela concludes the dialogue just before the bell rings for them to go to the next lesson: *I would choose the art center because art calms you. It calms you down. And you get to be able to explore your creative side and see what you can actually do. That's why.*

Dare We Dream?[3]
Concluding Thoughts

As we continue to grapple with the challenges facing our lives in what for many is one of the most unequal societies on the planet, we are reminded by clinical psychologist Pumla Gobodo-Madikizela's cry in her seminal works including *Dare We Hope?* (2014) and *A Human Being Died that Night* (2003), the latter which scours the apartheid legacy and the Truth and Reconciliation Commission (TRC) for answers that were implored thereafter. Written into her TRC pleas is an urgency to think through the politics of multi-culturalism, ravages in education and the devastation of crime. An expert on peacebuilding and reconciliation Gobodo-Madikezela's invitation endures when she wrote

> Listening to one another and acknowledging the experience of the loss on both sides would be a start. The task of picking up the pieces of a society shattered by violence is not easy. It needs patience. Our humanity is strongest when we are focused on that which unites us as human beings: compassion, and an ethos of care for one another, rather than giving in to fear and suspicion.
>
> (2014, p. 20)

Finally, we need to remain mindful that "reconciliation cannot be condensed into a quick-fix project, one that has to take place with a prescribed space of time" (Gobodo-Madikizela, 2014, p. 21). Dancing social cohesion and justice for us means a commitment to an individual and collective desideratum.

Notes

1. As part of our ethical practice the names of all the children have been anonymized to offer a layer of privacy to the children. We have also ensured that the pseudonyms used here are also not found in the class lists from which the project's children emanate.
2. A cogent example would include local high school principal Wesley Neumann's charge of guilty by the Western Cape Education Department for his refusal to reopen Heathfield High School at the height of the COVID pandemic. This in spite of widespread support from his students, parents, school's governing body and hundreds from surrounding poor, local communities. Was his action care or disrespect and to which constituency should this young leader give account? See also, " Petition to support Heathfield Principal" in *The Weekend Argus* on Sunday October 17, 2021, p. 6.
3. This subtitle purposely echoes author and TRC expert Pumla Gobodo-Madikizela's haunting book *Dare We Hope?* published by Tafelberg, a division of Media24Boeke Ltd, in 2014, in order to signal not a hopelessness but rather to reframe the desire for hope as an implicit call to action.

References

Africa, K. (2021). Petition to support Heathfield principal. *The Weekend Argus*. Sunday October 17, p. 6.
Antilla, E. (2004). Dance learning as practice of freedom. In L. Rouhianen, Antilla, E., Hamalainen, S., & Loytonen, T. (Eds.). *The same difference: Ethical and political perspectives on dance* (pp. 19–62). Helsinki: Helsinki-Theatre Academy of Finland.
Bharucha, R., (1984). A collision of cultures: Some western interpretations of the Indian theatre. *Asian Theatre Journal*, 1(1), 1–20.
Bourriaud, N. (2002). *Relational aesthetics*. Dijon: Les Presses du Réel.

Davie, E. (2005). *Unchain the child—abolish compulsory schooling laws.* Johannesburg-The free Market Foundation. Retrieved at www.freemarketfoundation.com/article-view/unchain-the-child-abolish-compulsory-schooling-laws

Gobodo-Madikizela, P. (2003). *A human being died that night: A South African story of forgiveness.* New York: Houghton Mifflin.

Gobodo-Madikizela, P. (2014). *Dare we hope? Facing our past to find a new future.* Cape Town: Tafelberg.

Loots, L. (2018). Embodied storytelling: Using narrative as a vehicle for collaborative choreographic practice – a case study of Flatfoot Dance Company's 2016 Homeland Trilogy (South Africa and Senegal). *South African Theatre Journal, 31*(1), 58–71.

Risner, D., & Stinson S. (2010). Moving social justice: Challenges, fears and possibilities in dance education. *International Journal of Education and The Arts, 11*(6), 1–26.

Shapiro, S. B. (2008). *Dance in a world of change: Reflections on globalization and cultural difference.* Champaign, IL: Human Kinetics.

Sheets-Johnstone, M., (2010). Why is movement therapeutic? *American Journal of Dance Therapy, 32*(1), 2–15.

Stinson, S. W., (2010). Questioning our past and building a future-Teacher education in dance for the 21st century. *Journal of Dance Education, 10*(4), 136–144.

Svendler Nielsen, C., Samuel, G. M., Wilson, L., & Vedel, K. (2020). "Seeing" and "being seen": An embodied and culturally sensitive arts integrated pedagogy creating enriched conditions for learning in multicultural school. *International Journal of Education & the Arts, 21*(2), 2–23.

Van Manen, M. (1990). *Researching lived experience: Human science for an action sensitive pedagogy.* New York: State University of New York Press.

10 Peacebuilding through Testimonial Theatre in the United States and Northern Ireland

Jennifer Blackburn Miller

Introduction

We are living in precarious times and we need to explore more methods of solving society's seemingly intractable problems. In addition to numerous environmental issues that threaten the very survival of life on Earth, there is growing polarization amongst its people. The polarization evidences increased conflict, which if not addressed, can become violent. In order to prevent violent responses to conflict and potential wars, we need to build peace between contesting groups of people. Communicative and cooperative intergroup relations are goals of conflict management and violence prevention. Theatre provides a context for facilitation of those goals in addition to creativity, which characterizes processes of successful conflict transformation (Carter, 2010; Cohen, Varea & Walker, 2011; Galtung, 2004). Facilitation of peacebuilding through applied theatre includes the goals of conflict management. Insights from those theatrical processes support the use of theatre as a means of peacebuilding education. This chapter focuses on the preliminary results from a case study about peacebuilding through a social justice Testimonial Theatre program in Philadelphia, Pennsylvania of the United States (US) and Derry/Londonderry, Northern Ireland (NI).

One way to improve intergroup relations is to develop empathy (Stephan & Finlay, 1999). Singer and Lamm (2009) define empathy as the "ability to share the affective experiences of others" (p. 81). The arts can be useful tools for transformative learning and perspective transformation, including the development of empathy and skills of conflict resolution (Bang, 2016). As noted by Hayes and Yorks (2007) and Scher (2007), community arts programs are uniquely situated to address various societal issues, including interracial conflict. Theater/Theatre of Witness (US/UK title) (TOW) falls under the domain of applied theatre.

Applied Theatre as Peace Education

Before introducing TOW further, it might help to share some examples and learning outcomes from applied theatre programs with a social justice and

DOI: 10.4324/9781003227380-10

peace education focus. Bell, Desai, and Irani (2013) discuss a storytelling project model through which young people create arts-based counter-stories to resist racism. This enables an integrated approach to teaching and learning about racism that offers hope, agency, and opportunities for imagining new possibilities and ways out of oppression. Harlap and Aristizabal (2013) used Theatre of the Oppressed activities with a variety of local participants in Derry/Londonderry, Northern Ireland. They note the following in response to the question: How do communities learn to use theatre as praxis for social justice? It awakens the imagination, it welcomes "mistakes" and invites experimentation, and it helps to model transformative community. They also mention, "the mentor learns as much from the apprentice as the apprentice learns from the mentor" (p. 33).

In her article about the community play (as conceived by Ann Jellicoe), Weston (2020) describes its effectiveness as a model for implicit and explicit political theatre practice. The kind of bonds that are created through collective responsibility (through the rehearsal process, performances, etc.), are similar to the feelings of community that are developed through collective political struggle. She notes: "What this demonstrates, is that the aspects of applied and community theatre that celebrate togetherness, unity, and ensemble are essential to the political efficacy of the work" (p. 175). Modirzadeh (2013) describes using documentary theatre in education as a tool for empathy building. The plays were based on oral histories of refugees in New York. She states: "The creation of beauty through attention to details of the personal rather than the general also stands as a reminder that those details that make one human are also universal, which in turn creates empathy in the viewer" (p. 56).

Some applied theatre practitioners focus on embodied pedagogy and embodied knowledge. Forgasz and McDonough (2017) used Augusto Boal's *The Rainbow of Desire* (1994) applied theatre techniques to explore the emotional aspects of teaching, learning, and embodied pedagogies. Through their experiences they learned three main things: (1) embodiment as a process of coming to know, (2) the challenges of engaging in embodied processes, and (3) the importance of developing skillful embodied practice. The challenges included vulnerability, resistance, and unfamiliarity. Butterwick and Selman (2012) learned a number of lessons from exploring somatic theatre processes and embodied knowing. Be attentive and use all the senses, assess the costs, risks, and benefits, be responsive to the community and do not impose recipes upon them, and be cautious, but also move forward. In addition, handle sensitive stories with care, inform participants ahead of time about what to expect (it might unleash powerful, surprising experiences), make sure there is individual and group self-care, create conditions for safety, and make the work count so that it informs action.

Perhaps one of the most extensive resources on peace education and applied theatre are *The Acting Together* volumes by Cohen, Varea, and Walker (2011). These authors documented the diverse artistic work and voices of people from more than 15 countries and a variety of cultures and conflict regions. It is worth sharing the lessons they learned from their project.

1. Performances are powerful: They embody a kind of power that can be crafted to contribute to the transformation of violent conflict.
2. Peacebuilding performances have the potential to support communities to engage with painful issues and to navigate among apparently conflicting and contradictory imperatives.
3. Performances in zones of violent conflict have the potential to cause great harm; precautions must be taken to minimize these risks.
4. Aesthetic excellence and sociopolitical effectiveness need not be competing imperatives; they are often mutually reinforcing.
5. Artist-based theatre, community-based theatre, rituals, and ceremonies all can be crafted to make substantive contributions to justice and peace.
6. The transformative power of the arts depends upon respect for the integrity of the artistic process.
7. Performances could have a greater impact on societies in conflict if more non-arts agencies and organizations recognized their peacebuilding potential and helped to extend their reach.
8. Peacebuilding performances bear witness to the human costs of war and oppression and to its gendered nature. They tell the stories not of heads of state and military leaders but rather of the children, women, and men whose lives are diminished by the fear and humiliation, the shame and dislocation that accompany violence (pp. 191–197).

TOW is another example of applied theatre, social justice theatre, and peace education. Testimonial Theatre is included under the performance "genre" of Documentary Theatre. Another term for it is Verbatim Theatre. These terms are often used interchangeably, which can be confusing (Maedza, 2013). Although there is literature by Drama scholars and critics about Documentary Theatre and the terms and plays associated with it (for example, Paget, 1987; Dawson, 1999; Claycomb, 2003; Hammond & Steward, 2008; and Forsyth & Megson, 2009), there is a dearth of empirical research about the impact of these programs.

Theoretical Framework

The theoretical framework for this study begins with Mezirow's (1978a, 1985, 1991a, 1994b, 2000, 2006) foundational theory. Daloz's (1986, 2012) psycho-developmental approach to transformative learning augments Mezirow's theory. Dirkx's (1997, 2000, 2001, 2006, 2008) emotional and spiritual approach to transformative learning complements Mezirow's and Daloz's approaches. Transformative learning through artistic ways of knowing that are extrarational, holistic, intuitive, creative, and embodied (Gardner, 1983; Greene, 1995; Eisner, 2002; Lawrence, 2005; Hoggan, Simpson, & Stuckey, 2009; Blackburn Miller, 2020) completes the framework.

Transformative Learning

Mezirow's foundational theory of transformative learning is the main theory for this theoretical framework (1978a, 1978b, 1985, 1989, 1990, 1991a, 1991b, 1992, 1994a, 1994b, 1995, 1996, 1997, 1998a, 2000, 2003, 2006). However, although his theory is useful for the TOW process, especially with regard to the disorienting dilemma and perspective transformation aspects, it is too critical and rational to be used alone to analyze TOW. Thus, Daloz's (1986, 2012) psycho-developmental approach to transformative learning will be used in addition. Daloz uses storytelling to help his students journey toward a more holistic and transformed view of the world. This is a very good fit for the TOW process.

Mezirow (1991a) is known as the founder of transformative learning theory. One of the main learning outcomes from this theory is perspective transformation. Central to perspective transformation is Mezirow's meaning perspectives and meaning schemes. A meaning perspective is "the structure of cultural and psychological assumptions within which our past experience assimilates and transforms new experience" (Mezirow, 1985, p. 21), and a meaning scheme is "the constellation of concept, belief, judgment, and feeling which shapes a particular interpretation" (Mezirow, 1994b, p. 223).

Mezirow notes various ways that perspective transformation can occur. Sometimes it can be painful, as a result of comprehensive and critical re-evaluation of oneself. He argues that the central element of perspective transformation is critical self-reflection (Mezirow, 1991a, 1994b). This is what may occur in the TOW process. Theatre powerfully affects people in this way because it has a gradual, indirect impact on their meaning schemes, which build up into a change in their meaning perspective, ultimately leading to a perspective transformation. Mezirow himself has said that a person does not have to experience all 11 phases of transformative learning to experience a perspective transformation (Kitchenham, 2008).

Another aspect of transformative learning theory that applies to TOW is the phase Mezirow added to the original 10-phase model, "renegotiating relationships and negotiating new relationships" (Mezirow, 1994b, p. 224). After TOW participants have a shift in perspective about the "other," they may change their relationship with those they interact with in that group, at least the ones they know they can trust. Regarding Mezirow's original 10-phase model, all of the phases could apply to the TOW process. The participants may not go through them all, or it may take them some time to go through them, but these phases certainly apply to the TOW process and the perspective transformation that may result.

In 2000, Mezirow revised and broadened his theory a bit more. With the revised theory, a perspective transformation consists of a meaning perspective that is a frame of reference. They both comprised habits of mind, which include perspectives (sociolinguistic, moral-ethical, epistemic, philosophical, psychological, aesthetic). These perspectives are each expressed as points of view, and these points of view each comprised clusters of meaning schemes. He also states that there are four types of learning: elaborating existing frames of reference, learning new frames of reference, transforming habits of mind, and transforming points of view (Kitchenham, 2008). This revised theory still aligns with the TOW learning process.

There are many specific transformative learning outcomes from the TOW process that were evident in the pilot study data. The audience bears witness to the participants' healing and transformation and develops a connection with them. This helps to humanize the "other," see the "other" as self, and see their common humanity. This also happens to the participants as they interact with each other. TOW is transformative in developing empathy in the audience and the participants. The cross-cultural interaction and communication creates awareness of the multiple angles/sides of conflicts. This reduces prejudice and promotes cross-cultural understanding. TOW also leads participants and audience members to engage in community social justice and peacebuilding work, which is an effect of inward transformative learning turned outward (Blackburn Miller, 2018).

In Daloz's (1986, 2012) view, the goal of transformative learning is lifelong personal development. Daloz focuses on a process of storytelling and how this can lead to a more holistic and transformed worldview. He often uses the metaphor of a journey tale to describe adult development. Stories also allow us to control and form the inchoate areas of our lives, and to give our lives meaning. Similar to Mezirow, Daloz feels dialogue and discourse are integral to the process of transformation. However, he concentrates on the process of storytelling between mentor and student, a mutual storying of lives, to guide development and transformation (Daloz, 1986, 2012). This emphasis on storytelling fits the TOW process very well.

Daloz (2012) offers three "maps" to describe adult development, without prescribing an end point to the transformational journey. First, he draws on phase theories of adult development, which focus on the tasks adults confront as they face problems associated with aging. Second, he looks at stage theories, which examine cognitive growth and one's ability to think outside one's cultural reference. Third, he uses Perry's (1968) model of intellectual and ethical development, which describes students journeying from naïve, simplistic thinking to complex, relativistic thinking over time. Although Daloz recognizes the importance of cognitive growth in transformative learning, he acknowledges the whole person in that growth (Daloz, 1986, 2012).

Emotional and Spiritual Learning

Dirkx's approach to emotional learning and soul work (1997, 2000, 2001, 2006, 2008, 2012) within transformative learning is also part of this theoretical framework. In adult education, there has been a shift in viewing emotions as an obstacle to reason and knowing, to a more integral and holistic way of being in the world (Dirkx, 2008). The idea of emotional intelligence

(Goleman, 1995) has also been discussed, as a way of regulating and managing emotions in the classroom and in one's life. "Allowing students to give voice to powerful affect is not getting it off their chests and getting it out of the way, but encouraging them to own and integrate these feelings and emotions within their sense of being" (Clark & Dirkx, 2008, p. 92). TOW gives participants the opportunity to do this. Various scholars within adult education have written about ways to incorporate emotion work into processes of adult learning; however, Dirkx's approach to this is through soul work and imaginal methods (Dirkx, 2001, 2006).

Dirkx (2001) states: "The purpose of the imaginal method or soul work is not to analyze and dissect these emotions and feelings but to imaginatively elaborate their meaning in our lives" (p. 69). This method contrasts with Mezirow's approach to transformative learning in that Dirkx encourages asking "what" questions, rather than "how" or "why" questions. "The imaginal method seeks a deeper understanding of the emotional, affective, and spiritual dimensions that are often associated with profoundly meaningful experiences in adult learning" (Dirkx, 2001, p. 70). Various art forms can be used to foster the life of the image in adult learning. That is why this method fits well with the TOW process.

Dirkx (2001) argues that personally significant and meaningful learning comes from an adult's emotional and imaginative connection with themselves and the world around them. The meaning given to emotions reflects broader psychological and sociocultural contexts. This process of meaning making is extrarational, not just reflective and rational (as Mezirow's theory suggests) (Dirkx, 2001). "Recent studies of transformative learning reveal extrarational aspects, such as emotion, intuition, soul, spirituality, and the body, as integral to processes of deep, significant change" (Dirkx, 2001, p. 68). Dirkx is similar to Daloz in that they both focus on the whole person in transformative learning. Dirkx's approach helps to support Sepinuck's meditative method of allowing the production to unfold naturally, and allowing her own intuition and spirituality to guide her through the process. This is also an important way the program is able to have a transformative impact on the participants.

Artistic Ways of Knowing

Artistic ways of knowing within transformative learning is also part of this theoretical framework. Theories about artistic and creative ways of knowing developed from theories on multiple ways of knowing. The *New Directions for Adult and Continuing Education* journal focused on *Artistic Ways of Knowing* in 2005. In the beginning of that publication, Lawrence discusses the limitations of traditional ways of constructing knowledge in adult education. She also talks about learning from diverse cultural perspectives through art, knowing self through art, accessing or uncovering hidden knowledge, learning through the arts, and art as a means for social change. At the end of this issue, Lawrence weaves the artistic themes together and notes the commonalities. All of the articles included the following: the arts leading to an awareness of self, an awareness of others, a context for learning, a means for social action, and a form of community building (Lawrence, 2005). This describes the TOW program very well.

Hoggan, Simpson, and Stuckey (2009) discuss the importance of artistic and creative ways of knowing, as well as symbolic and imaginal knowing, spiritual dimensions of knowing, and affective knowing. They focus on artistic and creative ways of knowing in relationship to transformative learning in adult education in their book *Creative Expression in Transformative Learning*. Gardner's (1983) theory of multiple intelligences also states that artistic ways of knowing are a form of intelligence and should be included in education.

The use of imagination is one important aspect of creative expression. "Access to or permission to use imagination is one of the key benefits of exploring through creative expression" (Hoggan et al., 2009, p. 22). Imagination helps us to "try on" possible alternatives, as Eisner (2002), Gardner (1993), and Greene (1995) suggest:

> Imagination, fed by sensing of experiences, allows us to see situations freshly, engenders visions of felt possibilities, liberates us from the literal, gives credence to alternatives, allows us to try things out – in our mind's eye – through practice or dress rehearsal, and provides us with new perspectives.
>
> (as cited in Hoggan et al., 2009, pp. 22–23)

This quote describes what happens when the TOW participants and audience members bear witness to each other's stories.

Greene (1995) states: "imagination is what, above all, makes empathy possible" (p. 3). One of the main goals of TOW is to humanize the "other" and see "other" as self. This is essentially a process of empathy development. Empathy requires self/other awareness (Singer & Lamm, 2009). Empathy can be induced and training can increase it (Stephan & Finlay, 1999). "Empathy is an important part of emotional intelligence and the latter is crucial for human relations" (Vrecer, 2015, p. 65).

Role-playing activities and theatre are another realm that allow for adopting different perspectives and opening one's awareness to other ways of seeing the world. Bassett and Taylor (2007) state that:

> When, rather than merely watching others do it, people engage in "make believe," they can often temporarily let go of a long-held perspective for another that may be new, different, and sometimes challenging. Engaging in role-play enables someone to be someone else, if only to a limited degree and for a little while… engaging in this intimate way with the "other" often leads the role-player to experience some shift in his or her own perspectives. Using non-rational parts of themselves allows people to access their imaginations and thereby perhaps experience a breakthrough or deepen their self-knowledge and understanding of others.
>
> (p. 355)

This quote shows the effectiveness of role-playing in perspective transformation, and the fact that this can have a significant impact on audience members. One does not have to officially be "role playing," the effects of role playing as an audience member can be just as powerful (it may even be subconscious). TOW participants are likely also affected by the stories of other participants in similar ways, when they first hear them.

Lawrence and Butterwick (2007) researched the effects of difference and oppression in an arts-based transformative learning study. They believe that the arts allow people to deeply express emotive and difficult issues. They also feel the arts can create opportunities for risky storytelling:

> Exploring oppression from a transformational learning perspective requires engaging with the subjective-objective dialectic, that is, it involves both the naming of lived experiences that are often painful and traumatic, and also a process of making sense of these experiences in order to collectively and individually take action to achieve social justice.
>
> (p. 411)

In their paper they reported the ways affective knowing, storytelling, and embodied knowing connect in Popular Theatre and become key components in creating transformational learning opportunities (Lawrence & Butterwick, 2007). This also describes certain aspects of the TOW process.

Wasserman's (2005) paper discusses the relational area of transformative learning and applies the theory to historically and socially defined group differences. The participants engaged in relational transformation after reflecting on their transformative experiences. This assisted them in expanding their stories of themselves, others, and "Us." Similarly, to weaken the dualities of "them and us," Tyler (2007) created a storytelling process for "trying on the other." She incorporated four theoretical strands into her experiment to create a group experience of "otherness." These studies support the use of theatre and storytelling for empathy development and humanizing the "other" through transformative learning experiences.

Each of the areas of this theoretical framework is needed to adequately describe the TOW process. Artistic ways of knowing in transformative learning addresses the extrarational, creative, and embodied aspects. Transformative learning theory draws on the psychological and developmental domains that capture the changes the participants and researcher are going through. Finally, emotional and spiritual learning within transformative learning embraces the emotions and spiritual aspects of the TOW experience. All the aspects of this theoretical framework interact with and support each other. Most importantly, they provide a lens through which to examine the TOW process.

Case Study of Participant Change

The purpose of this qualitative case study was to explore and describe the impact of the TOW program. In addition to the examination of a number of

TOW productions in both the primary and secondary contexts, the main focus of the study is on the individual changes of the participants and this author through their interactions with the program. The theoretical framework that served as the foundation for this study is transformative learning (Mezirow, 1978a, 1985, 1991a, 1994b, 2000, 2006; Daloz, 1986, 2012), emotional learning and soul work (Dirkx, 1997, 2000, 2001, 2006, 2008), and artistic ways of knowing (Gardner, 1983; Greene, 1995; Eisner, 2002; Lawrence, 2005; Hoggan, Simpson, & Stuckey, 2009; Blackburn Miller, 2020).

Research Questions

Q1: Why and how did the founder of TOW develop the program and what do the scripts look like across contexts?
Q2: How have the TOW participants changed through their involvement with the program?
Q3: How has the researcher changed through her involvement with the program?

This chapter will focus on research question two. This research uses a single case study methodology (Stake, 1995, 2000). Case study research is known by the thick description of phenomenon and the use of multiple approaches to triangulate conclusions (Stake, 1995; Yin 2018). A case study is a good approach for this research because TOW is a bounded, unusual case. It is also within a specific time frame that is contemporary (Yin, 2018). Its inception as an organization in 1991 until the present bounds the TOW program. However, this study focuses more specifically on the founder's work on inner-city violence in Philadelphia over the last 20 years, and her work in NI between 2009 and 2014. It is an unusual case in that there is very little empirical research about Testimonial Theatre programs, especially with non-actors.

To situate oneself in qualitative inquiry, as the research instrument, it is necessary to address the researcher's positionality. Due to their alignment with the purposes of the examined TOW program, the researcher focused on transformative educational practices (Mezirow, 1991a, 2000; Daloz, 1986, 2012), versus critical and emancipatory education (Freire, 1970; Horton & Freire, 1990; Boal, 2000). Transformative practices are a better fit for the TOW process because TOW focuses on individual change, whereas emancipatory practices focus more on social change. Also, TOW is more facilitator led, whereas emancipatory practices are more participatory.

Spirituality, soul, and emotions are important in adult learning (Dirkx, 1997, 2001). This is also part of the author's theoretical framework because these attributes can be found in TOW. Constructivism (Dewey, 1933) is the guiding philosophy, which means knowledge is constructed by learners' prior experiences (usually determined by their social and cultural environment). This perspective affects how learning is viewed in this research study. Artistic ways of knowing are respected and upheld, and there is wisdom in many different traditions and approaches to knowledge (Lawrence, 2005; Hoggan, Simpson, & Stuckey, 2009). It is important to study the arts and the impact they have upon learning, along with other educational outcomes.

The TOW Process

While TOW has some similarities to other forms of applied theatre, it also has many unique characteristics that have been developed by Teya Sepinuck over the years she has practiced developing this art form. The TOW process begins when Sepinuck chooses a social justice topic relevant to the community with whom she works. She then looks for community members involved with that topic and conducts "listening circles" with them. After this, she selects people to interview. That involves numerous one-on-one meetings (during which she takes verbatim notes). She then decides who is ready to work with the "other side" (the "other side" depends on the topic of the production). There are usually 6 to 10 people for each production. After they get to know each other informally, they work for about 8 to 10 months to develop the production.

The production script consists of excerpts from the verbatim interview transcripts. The performers work with Sepinuck to refine it into something they are comfortable performing. She also considers other artistic aspects like lighting, stage position, music, etc., that help to bring each story to life. Once the piece is complete, they perform and film the production. Sepinuck focuses especially on engaging audiences directly to explore the topic of the production. This happens through "talk backs" with the performers, where the audience can ask questions, after the performance or film screening is over. The film is often used for community education and workshops after the production is finished.

One of the keys to this approach, that develops empathy, is truthful storytelling, which is authentic and vulnerable. Many participants have experienced being a perpetrator or a victim (sometimes both). They need to be in an emotional condition and mindset where they can cooperatively work with the "other side." Even if they have already undergone therapy and healing, it can still be very emotional and challenging work.

Twelve Guiding Principles of TOW

Sepinuck wrote a book in 2013 in which she discusses the history of TOW and the various productions she has created, as well as her "method." Her 12 guiding principles are: (1) Not knowing, (2) Bear witness, (3) Find the medicine, (4) The blessing is at the center of the wound, (5) Deeply listen with the ears of your heart, (6) Become the vessel, (7) Hold the paradox, (8) Find the gold, (9) Take the problem and make it the solution, (10) Fall in love, (11) Trust the process, and (12) Everyone is me (i.e., see the "other" as self) (Sepinuck, 2013, pp. 227–235). Some of these won't make sense without further explanation, but they certainly reflect Sepinuck's meditative approach to her work.

Research Program and Setting

Sepinuck lives in Philadelphia, Pennsylvania, and has been creating TOW productions there for over 30 years. The author first discovered TOW in 2016 on a tour of The Playhouse in Derry/Londonderry, NI, where TOW had been housed for five years (2009–2014). The Playhouse Director, Pauline Ross, recounted the powerful impact the TOW productions had had on the divided community during the time Sepinuck had created them there with the aid of EU peace process funding. The Playhouse offers a variety of arts programs and serves as neutral territory for cross-community peacebuilding projects in Derry/Londonderry.

The Philadelphia/United States Context

Many inner-city conditions result from systemic racism and economic oppression. As a result, a large percentage of inner-city residents are racial minorities, especially "Black," and are of low socioeconomic status. Their financial opportunities are very limited and their communities suffer with crime, especially by disconnected youth, for a source of income. These structural conflicts are the roots of gang violence and incarceration of the community's members (Patterson, 2015). This is the case with inner-city Philadelphia. It is the poorest big city in the US (Saksa, 2017). Using data from the 2010 US Census and the 2012–2016 American Community Survey, Diebel, Norda, and Kretchmer (2019) provided the following statistics for race and ethnicity in Philadelphia: 42.9% Black, 35.3% White, 12.4% Hispanic, 6.9% Asian, 2.1% Mixed, and 0.5% Other. Philadelphia is also one of the most identity-segregated cities in the US (Comen, 2019).

This kind of environment leads to mistrust between community members, in addition to between them and its police. There is a need for community development and engagement to increase economic opportunities, provide job training, improve the quality of the schools, and increase the safety of the neighborhoods. In addition, on a broader scale, there is a need for racial reconciliation, to help remove and prevent institutionalized racism as well as for improvement of police–community relations. Preventing overt racism is also necessary, which is a process of racial reconciliation between community members at the individual level (Shearer, 1994; Hampton & Gullotta, 2004; Corcoran, 2010). TOW and other community arts programs are uniquely situated to address some of these issues.

The Northern Ireland Context

NI had difficulty maintaining social stability for centuries before its inception as a country within the United Kingdom in May 1921. The social instability began with the Anglo-Norman intervention in Ireland in 1167, and is still felt today. This intervention created two distinct people groups: the English and Scottish Protestant settlers, and the Irish Catholics. Most Irish Catholics have wanted to maintain their unity with the Republic of Ireland, whereas the English and Scottish Protestant settlers have wanted to remain loyal to England. This created a schism in NI society. The period of The Troubles began in the 1960s, when Irish Catholics began a civil rights movement to create equality in voting, housing, and employment. However, what began peacefully eventually became violent, and paramilitaries were formed on both sides. The unrest of The Troubles lasted for 30 years, officially ending with the Good Friday Agreement in 1998. However, there has been a long road to actual peace while needed changes in society and in the education system have been very slow (Tonge, 2002).

Northern Irish society is highly segregated. Even though The Troubles have ended, much segregation still exists (Carter, 2005). Segregation can be seen not only with housing but also with employment and education (Carter, 2007; Evans, 2012; Pavett, 2011). Since the education system has only partially integrated its students, this is one area where community arts programs step in to create cross-community opportunities wherein children and adults can make connections and build peaceful relationships. TOW productions and community workshops pursue that goal.

Research Sample and Sampling Procedures

The TOW narratives describe the historical, cultural, political, economic, and social conditions that shape the identities and worldviews of the participants, as well as the desired program outcomes. As a result of participating in an intensive five-day training with Sepinuck in 2017, and having attended three live productions and two film screenings, the author is a participant observer in this research.

The participant interviews are based on purposive and snowball sampling (Patton, 2015). The pilot study interviews helped to identify themes. Additional interviews and data collection help to validate these themes. The interviews investigate the participants' TOW experiences and learning outcomes.

Regarding the ethical concerns for this research study, the Penn State University Institutional Review Board (IRB) gave an expedited review. The participants' names were removed from their quotes to protect their identities, except for the NI TOW Producer. Intersectionalities like race, ethnicity, class, and gender need to be considered in social justice theatre productions like TOW. It is important that the researcher maintains awareness of these identity factors as potential issues and how they can influence the researcher–participant relationship and data outcomes in both locations (Karnieli-Miller, Strier, & Pessach, 2009).

Data Sources and Collection

The research sites are The Playhouse and other locations in NI, and various locations in Philadelphia. The Playhouse in Derry/Londonderry is where the founder developed all of the TOW productions during the five years she worked there. The Playhouse still conducts TOW workshops in the community with former TOW participants. The author was given access to the audience feedback forms from the productions, as well as three of the four scripts from the productions, which are kept in The Playhouse archives. One of the scripts is inaccessible due to privacy concerns, and it is not about The Troubles (the other three are). Semi-structured interviews were conducted with five participants and three staff members in NI.

Sepinuck gave the author four scripts from the Philadelphia productions that are all on a similar theme: the effects of inner-city violence on community members, families, prisoners, and police in Philadelphia. Semi-structured interviews were conducted with four participants and four staff members in Philadelphia. For all interviews in both locations, a brief background questionnaire was included. Program materials were also collected when the author attended TOW events in Philadelphia, and relevant cultural/historical materials were gathered in NI. In addition, the author has her own written reflections on her experiences as a participant and audience member in Philadelphia. The preliminary results for this chapter will be limited to the participant interviews.

Data Analysis

Many researchers are now turning to narrative analysis because stories reveal truths about human experience. Sometimes sorrowful or traumatic experiences can be processed more easily through storytelling. "Telling stories about difficult times in our lives creates order and contains emotions, allowing a search for meaning and enabling connection with others" (Riessman, 2008, p. 10). TOW is an example of this kind of storytelling. It is important to remember the inherent social nature of storytelling:

> To be understood, these private constructions of identity must mesh with a community of life stories, or "deep structures" about the nature of life itself in a particular culture. Connecting biography and society becomes possible through the close analysis of stories.
>
> (Riessman, 2008, p. 10)

In narrative analysis, there is an attention to the process of action. The researcher focuses on particular actors in certain places at certain times, all bound within a social context. During the analysis, the researcher is concerned with how the speaker uses language to communicate meaning and how they are making particular points to the audience. In narrative analysis, there is an interrogation of how and why the language is being used in a certain way (Riessman, 2008). As Riessman (2008) asks:

> For whom was this story constructed, and for what purpose? Why is the succession of events configured that way? What cultural resources does

the story draw on, or take for granted? What storehouse of plots does it call up? What does the story accomplish? Are there gaps and inconsistencies that might suggest preferred, alternative, or counter-narratives?

(p. 11)

Since there are so many ways to narrate experience, attention must be paid to how it is done.

Every research method has its own goals and purposes. In narrative analysis the particulars and context of the narrative come to the forefront. For instance, how does the audience affect what is told and what cannot be told? This applies to the TOW scripts, and also to the interviews with the participants. There are also a number of levels of interpretation. The narrator interprets their memory of past events while narrating, the researcher interprets what is said, and the reader interprets what is reported. This allows the research to include many voices and subjectivities (Riessman, 2008).

In thematic narrative analysis (Riessman, 2008), the researcher is interested in the content of *what* is being said. The focus is on the told events and experiences, not the telling. Thematic analysts generally do not attend to language, form, or interaction. The content of stories can unmask sociological concepts at work in everyday life, like how we understand ourselves in relation to society, and what that society is like. The researcher is looking for the thematic meanings and points. In this approach, prior theory serves as a reference to interpret the narrative. The researcher can also look for common thematic elements across participant narratives (Riessman, 2008). All of these points make sense for the TOW data analysis, which is why thematic narrative analysis was chosen for the TOW participant interviews.

Themes

Based on a preliminary data analysis, the following themes have emerged: empathy development, humanizing the "other," perspective transformation, personal healing from trauma/"finding the medicine" in their story, overcoming personal obstacles and challenges, creating a close "family-like" bond with other participants, developing personal strength and resilience, and personal transformation leads to social transformation. A selection of participant quotes illustrate the findings below.

Empathy Development

Researcher: "Do you feel that the influence that TOW has on empathy is lasting for people?"

> Oh yeah, without a doubt. I mean I'm still going into workshops with people I never thought I would be in the same room as... A couple of weeks ago we met with a group of American students at the Playhouse,

and I sat beside ___ and ___, and people were amazed that we could sit in the same room. I'm a serving police officer, ___ is a former paramilitary, and ___ is a former Republican [IRA]. That empathy still continues to allow us to work together and it's an actual fact, and I'm proud to say it, to be friends. In circumstances where people would think that those people would never be friends… never…

      (Participant A, personal communication, June 23, 2017)

Humanizing the "Other"

Only good stuff has come out of this… only good stuff. Incredible friendships, incredible empathy, and understanding. Now when I look at things, I look at them from all sides… not just tunnel vision.

If you've already humanized somebody, it's hard to dehumanize them. Before you get to judge somebody, if you've made some sort of connection, it's hard to go back on that connection. It's all about humanizing people.

      (Participant B, personal communication, June 3, 2017)

Perspective Transformation

Hearing their [police officers'] stories made me look at them as people. You know… Uh, I'd never even stopped to think about police as people. I mean, I know they was human beings, that's just, that's natural. But I'd never, never really looked at them as being people… you know, with feelings and emergencies and regrets, and you know, all the stuff that we all have. But when I listened to ___ at that time, and after that session was over with… I went and shook his hand and we embraced. I had never done that… I never shook the hand of a policeman.

That was a breakthrough for me with [production name]. That small gesture of a handshake. But it was a legitimate change in how I looked at him and the police.

      (Participant C, personal communication, September 27, 2018)

Personal Healing from Trauma/'Finding the Medicine'

Participant D claimed TOW (NI) was more healing than years of therapy:

I grasped the concept of TOW very early on. I could see the power of it for me personally, as well as where it could go. And I know that all the other guys absolutely connected at a very deep level with it.

There's something about the uniqueness of telling your story. Something very powerful about it.

But there's certainly something about the power of how we tell a story, and the impact that has on you as you tell that story. [the impact on the

audience and yourself] If it's working for you at a personal level, it's absolutely going to resonate with the audience, of course it is, of course it is…
(Participant D, personal communication, June 2, 2017)

Overcoming Personal Obstacles and Challenges

Teya had so much confidence in me, and believed in me and listened to me, and made me start believing in myself… and giving me confidence, through the Theatre of Witness. And Teya helped put us on that stage, and giving me my life back.

I couldn't believe it, and I did it! I got up on that stage! And every time we did a play, it was like I was getting rid of my wee skeletons. My fears… and starting to like who I was. And finding a voice, she gave me a voice, which I never, ever, ever had.
(Participant E, personal communication, May 3, 2018)

Creating a Close "Family-like" Bond with Other Participants

So lucky to have been involved in this, for as hard as it was… emotionally, I got to meet so many good people in that group. And that I not only just consider as friends, but kind of like family, and I would bend over backwards for any one of those people involved in this whole process with us. And I would, in a minute, drop of a dime, I would… if they needed help, I'd be heading there to help them. To form a bond like that is very special and I'm very lucky to have been picked to be able to experience that and be part of it.
(Participant F, personal communication, December 30, 2018)

Developing Personal Strength and Resilience

That's just how advocating is… when you're in front of people. They don't want you reading off a script, they want you to speak from your heart. And then you remember everything. It's easier to advocate for yourself when you've memorized it, instead of cramming it.

And so, if I wrote down the timeline and actually remember it, this way when I say it it's just like rehearsing the lines of my story… through Theater of Witness. It's important in that way. Um, it's also helped me with learning that it's my truth and I can say in front of everybody who's a complete stranger and I don't care about that. Because I'm here to speak my truth and you're here to hear the truth. And if you don't like it that's not my problem.
(Participant G, personal communication, November 8, 2018)

Personal Transformation Leads to Social Transformation

I'm using the same [TOW] storytelling technique to illustrate points in a training curriculum to officers in Poland, Romania, Ukraine, Italy, all the way around Europe. And we've seen that it is transformative. Using narrative and using true storytelling in context to illustrate lessons, and to illustrate points about how you treat minority communities. We have actually proved the transformative nature that it takes with the officers.

I train police officers in how to engage positively with these communities. And I use narrative in order to illustrate points from the lesson. So, in a two-day training course, I'll probably use about 10 stories from my past, from my background, to illustrate the negative side of treating people oppressively. So, I'm still using these techniques… years after [production name]. And I'm still working in Northern Ireland, we're still working in communities doing TOW workshops… in communities and schools. That's the longevity of this project.
(Participant A, personal communication, June 23, 2017)

Summary

This study showed that TOW is able to deeply impact the participants' lives when the whole process is handled with great care. Her background and skills, as well as her spiritual practices, helps Sepinuck in that work. Over the years, she developed the 12 guiding principles (listed earlier in this chapter), which became the foundation for doing TOW productions. Each rehearsal begins with quiet time, creating a safe space where participants can let go of what they came in with and embrace what is before them. Sepinuck has a variety of healing rituals and activities that she uses to bring the participants closer together and to help them understand each other better. Some examples the participants mentioned in their interviews were eye contact and breathing exercises that they did with partners. These were very effective at creating empathy. In addition, the deep listening and bearing witness to each other's stories as a small group helped prepare them to tell their stories to the audience, who in turn were there to bear witness to their suffering, strength, and common humanity. The TOW producer in NI sums the impact of TOW up best:

> People still talk about TOW. People still ask me is there going to be any more of it. And a politician, just 3 months ago, said to me… "we need more of TOW." Because the past won't go away. It's not going to go away, you know… And I think that TOW, it has such a cushion around it, a cushion of care and consideration and sensitivity, and that its primary aim, not only to create the empathy, but to safeguard everyone involved in it… their health and wellbeing is critical. And I do without reservation say I feel it has helped every single participant. It could not but make an impact.
> (P. Ross, personal communication, June 1, 2017)

Conclusion

Theatre can create the conditions for role playing and deep listening when each participant is willing to let those conditions affect them during that experience. TOW, in particular, helps people see other people as human beings—as people with hopes, desires, vulnerabilities, and individual lives. That perception enables the peacebuilding processes of empathy development and breaking down stereotypes. Peacebuilding is an ongoing process, like a garden that needs to be watered over and over by the arts and peace education programs inside and outside of schools for harvesting needed relationships and understanding. It is an endeavor worth undertaking though, for without it, empathy will not grow, but the weeds of prejudice and hatred will.

References

Bang, A. H. (2016). The restorative and transformative power of the arts in conflict resolution. *Journal of Transformative Education, 14*(4), 355–376.

Bassett, C., & Taylor, K. (2007). *Using role-play (and music, poetry, and drama) to challenge perspectives and understand "difference"*. Paper presented at the 7th International Transformative Learning Conference, Albuquerque, NM.

Bell, L. A., Desai, D., & Irani, K. (2013). Storytelling for social justice: Creating arts-based counterstories to resist racism. In M. S. Hanley, G. L. Sheppard, G. W. Noblit, & T. Barone (Eds.), *Culturally relevant arts education for social justice: A way out of no way* (pp. 15–24). Routledge.

Blackburn Miller, J. (2018). The transformative and healing power of theatre of witness. *Canadian Journal for the Study of Adult Education, 30*(2) 47–56.

Blackburn Miller, J. (2020). Transformative learning and the arts: A literature review. *Journal of Transformative Education, 18*(4), 338–355.

Boal, A. (1994). *A rainbow of desire: The Boal method of theatre and therapy*. New York: Routledge

Boal, A. (2000). *Theatre of the oppressed*. London: Pluto Press.

Butterwick, S., & Selman, J. (2012). Embodied knowledge and decolonization: Walking with theater's powerful and risky pedagogy. *New Directions for Adult and Continuing Education, 134*, 61–69.

Carter, C. C. (2005). Reaching out for "the other". In J. Canfield, M. V. Hansen, C. C. Carter, S. Palomares, L. Williams, & B. Winch (Eds.), *Chicken soup for the soul: Stories for a better world* (pp. 326–329). New York: Simon & Schuster.

Carter, C. C. (2007). Teacher preparation for peacebuilding in USA and Northern Ireland. In Z. Bekerman & C. McGlynn (Eds.), *Addressing ethnic conflict through peace education* (pp. 245–258). New York: Palgrave Macmillan.

Carter, C. C. (Ed.). (2010). *Conflict resolution and peace education: Transformations across disciplines*. New York: Palgrave Macmillan. doi: 10.1057/9780230107830

Clark, M. C., & Dirkx, J. (2008). The emotional self in adult learning. *New directions for adult and continuing education, 120*, 89–96.

Claycomb, R. M. (2003). (Ch) oral history: Documentary theatre, the communal subject and progressive politics. *Journal of Dramatic Theory and Criticism, 2*, 95–122.

Cohen, C., Varea, R. G., & Walker, P. (2011). Lessons from the acting together project. In C. Cohen, R. G. Varea, & P. Walker (Eds.), *Acting together: Performance and the creative transformation of conflict* (Vol. 2) (pp. 191–197). Oakland, CA: New Village Press.

Comen, E. (2019). Detroit, Chicago, Memphis: The 25 most segregated cities in America. *USA Today*. Retrieved from www.usatoday.com/story/money/2019/07/20/detroit-chicago-memphis-most-segregated-cities-america-housing-policy/39703787/

Corcoran, R. (2010). *Trustbuilding: An honest conversation on race, reconciliation, and responsibility*. Charlottesville: University of Virginia Press.
Daloz, L. A. (1986). *Effective teaching and mentoring: Realizing the transformational power of adult learning experiences*. San Francisco: Jossey-Bass.
Daloz, L. A. (2012). *Mentor: Guiding the journey of adult learners* (2nd ed.). San Francisco: Jossey-Bass.
Dawson, G. F. (1999). *Documentary theatre in the United States: An historical survey and analysis of its content, form, and stagecraft*. Westport, Conn: Greenwood Press.
Dewey, J. (1933). *How we think: A restatement of the relation of reflective thinking to the educative process*. Boston: D.C. Heath & Co Publishers.
Diebel, J., Norda, J., & Kretchmer, O. (2019). *Race and ethnicity in Philadelphia, Pennsylvania, PA*. Retrieved from https://statisticalatlas.com/place/Pennsylvania/Philadelphia/Race-and-Ethnicity
Dirkx, J. (1997). Nurturing soul in adult learning. *New Directions for Adult and Continuing Education, 74*, 79–88.
Dirkx, J. (2000). Transformative learning and the journey of individuation. *Eric Clearinghouse on Adult Career and Vocational Education*. https://eric.ed.gov/?id=ED448305
Dirkx, J. (2001). The power of feelings: Emotion, imagination, and the construction of meaning in adult learning. *New Directions for Adult and Continuing Education, 89*, 63–72.
Dirkx, J. (2006). Engaging emotions in adult learning. *New Directions for Adult and Continuing Education, 109*, 15–26.
Dirkx, J. (2008). The meaning and role of emotions in adult learning. *New Directions for Adult and Continuing Education, 120*, 7–18.
Dirkx, J. (2012). Self-formation and transformative learning: A response to "Calling transformative learning into question: Some mutinous thoughts," by Michael Newman. *Adult Education Quarterly, 62*(4), 399–405.
Eisner, E. (2002). *The arts and the creation of mind*. New Haven, CN: Yale University Press.
Evans, M. (2012, October 2). Uneasy peace, the segregated reality of Northern Ireland. *CBC News*. Retrieved from www.cbc.ca/news/world/uneasy-peace-the-segregated-reality-of-northern-ireland-1.1255828
Forgasz, R., & McDonough, S. (2017) "Struck by the way our bodies conveyed so much": A collaborative self-study of our developing understanding of embodied pedagogies. *Studying Teacher Education, 13*(1), 52–67. doi: 10.1080/17425964.2017.1286576
Forsyth, A., & Megson, C. (Eds.). (2009). *Get real: Documentary theatre past and present*. London: Palgrave Macmillan.
Freire, P. (1970). *Pedagogy of the oppressed*. New York: Herder and Herder.
Galtung, J. (2004). *Transcend and transform*. Boulder, CO: Paradigm.
Gardner, H. (1983). *Frames of mind: The theory of multiple intelligences*. New York: Basic Books.
Gardner, H. (1993). *Multiple intelligences: The theory in practice*. New York: Basic Books.
Goleman, D. (1995). *Emotional intelligence: Why it can matter more than IQ*. New York: Bantam Books.
Greene, M. (1995). *Releasing the imagination: Essays on education, the arts, and social change*. San Francisco: Wiley.
Hammond, W., & Steward, D. (2008). *Verbatim verbatim: Contemporary documentary theatre*. London: Oberon.

Hampton, R. L., & Gullotta, T. P. (Eds.). (2004). *Promoting racial, ethnic, and religious understanding and reconciliation*. Washington, DC: Child Welfare League of America.

Harlap, Y., & Aristizabal, H. (2013). Using theater to promote social justice in communities: Pedagogical approaches to community and individual learning. In M. S. Hanley, G. L. Sheppard, G. W. Noblit, & T. Barone (Eds.), *Culturally relevant arts education for social justice: A way out of no way* (pp. 25–35). New York: Routledge.

Hayes, S., & Yorks, L. (2007). Lessons from the lessons learned: Arts change the world when…. *New Directions for Adult and Continuing Education, 2007*(116), 89–98. doi:10.1002/ace.279

Hoggan, C., Simpson, S., & Stuckey, H. (2009). *Creative expression in transformative learning: Tools and techniques for educators of adults*. Malabar, FL: Krieger Publishing Co.

Horton, M., & Freire, P. (1990). *We make the road by walking: Conversations on education and social change*. Philadelphia, PA: Temple University Press.

Karnieli-Miller, O., Strier, R., & Pessach, L. (2009). Power relations in qualitative research. *Qualitative Health Research, 19*(2), 279–289.

Kitchenham, A. (2008). The evolution of John Mezirow's transformative learning theory. *Journal of Transformative Education, 6*(2), 104–123. doi:10.1177/1541344608322678

Lawrence, R. L. (2005). Knowledge construction as contested terrain: Adult learning through artistic expression. *New Directions for Adult and Continuing Education, 2005*(107), 3–11. doi:10.1002/ace.184

Lawrence, R. L., & Butterwick, S. (2007). *Re-imaging oppression: An arts-based embodied approach to transformative learning*. Paper presented at the 7th International Transformative Learning Conference, Albuquerque, NM.

Maedza, P. (2013). *Theatre of testimony: An investigation in devising asylum*. [Master's dissertation, University of Cape Town]. https://open.uct.ac.za/handle/11427/6848

Mezirow, J. (1978a). *Education for perspective transformation: Women's re-entry programs in community colleges*. New York: Teacher's College, Columbia University.

Mezirow, J. (1978b). Perspective transformation. *Adult Education, 28*, 100–110.

Mezirow, J. (1985). A critical theory of self-directed learning. In S. Brookfield (Ed.), *Self-directed learning: From theory to practice – New directions for continuing education, 25*. San Francisco: Jossey-Bass.

Mezirow, J. (1989). Transformation theory and social action: A response to Collard and Law. *Adult Education Quarterly, 39*(3), 169–175.

Mezirow, J. (1990). *Fostering critical reflection in adulthood*. San Francisco: Jossey-Bass.

Mezirow, J. (1991a). *Transformative dimensions in adult learning*. San Francisco: Jossey-Bass.

Mezirow, J. (1991b). Transformation theory and cultural context: A reply to Clark and Wilson. *Adult Education Quarterly, 41*(3), 188–192.

Mezirow, J. (1992). Transformation theory: Critique and confusion. *Adult Education Quarterly, 42*(4), 250–252.

Mezirow, J. (1994a). Response to Mark Tennant and Michael Newman. *Adult Education Quarterly, 44*(4), 243–244.

Mezirow, J. (1994b). Understanding transformation theory. *Adult Education Quarterly, 44*(4), 222–232.

Mezirow, J. (1995). Transformation theory of adult learning. In M. R. Welton (Ed.), *In defense of the life-world* (pp. 39–70). New York: State University of New York.

Mezirow, J. (1996). Contemporary paradigms of learning. *Adult Education Quarterly, 46*(3), 158–172.

Mezirow, J. (1997). Transformative learning: Theory to practice. *New Directions for Adult and Continuing Education, 74*, 5–12.
Mezirow, J. (1998a). Cognitive processes: Contemporary paradigm of learning. In P. Sutherland (Ed.), *Adult learning: A reader* (pp. 2–13). London: Kogan Page.
Mezirow, J. (1998b). On critical reflection. *Adult Learning Quarterly, 48*(3), 185–198.
Mezirow, J. (2000). *Learning as transformation: Critical perspectives on a theory in progress.* San Francisco: Jossey-Bass.
Mezirow, J. (2003). Transformative learning as discourse. *Journal of Transformative Education, 1*(1), 58–63.
Mezirow, J. (2006). An overview of transformative learning. In P. Sutherland & J. Crowther (Eds.), *Lifelong learning: Concepts and contexts* (pp. 24–38). New York: Routledge.
Modirzadeh, L. (2013). Documentary theater in education: Empathy building as a tool for social change. In M. S. Hanley, G. L. Sheppard, G. W. Noblit, & T. Barone (Eds.), *Culturally relevant arts education for social justice: A way out of no way* (pp. 47–57). New York: Routledge.
Paget, D. (1987). 'Verbatim theatre': Oral history and documentary techniques. *New Theatre Quarterly, 3*(12), 317–336.
Patterson, O. (2015, May 9). The real problem with America's inner cities. *The New York Times.* Retrieved from www.nytimes.com/2015/05/10/opinion/sunday/the-real-problem-with-americas-inner-cities.html
Patton, M. Q. (2015). *Qualitative research and evaluation methods: integrating theory and practice* (4th ed.). Thousand Oaks, CA: Sage.
Pavett, D. (2011, November 29). Northern Ireland teaches us the dangers of segregated schools. *The Guardian.* Retrieved from www.theguardian.com/commentisfree/2011/nov/29/northern-ireland-segregated-schools-peter-robinson
Perry, W. G. (1968). *Forms of intellectual and ethical development in the college years: A scheme.* New York: Holt, Rinehart and Winston.
Riessman, C. K. (2008). *Narrative methods for the human sciences.* Thousand Oaks, CA: Sage.
Saksa, J. (2017, November 15). Pew report: Philly's poor have been stuck in the inner city, separated from suburban job growth. *Whyy.* Retrieved from https://whyy.org/segments/pew-report-phillys-poor-stuck-inner-city-separated-suburban-job-growth/
Scher, A. (2007). Can the arts change the world? The transformative power of community arts. *New Directions for Adult and Continuing Education, 2007*(116), 3–11. doi:10.1002/ace.272
Sepinuck, T. (2013). *Theatre of witness: Finding the medicine in stories of suffering, transformation and peace.* London: Jessica Kingsley.
Shearer, J. M. (1994). *Enter the river: Healing steps from white privilege toward racial reconciliation.* Scottsdale: Herald Press.
Singer, T., & Lamm, C. (2009). The social neuroscience of empathy. *Annals of the New York Academy of Sciences, 1156*(1), 81–96.
Stake, R. E. (1995). *The art of case study research.* Thousand Oaks, CA: Sage.
Stake, R. E. (2000). Case studies. In N. K. Denzin & Y. S. Lincoln (Eds.), *Handbook of qualitative research* (pp. 435–454). Thousand Oaks, CA: Sage.
Stephan, W. G., & Finlay, K. (1999). The role of empathy in improving intergroup relations. *Journal of Social Issues, 55*(4), 729–743.
Tonge, J. (2002). *Northern Ireland: Conflict and change* (2nd ed.). New York: Pearson.

Tyler, J. A. (2007). *How did you hear that? A storytelling process for "Trying on the Other" in three rounds.* Paper presented at the 7th International Transformative Learning Conference, Albuquerque, NM.

Vrecer, N. (2015). Empathy in adult education. *The Andragogic Perspectives, 3,* 65–73.

Wasserman, I. C. (2005). *Expanding stories of ourselves, others and us in dialogue: A relational approach to transformative learning in the engagement of diversity.* Paper presented at the 6th International Transformative Learning Conference, East Lansing, MI.

Weston, S. (2020) 'Being part of something much bigger than self': The community play as a model of implicit and explicit political theatre practice. *Research in Drama Education: The Journal of Applied Theatre and Performance, 25*(2), 161–177.

Yin, R. K. (2018). *Case study research and applications: Design and methods* (6th ed.). Thousand Oaks, CA: Sage.

11 Political Humor and Peace Education

Syed Sikander Mehdi

Introduction

How to diminish violence and unfreedom and enhance peace and happiness has always been an issue of great concern to the visionaries and political activists. This concern often produced new ideas and perspectives, projected images of new futures, launched titanic movements, and brought about spectacular changes in the societies struggling for peace and change. Though little acknowledged, the changes that took place at international, regional, and local level in the modern times are profound. These include the collapse of empires, including colonial empires, fall of absolutist monarchies and totalitarian regimes, abolishment of the institution of slavery, emergence of the European Union in an age of nation-states, no use of nuclear weapons in wars after Hiroshima and Nagasaki, and almost an end of inter-state wars. In addition, the launch and spread of movements for peace, justice, democracy and freedom, human rights, development, human security, and happiness have considerably impacted political and social thinking, practices, and policies. To a certain extent, all this could be possible because of the peace teachings along with peace initiatives of philosophers, scholars, and leaders of peaceful change.

However, the journey to peace is an endless and timeless journey. The train is perpetually on the move from one station to another. There is no final destination, no last station. When one river is crossed, another comes in sight; and when one mountain is scaled, another moves in. At the doors of every new age, the unresolved issues of the past are delivered. Soon after, new challenges also present. To tackle these, pushing of the alternate knowledge frontiers, sharpening of available tools, inventing of new tools and innovative strategizing are minimal prerequisites.

It is in this context that the role of peace education in promoting peace in these changing and challenging times needs to be examined. This need has arisen because traditional peace education alone cannot deliver. Worse still, peace studies programs in universities and peace research centers in many countries are simply reproducing the official narratives of the states and selling unpeace in the name of peace. Again, the amazing peace initiatives on the

DOI: 10.4324/9781003227380-11

streets, on the stage in the theatres, in films and art galleries, in fiction and poetry, and in music and dance still remain somewhat unacknowledged and unsung. Formal peace education programs seem to be too preoccupied with their own traditional and loaded programs to provide time and space to the ever-enlarging domain of informal peace education. Likewise, focused studies on the peace role and peace potentials of performing arts are few and far between. Keeping this in view, this chapter discusses the peace potentials of political humor and recommends its larger application as a powerful political tool and as an agency of nonformal peace education to contain and control violence all around.

These are, indeed, violent times. Besides direct military rule and military sponsored, patronized or backed regimes, several other bizarre political systems in the developed and developing countries, all claiming to be democratic, tend to demonstrate authoritarian tendencies. A number of them try to silence the voices of dissent and run their political systems by showing and using force. In addition, proliferation of weapons of mass destruction and other deadly weapons, rise of militarism, extremism, intolerance and discrimination, neglect of human security and wellness issues, widespread poverty and expanded inequality have increased human vulnerabilities manifold. By and large, vulnerability and slavery of all kinds are being produced by power-over political systems at all levels of governance. These undermine human well-being and happiness, and endanger the future as well as the present world. "The future of the world," Nobel Laureate Amartya Sen rightly says, "is intimately connected with the future of *freedom* in the world" (Sen, 2006, p. 27). It is therefore important to confront the twin threats to freedom, which are violent political systems and modern slavery. It is equally important that the diverse peace agencies, including the performing arts, are put into action to help transform this violent world into a "nest-world."

Setting Up Nests and Tearing Down the Nets

Though there is the difference of only one letter "S" in the two terms nest and net, these are worlds apart. Nests are cradles and homes, enclaves of peace, security, wellness, and happiness. These are schools teaching the art of sharing, caring, living, and growing together. They are, indeed, the little heavens where the mother and father birds protect their little ones, feed them, sing the songs of love into their ears, talk about their own experiences and joys and pains of life, caution about the lurking dangers, and prepare them to fly into the free and all-welcoming blue sky. A day comes, when the little ones fly away in search of larger freedom, and get ready to deal with the ecstasy and torment of the unknown. In due course, these little ones set up nests for their own little ones, feed them, train them to fly, and provide security and hope. In the kingdom of the nests, the mother birds and father birds feed and protect their little ones. Never ever are the nests reduced into Plato's caves. They are always the launching pads for larger freedom.

Nets, on the other hand, are the traps laid by power. These are the hunters, cagers, and destroyers of ideas and dreams for freedom and change. The nets are the trafficking mechanisms and prison houses, where the people are intended to be kept until dead. These nets are used to disturb the peace and tranquility of the rivers and oceans, pick up the swimming, dancing fish from their free and natural environ and habitat, put them out of water and offer the choice to buy life, accept servitude and float in the aquarium or languish and die. However colorful and attractive an aquarium full of water may be, it's a prison house for the fish. For the fish, life and joy of life are in the rivers and the oceans to which they belong, and where freedom is; and for the birds, life and joy of life are not in the cages, but in the nests, where freedom launches. Likewise, life and joy of life are there for the humans in the "nest-world" and not in the crowded "net-world" (Mehdi, 2020a, pp. 83–84).

Asking peace education to set up the nests and tear down the nets everywhere will be asking for too much. After all, peace education is not the genie out of the bottle. Nor is it capable of delivering what a happy, resourceful, and liberated genie can after gaining freedom. Neither is it a magic wand that may swash away all the dirt and put a shine on everything it handles. As such, substantive and qualitative change in the political behavior of the states will not be possible in a haste. Neither can traditional peace education alone transform the violent and oppressive power system. Nor can it dismantle the powerful authoritarian states in one go. Moreover, its job is to sow the seeds and prepare the ground for change. To accomplish this, both formal and informal peace education have to work imaginatively and creatively, and very hard for months, years, and decades, to promote larger awareness of the promise of a "nest-world" and the danger of a "net-world," and to convince that the "nest-world" is possible as well as desirable.

"Peace," observes Ian Harris, a distinguished American peace educator and scholar "is a practice of love" (Harris, 1988, p. 7). Pointing out that bringing "peace to this world is a complex activity that ranges in scope from political leaders negotiating arms agreements *to* lovers amicably settling disputes," Harris adds:

> Teachers have certain cognitive and affective goals for their students. Teachers may want their students to become aware of the role of violence in their lives, but awareness does not necessarily lead to action. What happens as a result of a particular international act is quite outside a teacher's control. Most peace educators have fairly traditional goals—hoping that their students will become more informed, think critically, learn the skills of conflict management, and use their rights as citizens—and are not sure what results their peace education activities will have.
> (1988, pp. 186–87)

More than 30 years after the publication of the first edition of Harris' pioneering study on peace education and storming of the academia and research institutes by peace and conflict studies during this period, along with globalizing of peace movements, it is clear that peace education needs to act proactively outside the classrooms as well. It needs to reach out to the people outside, strengthen the constituencies of peace worldwide, and create new peace constituencies. Ela Gandhi, the South African peace activist and former Chancellor of the Durban University of Technology, rightly observes that "Hitler would not have been able to run his reign of terror without his formidable band of followers." She says that the thinking that "elimination of one person, a Saddam Hussein or a Bin Laden, will in any way change the situation is barking up the wrong tree." "Acts, whether of terror or goodness," she points out, "can only be achieved if one has a band of followers" (Gandhi, 2014, pp. 65–66). Peace education needs to take note of this wise observation and work consciously for the enlargement of peace constituencies and for the broadening and enriching of peace contents and themes. Likewise, it needs to positively and proactively respond to the new and innovative initiatives taken in the recent years to build peace.

One such initiative was taken up by the UN, when it initiated the Program of Action on a Culture of Peace in 1999, and adopted a Declaration of the International Decade for the Promotion of a Culture of Peace and Nonviolence for the Children of the World 2001–2010. Commenting on it, a book description on the book entitled *Peace Education: Past, Present and Future*, edited by Jeannie Lum, says that this change "represented a paradigm shift away from the prevailing conceptualization of peace as 'the absence of war' to one of 'creating cultures of peace', and indicated a significant opening for peace educators and the expansion of their mission and field in peace research and scholarship" (Lum, 2017, p. 1).

In an excellent article published in 2014, Jeannie Lum, former editor of *The Journal of Peace Education*, writes at length about the changing times and the changing world, and the need for peace education to notice the changes and come out of its traditional mold and traditionalist approach to the issues of war and peace. She says that the "challenges for visioning a model for global educational leadership in the twenty-first century are uniquely different from those thus far assumed in the outgoing discourse about what determines 'success' in education, leadership, and administration." She points out:

> With the revelations of climate change, limited natural resources, the reality of nuclear, environmental, and industrial threats to survival of the human species in the past fifty years having finally reached a tipping point, a paradigm shift to a global mindset creates what appears to be a near impossible task.
>
> (Lum, 2014, p. 96)

However, Jeannie Lum is an optimist and she believes that the hurdles on the way are removable. She puts forward arguments and examples to explain as to how can this impossible task be made possible.

Emphasizing the need for "a revisioning, re-culturing, retooling, and reorienting of values in educational leadership for building cultures of peace," Jeannie Lum adds:

> The typical concerns of educational leaders (teachers and administrators), for example, curriculum content, school organization, discipline, classroom management, assessment and evaluation, policy decisions, relations with the community, parent involvement, student performance, and so on have values underlying and guiding the decision making and choices made in all of these areas. It's this level of taken-for-granted values that need to be consciously articulated and critically reflected upon in order to make the transformations needed.
>
> (Lum, 2014, p. 114)

Jeannie Lum further states that "a fundamental sensibility of the interconnectedness of all life systems of the earth and cosmos" need to be acknowledged and advises: "It is time for educational leaders to take that transdisciplinary leap into global visioning to cultures of peace in schooling'" (Ibid.). Along with the recommendations offered by her, peace education needs to try out different tools and methods of building the "nest-world." It is in this context that theatrical skills have been developed and used as peace education.

The Theatrical World of Laughter

The world of laughter is a crowded world. It is stuffed with jokes, humorous stories, one-liners, cartoons, comedy plays in print and on the stage in theatres and open spaces under the sky, comedy movies, comedy shows on TV channels, cartoonish graffiti, and political humor on social media. All these, and especially jokes and humorous stories are abundantly available online. These cover a variety of topics and themes, professions, and relationships. By and large, humor continues to be popularly viewed as a sort of innocent, harmless activity to portray and project hilarious situations for fun sake and to release tension and make academic, business, literary, political, sexual, and social discussion and discourse more lively and spicy. The realization is rather slow to grow that humor is a performing art and like music, painting, and poetry, can play a remarkable transforming role. As a matter of fact, it's not only political humor but also other performing arts that were given little space by peace education and peace research until very recently. Recommending that "attempts to halt and reverse the cycle of violence draw on the widest possible range of peacemaking instruments and mechanisms," Peter van den Dungen, an eminent peace historian and former General Coordinator of International Network of Museums for Peace (INMP), observes "In this context, the potential contribution of the arts has traditionally been ignored or marginalized, and also today is insufficiently appreciated (Van den Dungen, 2008, p. xvi).

The importance of performing arts in peacebuilding is further appreciated when realized that there are many cultural worlds in this one world and there are many peaces (Pearce & Dietrich, 2019; Wolfgang & Wolfgang, 2006), and Raimon Pannikar's famous remark "without interculturality, peace is only utopia" is notable (Pannikar in Esteva, 2011, p. 571). Little wonder therefore that important studies highlighting the bonding and liberating role of music as a performing art and on its contribution to the movements against unpeace and unfreedoms are being produced (Urbain, 2011; Garcia, 2011; Boyce-Tillman, 2011; Galtung, 2008; Whitehead, 2008; Skyllsted, 2008). Similarly, peace teaching and the liberating role of paintings are being highlighted. In particular, Pablo Picasso's immortal painting Gernika and paintings on the Berlin Wall are being increasingly referred to.[1,2] Nevertheless, much more needs to be done to highlight the important role that the performing arts can play in the struggle against injustice, violence, and authoritarianism. For instance, serious discussion and focused studies on the power and peace-potential of political humor is required.

Such a call is not untimely. Undemocratic forces are powerful enough and they seem to be gathering more strength. They need to be resisted with all resources, tools, and firm resolve. As such, the need to examine the relevance of political humor for the movement for peace and freedom, and its possible intervention as an active player in the power game. It is heartening to note that there is not a dearth of material on humor, nor is research on humor too scanty. Books on humor abound. Likewise, research articles are regularly published in international journals like *Humor: International Journal of Humor Research*, *Studies in American Humor*, and *The European Journal of Humor Research* and occasionally in several other social science journals. What is problematic is the absence of focus on political humor as an energy and symbol of resistance. There are all sorts of websites on laughter, including Laughter on Call (laughteroncall.com) and Laughter Online University (www.laughteronlineuniversity.com). All the sites are flooded with jokes on human relationships and activities, professions, and peoples. In addition, a large number of joke books are available for the people of different age groups. They cover a wide variety of topics and themes including sex, professions, politics, and so on. Equally important, new jokes, like the jokes about COVID-19 and the somersaults of former US president Donald Trump and Indian Prime Minister Narendra Modi continue to pour in. Since human creativity is boundless, the crafting of jokes is endless.

Peace Education

Likewise, the field of peace education is vast and ever expanding. Its recognition is worldwide as it covers a variety of themes, topics, and issues relating to human rights, human security, human development, gender equality, freedom, democratic governance, and so on. Moreover, peace education resources are being regularly compiled in the form of directory, bibliography, and encyclopedia (Harris, 2009). For instance, A *Directory of Peace Education Resources* was produced in 2012 by the National Centre for Peace and Conflict Studies, University of Otago, New Zealand.[3] *Where to Study Peace Education: A Global Director* is another resource. It was planned and initiated by the Global Campaign for Peace Education in collaboration with the International Institute on Peace Education and Peace Education Initiative at the University of Toledo. It focuses on "programs, courses and trainings *specific to research and the study of peace education, and the preparation of formal and non-formal educators to teach for peace.*" Its list of programs on peace education offered by different universities and institutes is indicative of the vastness of this academic field.[4] Nonviolence is a central topic, value, and strategy studied in the field.

Political Humor and Peace

Nonviolence is doubtless a major component of peace education studies. Over the years and especially since the 1960s, a number of important studies on nonviolence and nonviolent action, and on the nonviolent struggle of leaders like Mahatma Gandhi, Martin Luther King Jr., Rosa Parks, Nelson Mandela, Abdul Ghaffar Khan and several others for freedom, human rights and civil liberties, democracy, peace, and justice have significantly enriched peace education. What, however, is still noticeably and largely missing are a good collection of focused and rigorous works on humor as a political tool. In fact, its use in the nonviolent and peace movements are very often missing from even the well-researched studies on such movements. Writing the introduction of a study on politics of humor, Martina Kessel (2012) points out how uses of humor are missing in accounts of big issues like war and other political conflicts.[5] However, and as the following section shows, humor has many colors, and their contribution in extending the frontiers of applied theatre is not insignificant.

Applied Theatre and Many Colors of Humor

Humor has many colors. Moreover, it has several uses that have peacebuilding roles in and beyond theatrical contexts. As a performance, it facilitates embodied communication, identity clarification, conflict response, and affective reactions. As an interpersonal strategy, humor enables intrapersonal as well as group processes that enhance human abilities such as development of self-knowledge and personal transformation in a situation (Amir, 2019). Embodied communication occurs during physical expression in a performance. It facilitates thinking and feeling by the performance observer, possible interactor, and performer. Atmospheric competence refers to the instructor's ability to assess the social and physical conditions of learning for decisions about how to optimize the instruction in a particular milieu (Wolf, 2019). That happens through keen attention to embodied as well as linguistic communication. Educators need awareness of how embodied teaching affects learners (Lim, 2021). Performance of embodied communication has the power of advancing uptake of the expressed message and multidimensional responses to it, including emotional, cognitive, physical, and social reactions, in all contexts where the senses receive the performance stimulus. Embodied communication affects the conception of self-in-the-world, which shapes personal and social identity (Sekimoto, 2012). Humor influences personal and group identity. Jokes express the boundaries of identities, who is in and who is out (Kessel, 2012). They locate the teller and subjects of jokes in social and political identities. The expression of in-group identities orients the listeners of jokes towards the shared perspectives, behaviors, and actions that have characterized that group (Vucetic, 2004). The expression of in-group identity and shared culture demarks the out-group as other. Ideas about difference are fertile ground for conflict when the seeds of mutuality are not cultivated and while indifference to the needs of the othered grows. Use of humor about oppressive dominators highlights their behaviors and builds community for the dominated, which can stimulate change efforts by those in either role. Humor is a catalyst of peaceable conflict resolution when the performance partially or fully meets the needs of individuals or groups without the use of force. Psychological needs, such as feeling safety in expression of dissatisfaction, identity with a group that aids self-definition, and stress relief exemplify need fulfillment through experience with humor (Zelizer, 2010). There are several contexts, besides theatre performance, that employ the affective uses of humor for stimulating well-being.

Although performance of humor can be a theatrical skill, humor has wide usage across professions as well as in contexts of entertainment. For several purposes, people use humor in performance of their professional roles as manager, teacher, and health-care provider, among others. A brief description here illustrates how analysis and strategic use of humor avoids harm in goal accomplishment. Managers have used positive humor for reduction of stress that affects the organization's members. Research has identified how leadership humor positively influences the behaviors of their subordinates in the organization (Cooper, Kong & Crossley, 2018). The quality of the relationship with the managers has influenced the amount of positive emotions stimulated by management's use of humor. Studies have shown that higher quality relationships are more positively affected by humor expression of management than lower quality relationships (Robert, Dunne & Iun, 2016; Wijewardena, Härtel & Samaratunge, 2017). However, gender identity mediates the evaluation of humor usage in the workplace. Humorous females have been perceived as more disruptive while humorous males have been evaluated as more functional at work (Evans, Slaughter, Ellis, & Rivin, 2019). The dynamics of differentiated evaluations in the workplace have roots in the educational settings that enable differential treatment based on identities. Proactive work needs to occur in all contexts for elimination of inequitable treatment, including who gets to use humor. Accomplishment of that goal must occur in programs for professional preparation.

Inclusion of instruction about humor usage in the professions has been stimulated by research. Pertinent to peace education for advancement of well-being and human development are the studies of humor in health care and teaching. The use of humor in health care has enhanced emotion management, interpersonal connections, and teamwork of providers (Dean & Major, 2008). Patient benefits from the experience of humor during pursuit of wellness include a reduction of stress, counteraction of depression, and increased tolerance of pain (Gremigni, 2012; Lapierre, Baker & Tanaka, 2019). Patients use humor to project their good persona during interactions with nurses (McCreaddie & Wiggins, 2009). In recognition of how humor has been found helpful in pursuit of wellness, Hussong and Micucci (2021) identified factors that clinicians consider in their use of humor with patients, including gender, culture, mood, and personality traits. Research on the use of humor in university science courses found that student identities affected their appreciation, or not, of jokes by their instructors (Cooper, Nadile & Brownell, 2020). Similarities of the humor styles, as determined by socioeconomic and cultural factors, need consideration (Mendiburo-Seguel & Heintz, 2020; Van Praag, Stevens & Van Houtte, 2017). Fluency in the language and its register that expresses humor influences its perception of its usage. Hence, in addition to other identity factors, careful use of humor involves consideration of its effects with an audience who has diverse language skills and cultural norms. With these factors in mind, thoughtful use of humor in transition times between formal lessons, as well as appropriate applications within instruction, has strengthened rapport between students and their instructors (Victoria, 2019). Indeed, the use of positive humor, which does not negatively affect its audience, has enhanced student engagement in learning (Bakar & Kumar, 2019; Pretorius, Koen & Schall, 2020). Research on the association between humor by teachers and student learning found positive effects when the humor was related, versus unrelated, to the course contents (Bieg & Dresel, 2018). The type of humor teacher use and the classroom climate it influences were identified as influential factors what type of humor adolescents learned (Chiang, Lee & Wang, 2016). Hence, attention to humor types taught through instructor modeling needs consideration. When negative humor about oneself and others is modeled or accepted, it can solidify as a means of communication. Instruction for humor use in conflict resolution includes development of student communication with creativity that helps them see situations in a new way (Wisler, 2010). Skills of conflict resolution fostered in formal and nonformal education are creativity in problem-solving and communication through humor (Sclavi, 2008; Smith, Vernard Harrington, & Neck, 2000). Research identified how strategic use of humor by negotiators helps them avoid circular argumentation and deadlocks by altering the content and process of the conflict communication (Maemura & Horita, 2012). Skills of conflict communication and management through creative use of humor have been developed through role playing in courses and applied theatre.

In the light of the above, one may add here that the link between humor and peacebuilding is neither weak nor invisible (Bonomi, 2010; Davidheiser, 2006). It is strong. Especially the link between political humor and peace has grown stronger since the advent of the twenty-first century. It is partly due to the upsurge of social and political activism, attracting larger popular participation. These include the anti-capitalist demonstrations against World Trade Organization (WTO) in Seattle (1999) and the World Social Forum Summit in Porto Alegre (2001), worldwide protests against Iraq war in 2003, outbreak and spread of Arab Spring from Tunisia (2010) to Egypt, Libya, Bahrain, Yemen, and Syria, anti-austerity movement, also referred to as 15-M movement in Spain (2011), which inspired Occupy movements worldwide, the Black Lives Matter Campaign (2014), Me Too call outs and movements against dictatorial regimes in several developing countries. A number of these and other popular protest movements used social media and effectively made use of performing arts, including political humor. Subsequently, peace education's interest in arts and peace, and especially in the performing arts, has increased during the first two decades of twenty-first century. However, a solid bonding between political humor and peace education is still awaited. This bonding should take place soon because these are very difficult times with escalating political, among other, conflicts.

Perhaps it will not be an exaggeration to say that the undemocratic regimes of our times are mightier and more organized than before. They have a hold on the masses through the use of technologies, propaganda machines, and newer strategies for mass exploitation, suppression, and silence. They thrive on the fear of the masses. It is this fear, which spreads like a plague, that paralyses the mind, body, and soul of the people, which facilitates power to suck in the spirit of liberty, and which needs to be confronted. In such challenging times, Political humor may offer a defiant response, because it may diminish the fear of the masses by making fools of absolutist rulers. Consequently, it may strengthen the movements for peace, justice, and freedom everywhere. Study and research on these lines may help build a peace perspective on political humor. Works focusing on political humor and peace may eventually contribute a new chapter to peace education studies.

Ralph Waldo Emerson, an eminent American poet and essayist, famously said that "The earth laughs in flowers" (Emerson, 2021, p. 1) but laughter isn't always flowery or velvety. Neither is it always innocent and harmless, nor always employed for fun only. It can be merciless, unsparing, sadistic, and even malicious, spreading laughing poison all around, and hurting its targets. It can target the absolutist regimes directly, and it's capable of hurting individuals, groups, communities, professions, and institutions behind the tyrannical rulers. The moment a resistance movement sprinkles political humor, it begins to empower the powerless. By laughingly exposing the ugliness in the corridors of power, laughter can undermine the confidence and support system of the powerful. Often the show starts by putting the iceberg upside down and hilariously revealing the ugliness at the bottom or showing the vulgarity and fragility of power by removing the masks from the face of power.

Political humor is a hidden tool. It may seem fragile, insignificant, and inconspicuous, but it can ignite a flame that may spread like a wild bushfire. Furthermore, political humor blossoms during stifling times. The more powerful an individual is, the more dominating a group acts, the more imposing a profession is, the more stifling the environment is, and the more dangerous the situation for freedom and defiance is, the more irresistible the temptation to laughingly target the individual, group, or system. History tells us that a resistance movement is always born when the going gets tough, and it gains momentum when the going gets tougher. During such times, political humor can come forward to provide courage and strength to the movement against the tyranny of the so-called one and the only truth.

Political humor is not only effective, it is also infectious and an agency without borders. While the substance of hilarious stories may remain the same and the hidden message may remain intact, local color and flavor is often added when it reaches a new land and a new environ. Humor is colorful, inter-relational, interconnected, globalizing, and the world's powerless masses' laughing weapon. Though its power doesn't grow out of the barrel of a gun, it's capable of blunting the gun. Though still insufficiently noticed, researched, and studied, this is what political humor has been doing since the introduction of its smart use in the theatres from ancient times.

Theatre and Political Humor

Theatre has been a popular retreat for thousands of years. It's a place visited by people of different classes, political views, ethnicities, religions, and regions. Every year, millions of people from all over the world visit these theatres. They visit theatres of their choice as there are different kinds of theatres like open air theatres, black box or studio theatres, small and large drama theatres, street theatres, and theatres of the absurd. These are the learning places and academies of ideas (Elam, 1997). Here, commentaries are offered bluntly or subtly on international, national, and local issues and on political, social, and economic issues. Furthermore, a theatre is a place where the audience is in direct contact with the actors on the stage and it expresses its appreciation or displeasure right on the spot. In order to ensure larger attendance of the people, stories, songs, music, and actors are generally carefully selected. After all, it's the story, dialogue, songs, dance, and acting that pull the crowd.

Further, these theatres have always been used by the powerful to protect and further entrench the status quo, instill fear in the people, promote the culture of obedience and conformism, and narcotize the masses through the projection of romance, religious and nationalistic passion, and application of vulgar humor in speech and physical movement on the stage. On the other hand, the passion for freedom and spirit of non-conformism have often led brave people to bypass the visible and invisible restrictions, reject the fabulous offers of the powerful, face insecurities, humiliation, imprisonment, execution, and exile, and use political humor to say their say. They offer passionate presentation and performance, provide center stage to political humor, and courageously satirize the futility and absurdity of war and authoritarianism.

War and authoritarianism are two foci of peace education and peace research. Both have also been major topics in different formats of political humor, for thousands of years. Take, for example, the anti-war comical play *Lysistrata*. It was authored nearly 2,500 years ago by Aristophanes, a prolific comic playwright of ancient Greece. He is commonly referred to as the Father of Comedy. His play *Lysistrata* was first staged in 411 BCE. It is a comic account of an extraordinary woman named Lysistrata, "a strong Athenian woman with a great sense of individual responsibility," who shared her unique plan to end the interminable Peloponnesian war between Athens and Sparta with women from different city states of Greece, and with support from the Spartan Lampito. She urged the women to deny sex to their men folk in order to force them to bring the war to an end. The women agreed and the word of revolt was spread. Soon after the old women of Athens seized control of the nearby Acropolis, which held the state treasury, in order to deny the men the financial resource to fund their war for long.[6]

Besides *Lysistrata*, there are numerous other plays that sprinkle laughter on the stage and ridicule war, along with violent thinking and practices. It is the task of peace education to discover such comedy plays, bring them into mainstream of peace teaching and research, and also arrange their frequent staging in different countries. *Arms and the Man* is one such play, which deserves more attention than it currently seems to be receiving.

This play was written in 1894, 20 years before the start of the first world war. It was set in the background of the four month long Serbo-Bulgarian war during November 1885 to March 1886. In the play *Arms and the Man*, subtitled "An Anti-Romantic Comedy," Shaw mocks the foolishness of glorifying war and hilariously exposes the absurdity of elitism and class factor in romance and marriage. The story revolves around Raina Petkoff, a young Bulgarian woman engaged to Sergius Saranoff, one of the heroes of the Serbo-Bulgarian war, and Captain Bluntschli, a Swiss mercenary soldier in the Serbian army who had escaped from a horrendous battle after being under fire for three days. Though both Sergius and Bluntschli were returnees from a bloody battle, the former, a war hero, wasn't presented by Shaw as a war hero, neither Buntschli as a coward war deserter. The hilarious march of events and satirical dialogues introduced by Shaw completely change the table. As a person totally opposed to violence and war, the playwright presents Bluntschli as a soldier with a human heart, who is not embarrassed to escape from the battle to save his life, and who would prefer to keep chocolates instead of ammunition in his cartridge belt. The playwright also drives Sergius to his senses, who finally sees the horrors of war and says: "And how ridiculous! Oh, war! war! The dream of patriots and heroes! A fraud, Bluntschli, a hollow sham" (Encyclopedia. Com, n.d., p. 28).

This anti-war and anti-militarism comedy play was first performed in London in 1894 and first published four years later in a collection entitled *Plays Pleasant*. It was authored by George Bernard Shaw. His play *Arms and the Man* continues to be staged in different countries. Moreover, its relevance for the contemporary times is generally acknowledged in peace circles, but the play deserves more popular attention. Clearly the field of peace education needs to offer more space to this and many other anti-war and anti-authoritarianism political comedies because such plays may provide food for thought and channel wild anger and anguish into powerful movements against war, violence, and authoritarianism. Likewise, the relevance of political comedy movies for peace education need to be highlighted. The point may be illustrated by referring to Charlie Chaplin's movie *The Great Dictator*.

Charlie Chaplin's Movie: The Great Dictator

Charlie Chaplin was a British comic actor, film maker, and composer. He attained worldwide fame during the silent film era. He is considered to be the greatest comic artist of film screen. *The Great Dictator* was his first talking film. This movie, which satirizes Adolf Hitler and Nazism, and condemns anti-Semitism, was released in New York on October 15, 1940. Chaplin had acted in the film and also directed it. It was his most successful film at the box office and regarded a classic for all times. Explaining why *The Great Dictator* should be regarded a classic, film critic K. Austin Collins says:

> It's startling in its depictions of violence, which stand out less for their outright brutality than for how memorably they depict the Nazis' betrayal of everyday humanity. And it's renowned as well as for its resourceful and original humor, which combines Chaplin at his most incisive and balletic with raucous displays of verbal wit.
>
> (Collins, 2019, p. 4)

The movie is set in a fictitious country, Tomania (Germany), and it revolves around two major characters—Adenoid Hynkel (Adolf Hitler) and the Jewish barber. Both the roles were played by Charlie Chaplin. The barber was wounded in the war. He was hospitalized for a long time and he has lost his memory. Twenty years after the war, he returns to his country, Tomania. He is unaware of profound changes introduced in his country by Adolf Hitler—the ruthless dictator and campaigner of an anti-Jewish murderous campaign. The barber goes back to his shop in a Jewish ghetto. The resemblance between him and Hitler is so striking and so close that the great dictator's storm troopers arrest Hitler instead of the Jewish barber. Mistaken to be the great dictator, the barber is respectfully taken to address a huge mass meeting, where he declares that he has changed and has no interest in violence, hatred, and intolerance. The plot of the movie is interwoven with hilarious comic scenes, funny situations, and sarcastic dialogues. It is a classic comedy movie.

However, and by any standard, *The Great Dictator* is a very serious movie. It ridicules Nazi anti-Semitism, humorously and strongly attacking the concept of the superior German race, while it condemns the rise of European fascism. The opening and concluding statements clearly express the intent of making the movie. Before the start of the film, a statement on the screen says: "This is a story of a period between two world wars—an interim in which Insanity cut loose, Liberty took a nose dive, and Humanity was kicked around somewhat" (Benjamin, 1942, p. 4) The film ends with the concluding remarks of the barber, who was accidently put on the seat of power. Indeed, the whole text should form part of the content of several peace education courses. Part of the text is as follows[7]:

> I'm sorry, but I don't want to be an emperor. That's not my business. I don't want to rule or conquer anyone. I should like to help everyone— if possible—Jew, Gentile—black man—white. We all want to help one another. Human beings are like that. We want to live by each other's happiness—not by each other's misery. We don't want to hate and despise one another. In this world there is room for everyone. And the good earth is rich and can provide for everyone. The way of life can be free and beautiful, but we have lost the way.
>
> (The Final Speech from The Great Dictator, 2018)

Humorous plays like *Lysistrata* and *Arms and the Man*, and comedy movies like *The Great Dictator* and numerous others that bask in political humor need to be taken seriously. They focus on issues concerning slavery and freedom, war, violence and peace, injustice and justice, authoritarianism and democracy, inequality and equality, and stifling of independent voices and giving voice to the voiceless. Many such movies remain buried in the dust of time. These should be rediscovered and discussed in the classrooms and outside. This is a task that calls for the attention of peace educators. Likewise, the study of power- and peace-potentials of political jokes, scattered all over on the internet and in print, can be taken up by peace education.

Political Jokes

Political jokes are a vital part of political humor. They distinguish political humor as an energetic, pro-active, resilient performance. They are in vogue everywhere. These jokes are cracked in the parliament houses, court rooms, press conferences, social gatherings, public meetings, conferences, class rooms, and so on. They are also part of stage comic shows and comedy shows in media. In the darker times, when the common people languish under the boots of authoritarian regimes, political jokes appear as shining stars in the sky. Like the celestial stars, they diminish the vast darkness and often show the way to be taken in tormenting times.

Political jokes may look very fragile, weak and of no significance, but they have the power to upset the power game. A political joke may pave the way to delegitimize the absolutist ruler on the seat of power. Equally importantly, a political joke may extinguish the fiery confidence of the absolutist ruler. It's therefore important that peace education takes due notice of the power- and peace-potentials of political jokes and research on their uses. An analysis by Anagondahalli and Sahar (2014) of political jokes during the presidency of Hosni Mubarak in Egypt and the revolution that ended his 30 years of repressive rulership identifies the humor functions of relief and empowerment that became widespread.

> Before the revolution, humor, therefore, helped maintain a delicate balance in the passive social activism of the Egyptian people; it performed a "safety valve" function for protestors, by giving them an outlet for their complex amalgam of experienced emotions, while at the same time protecting them from the consequences of expressing such emotions. During the revolution, humor clearly reversed the status of the players; the powerless public became powerful by openly ridiculing Mubarak.
> (Anagondahalli & Sahar, 2014, p. 28)

Conclusion

Theatrical performances with humor have advanced several political goals of peacebuilding. Participation in as well as observance of such performances in applied theatre constitute nonformal peace education when the participants experience peacebuilding. The performances have entailed methods of constructing positive social interactions between contesting group members. They contributed to psychological well-being when the performance productions reduced the tensions between groups during their cooperative and creative interactions (Martin et al., 2003). In post-conflict Rwanda, for example, production of improvisational comedy with contesting, thus othered, ethnic groups demonstrated peacebuilding as well as performance skills (McFarren, 2011). Ed Greenberg, an instructor and producer of comedy in post-conflict Rwanda, explained that production of comedy and social change occur through "developing skills as a better listener, a more trusting partner, a less judgmental participant in a group creative process, [and] a more confident creative force" (as cited in McFarren, 2011, p. 166). As a strategy of violence avoidance, humor that bridges ethnic divisions forefronts a common heritage and geographic identity in a shared relationship through humor performance such as jokes (Merchant, 2013). The mutuality in the relationship supports cooperative and collective interactions. Stimulation of change characterizes applied theatre with political goals. Street theatre in the context of a carnivalesque event, enables satire and parody in a celebratory milieu, which is safer from forceful and violent disruption than other types of protests in public. Satire has been used worldwide for bringing attention to a political issue whereas comedy has been more commonly used to joke about political figures (Gibson, 2019). ChanChirā Sombatphūnsiri (2015) describes how humor enabled theatrical protests about political conflict in Serbia during the leadership of Slobadan Milošević. "Pardodied obedience" became a humorous protest action in 1990s Serbia (Sombatphūnsiri, 2015, p. 26). Critical analysis of oppression sources and communication about them are primary goals of peacebuilding education. The development of critical consciousness in theatre is a goal that Augusto Boal (2006) supported through empowerment of the actors, and spect-actors (theatrical participant spectators) in image as well as forum theatre. Use of aesthetics for embodied thinking towards change through direct action and legislation is both ethical and political (Boal, 1998). It is ultimately educational and crucially needed.

There is another important point that needs to be stressed here. It is this: while inter-state war has almost ended, no end of unpeace and unfreedom is in sight. The vulnerability and insecurity of the common people abound. The traditional power systems and structures at all levels remain violent, powerful, and intact. Worse still, the anti-democratic forces are becoming more powerful as democracy continues to rest in what the University of Ontario Professor Ronald Wintrobe calls the "inaction zone" (Wintrobe, 1998, p. 247). Again, global challenges like climate change, arms races and arms sales, cyber violence, widespread inequality, proliferation of slavery of all kinds, and taming of both print and electronic media, judiciary and academia have built up mountains in front of the movement for peace and change in many countries. Given the state of affairs, it's important that peace education pools all available tools and resources to accelerate the pace and process of transforming the savage "net-world" into the "nest-world." In this connection, the largest possible involvement of common people in the struggle against war, violence and authoritarianism is required. To achieve this, the constituencies of peace will need to be continuously enlarged and new peace constituencies regularly established. At the same time, the well-entrenched power systems and absolutist states will be required to be challenged and confronted. These are not easy tasks. By any count or criterion, these are huge tasks. As such, both formal and informal peace education will have to be in the forefront, along with peace movements, to meet the challenges ahead. In order to achieve these goals, peace education will have to be more actively and creatively provided outside as well as inside classrooms. It must have more space for and facilitation of performing arts as game changers and peace-builders. Keeping this in view, peace education will have to be taken out of schools and into open public spaces. Perhaps political humor as a performance can serve as its bridge between the classrooms and open public spaces.

Notes

1 On April 26, 1937, the German and Italian forces heavily bombed the Basque town of Gernika in Spain, and completely destroyed it in three hours. This tragedy of Gernika has been immortalized by the famous painting of the Spanish painter and sculptor Pablo Picasso. The painting, 11 and a half foot tall and almost 26

foot wide and painted in black and white, depicts the carnage through people, animals and buildings wrenched by violence. This immense mural is, indeed, a peace teacher. It continues to tell the world what violence and war really mean (Mehdi, 2020b; and www.amnesty.org.uk/blogs/journalist-and-human-rights/nazi-bombing-guernica, last accessed on October 17, 2021).
2 The Berlin Wall was built in 1961 at the height of the Cold War and it fell in 1989. About five years before its fall, the French artist Thierry Noir registered his anger against the Soviet totalitarianism and its control over several Eastern European countries including East Germany. In 1984, he painted illegally and ferociously on the Western side of Berlin Wall and attacked the Soviet repression through cartoonish graffiti. Commemorating the 100th anniversary of the Statue of Liberty on July 4, 1986, Noir and Cristoph Bouchet put up 42 Statue of Liberty paintings on the Berlin Wall. The Berlin Wall fell in 1989, but a 1,316-mile long remnant of the wall has been preserved and decorated with more than a hundred historical and historical murals directly painted on the wall. It is known as East Side Gallery. It is world's first wall museum. This museum has superb historical, visual, and symbolic value for liberation struggle anywhere in the world (Mehdi, 2020a).
3 This directory is a living or dynamic document. It is continually updated https://podcasts.otago.ac.nz/nzpeace-ed/peace-education-directory/, last accessed on October 17, 2021.
4 Its listings "fall into two broad categories: (1) the study of education (systems, philosophy, pedagogy) and its role in building peace, and (2) teacher and learning facilitator training and preparation in peace education (theory, methodology, pedagogy)," www.peace-ed-campaign.org/view/peace-education-directory-study-peace-ed/, last accessed on October 17, 2021.
5 Nevertheless, Martina Kessel does stress the importance of political humor in the introduction to a study co-edited by her and says that "humour is an important means to negotiate identity and belonging, and in the twentieth century, comics and funny magazines sold extremely well while cheerful radio shows and films attracted a huge audience both in the democratic and authoritarian societies" (Kessel 2012, p. 3).
6 For details, see www.ancient-literature.com/greece_aristophanes_lysistrata.html, last accessed on October 17, 2021.
7 For full text, see www.charliechaplin.com/en/articles/29-the-final-speech-from-the-great-dictator-, last accessed on October 17, 2021.

References

Amir, L. (2019). *Revisiting philosophic ideals: Philosophy, humor, and the human condition.* (pp. 97–117). Cham: Palgrave Macmillan. doi: 10.1007/978-3-030-32671-5_4

Anagondahalli, D., & Sahar K. (2014). Mubarak framed! Humor and political activism before and during the Egyptian Revolution. *Arab Media & Society*, 19 Retrieved at www.files.ethz.ch/isn/184970/20140924113801_Khamis_HumorandPoliticalActivism_Final.pdf

Bakar, F., & Kumar, V. (2019). The use of humour in teaching and learning in higher education classrooms: Lecturers' perspectives. *Journal of English for Academic Purposes*, 40, 15–25. doi: 10.1016/j.jeap.2019.04.006

Benjamin, K. (February 17, 1942). *Chaplin's 'The Great Dictator' remains a hit*. Retrieved at https://blogs.shu.edu/ww2-0/1942/02/17/chaplins-the-great-dictator-remains-a-hit/

Bieg, S., & Dresel, M. (2018). Relevance of perceived teacher humor types for instruction and student learning. *Social Psychology of Education*, 21(4), 805–825. doi:10.1007/s11218-018-9428-z.

Boal, A. (1998). *Legislative theatre: Using performance to make politics.* (A. Jackson, Trans). London: Routledge.

Boal, A. (2006). *The aesthetics of the oppressed.* (A. Jackson, Trans). London: Routledge

Bonomi, B. (2010). A funny way to fight: Comedians battle for peace. *National News, Arts & Culture,* May 12, 2010. Retrieved at www.thenationalnews.com/arts-culture/a-funny-way-to-fight-comedians-battling-for-peace-1.572684

Boyce-Tillman, J. (2011). Making musical space for peace. In F. Laurence & Urbain, O. (Eds.), *Music and solidarity: Questions of universality, consciousness, and connection* (pp. 185–201). New Brunswick, NJ: Transaction Publishers.

Chiang, Y., Lee, C., & Wang, H. (2016). Effects of classroom humor climate and acceptance of humor messages on adolescents' expressions of humor. *Child & Youth Care Forum,* 45(4), 543–569.

Collins, K. A. (2019, October 18). What Charlie Chaplin got right about satirizing Hitler. *Vanity Fair.* Retrieved at www.vanityfair.com/hollywood/2019/10/satirzing-hitler-charlie-chaplin-great-dictator

Cooper, C. D., Kong, D. T., & Crossley, C. D. (2018). Leader humor as an interpersonal resource: Integrating three theoretical perspectives. *Academy of Management Journal,* 61(2), 769–796. DOI: 10.5465/amj.2014.0358

Cooper, K. M., Nadile, E. M., & Brownell, S. E. (2020). Don't joke about me: Student identities and perceptions of instructor humor in college science courses. *Journal of Microbiology & Biology Education,* 21(1). doi: 10.1128/jmbe.v21i1.2085

Davidheiser, M. (2006). Joking for peace. Social organization, tradition, and change in Gambian conflict management. *Cahiers d'études africaines [African Study Papers]* XLVI (4), 835–859.

Dean, R. A., & Major, J. E. (2008). From critical care to comfort care: the sustaining value of humour. *Journal of Clinical Nursing,* 17(8), 1088–1095 doi: 0.1111/j.1365-2702.2007.02090.x

Elam, H. (1997). *Taking it to the streets: The social protest theater of Luis Valdez and Amiri Baraka (Theater—theory/text/performance).* Ann Arbor: University of Michigan

Emerson, R. W. (2021). Quote of the day. Brainy Quotes. Retrieved at www.brainyquote.com/quotes/ralph_waldo_emerson_105196

Encyclopedia.Com. Arms and the man. Arts. Retrieved at www.encyclopedia.com/arts/educational-magazines/arms-and-man#THEMES

Esteva, G. (2011). Intercultural inspiration: The life and work of Raimon Pannikar. In Dietrich, W., Echavarria Alvarez, J., Esteva, G., Ingruber, D. & Koppensteiner, N. (Eds), *The Palgrave international handbook of peace studies: A cultural perspective* (pp. 570–585). New York: Palgrave Macmillan

Evans, J. B., Slaughter, J. E., Ellis, A. P. J., & Rivin, J. M. (2019). Gender and the evaluation of humor at work. *Journal of Applied Psychology,* 104(8), 1077–1087.

Galtung, J. (2008). Peace, music and arts: In search of interconnections. In O. Urbain (Ed.), *Music and Conflict Transformation: Harmonies and dissonance in geopolitics* (pp. 53–60). London: I. B. Tauris & Co Ltd.

Gandhi, E. (2014). Building a global culture of peace and nonviolence. *Peace & Policy: Dialogue of Civilization for Global Citizenship,* 19, 58–66.

Garcia, M. E. P. (2011). Music and human rights: Towards a paradoxical approach. In F. Laurence & O. Urbain (Eds.), *Music and solidarity: Questions of universality, consciousness, and connection* (pp. 117–130).New Brunswick, NJ: Transaction.

Gibson, J. M. (2019). *Introduction to the psychology of humor.* Abingdon: Routledge.

Gremigni, P. (2012). Is humor the best medicine? In P. Gremigni (Ed.), *Humor and health promotion* (pp. 149–166). Hauppauge, NY: Nova Biomedical.

Harris, I. 1988. *Peace education*. North Carolina: McFarland & Company, Inc.
Harris, I. October 2009. A select bibliography for peace education. *Peace & Change: A Journal of Peace Research*, 34(4), 571–576.
Hussong, D. K., & Micucci, J. A. (2021). The use of humor in psychotherapy: Views of practicing psychotherapists. *Journal of Creativity in Mental Health*,16(1), 77–94.
Kessel, M. (2012). Introduction. Landscapes of humour: The history and politics of the comical in the Twentieth Century. In M. Kessel & Merziger, P. (Eds.), *The politics of humour – laughter, inclusion and exclusion in the twentieth century* (pp. 3–21). Toronto: University of Toronto.
Lapierre, S. S., Baker, B. D., & Tanaka, H. (2019). Effects of mirthful laughter on pain tolerance: A randomized controlled investigation. *Journal of Bodywork and Movement Therapies*, 23(4), 733–738. doi:10.1016/j.jbmt.2019.04.005
Lim, F. (2021). *Designing learning with embodied teaching: Perspectives from multimodality*. New York: Routledge.
Lum, B. J. (2014). Global values in educational leadership toward creating cultures of peace. *Peace & Policy: Dialogue of Civilization for Global Leadership*, 19, 96–118.
Lum, B. J. (2017). *Peace education, past, present, and future*. Routledge Book Description. Retrieved at www.routledge.com/Peace-Education-Past-present-and-future/Lum/p/book/9780367074340
Maemura, Y., & Horita, M. (2012). Humour in negotiations: A pragmatic analysis of humour in simulated negotiations. *Group Decision and Negotiation*, 21(6), 821–838.
Martin, R. A., Puhlik-Doris, P., Larsen, G., Gray, J., & Weir, K. (2003). Individual differences in uses of humor and their relation to psychological well-being: Development of the Humor Styles Questionnaire. *Journal of Research in Personality*, 37, 48–75. DOI:10.1016/S0092-6566(02)00534-2
McCreaddie, M., & Wiggins, S. (2009). Reconciling the good patient personal with problematic and non-problematic humour: A grounded theory. *International Journal of Nursing Studies*, 46(8), 1079–1091. DOI: 10.1016/j.ijnurstu.2009.01.008
McFarren, C. K. (2011). Laughter diplomacy: Transcultural understanding at play in Rwanda. *Theatre Topics*, 21(2), 163–173.
Mehdi, S. S.. (2020a). Memory, freedom and power. *Strategic Thoughts: A Journal of International Affairs*,1, 80–98.
Mehdi, S. S. (November 10, 2020b). *Aerial bombing and memorials and museums for peace*. Paper presented at the No Gun Ri Global Peace Forum, South Korea.
Mendiburo-Seguel, A., & Heintz, S. (2020). Who shows which kind of humor? Exploring sociodemographic differences in eight comic styles in a large Chilean sample. *Scandinavian Journal of Psychology*, 61(4), 565–573. DOI: 10.1111/sjop.12629
Merchant, M. (2013). African scholar explains how jokes, humor can be used to avoid conflict. *University Wire*, 2013-October-25, 1.
Pearce, J. V., & Dietrich, W. (2019). Many violences, many peaces: Wolfgang Dietrich and Jenny Pearce in conversation. *Peacebuilding*, 7(3), 268–282.
Pretorius, J., Koen, M., & Schall, R. (2020). Using intentional humour in a higher-education classroom: Connecting with, and building on Lovorn and Holaway. *European Journal of Humour Research*, 8(2), 146–165. DOI: 10.7592/EJHR2020.8.2.Pretorius
Robert, C., Dunne, T. C., & Iun, J. (2016). The impact of leader humor on subordinate job satisfaction. *Group & Organization Management*, 41(3), 375–406.
Sclavi, M. (2008). The role of play and humor in creative conflict management. *Negotiation Journal*, 24(2), 157–180.

Sekimoto, S. (2012). A multimodal approach to identity: Theorizing the self through embodiment, spatiality, and temporality. *Journal of International and Intercultural Communication, 5*(3), 226–243. doi: 10.1080/17513057.2012.689314

Sen, A. (2006). The future and our freedoms. In V. Martinez Guzman and Sonia Paris Albert, S. P. (Eds.), *Amartya K. Sen Y La Globalizacion* (pp. 27–36). Castello De La Plana: Universitat Jaume 1.

Skyllsted, K. (2008). Managing conflicts through music: Educational perspectives. In O. Urbain (Ed.), *Music and conflict transformation: Harmonies and dissonance in geopolitics* (pp. 172–183). London: I. B. Tauris & Co Ltd.

Smith, W. J., Vernard Harrington, K., & Neck, C. P. (2000). Resolving conflict with humor in a diversity context. *Journal of Managerial Psychology, 15*(6), 606–625.

Sombatphūnsiri, J. (2015). *Humor and nonviolent struggle in Serbia*. Syracuse, New York: Syracuse University.

The Final Speech from The Great Dictator. (2018). *CharlieChapman.com*. Retrieved at www.charliechaplin.com/en/articles/29-the-final-speech-from-the-great-dictator-

Urbain, O. (2011). Inspiring musical movements and global solidarity: *Playing for Change, Min-On* and *El Sistema*. In F. Laurence & O. Urbain (Eds.), *Music and solidarity: Questions of universality, consciousness, and connection* (pp. 11–29).New Brunswick, NJ: Transaction.

Van den Dungen, P. (2008). Foreword. In O. Urbain (Ed.), *Music and conflict transformation: Harmonies and dissonances in geopolitics*, (pp. XV–XVI. New York: LB. Taurus & Co Ltd.

Van Praag, L., Stevens, P. A. J., & Van Houtte, M. (2017). How humor makes or breaks student-teacher relationships: A classroom ethnography in Belgium. *Teaching and Teacher Education, 66*, 393–401. doi: 10.1016/j.tate.2017.05.008

Victoria, M. (2019). The use of humour in the off-task spaces of the language classroom. *ELT Journal, 73*(2), 186–196. doi: 10.1093/elt/ccy054

Vucetic, S. (2004). Identity is a joking matter: Intergroup humor in Bosnia. *Spacesofidentity.net, 4*(1). Retrieved at https://soi.journals.yorku.ca/index.php/soi/article/download/8011/7167/0

Whitehead, B. (2008). We shall overcome: The role of music in the U.S. Civil Rights Movement. In O. Urbain (Ed.), *Music and conflict transformation: Harmonies and dissonance in geopolitics*. (pp. 78–92). London: I. B. Tauris & Co Ltd.

Wijewardena, N., Härtel, C., & Samaratunge, R. (2017). Using humor and boosting emotions: An affect-based study of managerial humor, employees' emotions and psychological capital. *Human Relations (New York), 70*(11), 1316–1341.

Wintrobe, R. (1998). *The political economy of dictatorship*. New York: Cambridge University.

Wisler, A. (2010). The use of humor in the conflict resolution classroom. *Journal for the Study of Peace and Conflict, 2010*, 19–27.

Wolf, B. (2019). Atmospheres of learning: Atmospheric competence. In *Atmosphere and aesthetics* (pp. 209–221). Cham: Springer International.

Wolfgang, D., & Wolfgang, S. (2006). A call for many peaces. In W. Dietrich, Alvarez, J. E. & Koppensteiner, N. (Eds.), *Schlusseltexte der friedensforschung [Key texts of peace studies]* (pp. 282–301). Vienna: LIT VERLAG GmbH & Co.

Zelizer, C. (2010). Laughing our way to peace or war: Humour and peacebuilding. *Journal of Conflictology, 1*(2). Retrieved at https://culturesmith.com/files/Craig_Zelizer_Humor_and_Conflictology_vol1iss2-17700.pdf

Conclusion

Candice C. Carter

Education for peace responds to the need for thriving, as well as surviving. Conditions of life on earth and beyond it where humans interactively have impact have increased the goals for developing and building up peace. Beyond traditions of teaching peace, through spirituality, culture, modeling, and schooling, expanded awareness of peace education's importance has resulted from potential, existing, and outcomes of human violence, along with ecological degradation. This urgency of learning about how to obtain and sustain peace is partial motivation for expanding peace education into contexts beyond instruction in schools and spiritual institutions to other venues for facilitating peacebuilding capabilities. Sites of aesthetic interaction are appropriately among these.

While there are several reasons why the arts have been appropriate and optimal means of expressing, teaching, and facilitating peace, emphasis here is on the importance of performativity in bringing about and building up peace. Peace is a performance in those pursuits. It entails cognitive, sensorial, spiritual, and physical processes that are purposefully done for having the condition of peace. Many of these processes are not "normal" everyday actions, especially as responses to conflict. On the contrary, they often involve altered thoughts and behaviors that have been recognized, analyzed, and recommended as steps toward peace. Since peace is a performance of purposeful interactions that is not widely taught in formal education of modern schools, theatrical experiences elsewhere have enabled such instruction. Learning through involvement in theatre and dance, especially in their applied models, have provided needed performance instruction. Development of sensorial and emotional acuity, that participation in theatrical arts can stimulate, has a role in creation of an expressive performance.

Performance creation and participation can cultivate several peacebuilding processes, such as creative thinking, which is needed in alternative dispute resolution. The courage to be different or identify the source of oppression through use of creative expression in performing arts, is a needed disposition in contexts of potential or extant violence, among other threats to peace.

DOI: 10.4324/9781003227380-12

The confidence that learners of performance develop becomes evident in additional aspects of their lives, beyond the performance venue. The connection with the "other" that performance enables, raises self-awareness and social understanding. The disposition of mutuality that supports peace can develop while creating performance together, especially when it is done in partnership with the "other" or the "director." It has additionally facilitated empathy, which is the foundation of caring interactions that characterize peacebuilding. While improvising in skits about conflicts, for instance, students of this educator and others have created alternatives to conflict interactions in their lives, as proactive responses to escalating aggression. They often conveyed empathy with nonviolent discourse and nonthreatening physical stances, wherein the needs of the aggressor were the focus of their performative attention (Rosenberg, 2000). Students must have several opportunities to create performances of the knowledge and skills they obtain in peace education. The skills of analyzing aggression and creating caring responses to it, that are taught in peace literacy (Chappell & Clough, 2019), need practice across contexts, to build confidence for performance of those peace skills in situations they will face throughout their lives. Integration of those opportunities across subject areas, as well as in arts-focused courses, and venues outside of schools, has enabled performance of peace in childhood through adult education. In these opportunities, they can develop capabilities for enacting the roles of personal, social, and political peace. When taught about them, they learn ideologies that performance of peace express.

There are several ideas about arts that have been explicitly taught, gleaned through informal curriculum and observation of performance, as well as developed through life's interactions. These include, among others, arts as living, emotion, spirituality, communication, learning, conflict response, relief, healing, cultural expression, socialization, identity clarification, connection, otherness, whiteness, colonization, and resistance. The contributors to this book apply in performing arts these ideas and theories that underly peace processes. *Pedagogy of the Oppressed* (Freire, 1970), *Theatre of the Oppressed* (Boal, 2000), and conflict transformation (Galtung, 2004; Lederach, 2003), for example, are theoretical frameworks that have been illustrated in several of their chapters. The theoretical foundations of peacebuilding instruction through theatrical arts support facilitation of holistic learning.

The contents of this book describe facilitation of experiential and holistic education, in formal-and nonformal-learning situations, that involved: interdisciplinary and transdisciplinary instruction, sensorial stimulation, liminal-difference states, embodied awareness, extrarational learning, mimetic instruction, dialogical pedagogy, presence, aesthetic knowledge, imagination, empathy, vulnerability, valuing, and praxis. Those facilitations in a range of settings demonstrate the breadth of possibilities for peacebuilding instruction through theatrical arts and its potential for accomplishing learning for, by, and of peace. Learning how to stop and avoid violence, heal from harm, transform conflict, build, and enhance relationships, along with teach about and take action for peace are some of the for-peace processes that this book's contributors described. The learning by-peace examples involved instruction characterized by peacebuilding processes such as elicitation, inclusion, caring, mutuality, empowerment, curriculum relevancy, problem solving, imagination, creativity, illustration, storytelling, and dialogue. Learning of peace involves awareness of how it has existed in different situations and cultures, including contexts of it in the past, present, and future. Given the limited contents of this book, due to many pandemic-related challenges at the time of its development, there is a need for further description of holistic arts as peacebuilding education and as a source of peace itself.

Nature's aesthetics functions stimulate the condition of peace and performative responses to it by humans. Connectivity with and care of Nature, along with artistic responses to it, are aspects of traditional land-based living and learning. The respect for and oneness felt with Nature that Indigenous cultures cultivate through holistic learning with embodied, sensorial, spiritual, cognitive, and aesthetic interactions are profound. Vicky Kelly provides insight to her understanding from that process.

> This sensitizing of our aesthetic sensibility creates an instrument that allows us to learn to entrain with the sounding of acoustic ecologies of being. Traditionally an Indigenous Knowledge Holder is one who has learned to hold knowledge such that they become resonant to and with the created world, or more specifically to the environmental and spiritual ecology of their traditional territory or lands.
> (Kelly, 2019, p. 19)

Reverence for all the beings in Nature and the land where they live builds peace through ethical relationality, which performance of Indigenous rituals and ceremonies often express. Peacebuilding education in schools and performance contexts needs not only authentic inclusion of information about Indigenous, as well as other cultural performances that convey peace. Greater inclusion in schools, where it exists, of Indigenous pedagogies that involve storytelling and artistic expressions may build peace through reconnection, relationality, and healing with Nature, and intercultural understanding. Interconnections between and beyond reified disciplines and worldviews are crucial for peacebuilding through education.

Future Directions

Educating for peace and theatrical arts have potential for expansion inside as well as outside of schools. Their curriculum partnership and support for each other when taught separately has demonstrated the strength of their nurturing power for holistic human development. Theatrical arts and peace education advance each other's implementation and provide for life skills that discipline-based curricula in many "modern" schools lack where there is sparse provision of instruction in theatrical arts. While inclusion of the theatrical arts in schools, hopefully, expands in all levels of education, due to greater recognition of its value, it can advance goals of peace education. Research on the enacted partnership of instruction in theatrical arts and peace education will continue to be supportive as well as informative of how the instructional goals are accomplished, or hindered.

There are several goals of peace education due to its contextual responsiveness. Although its pedagogies address the particular learning goals of each context, there are recommendations available for the outcomes of its facilitation. The Standards for Peace Education that researchers from around the world developed, in response to the standardization movement in education, identify knowledge, skills, and dispositions that have been instructional goals for student learning (Carter, 2006, 2008). The appendix of this book includes those standards for support in setting instructional goals that can be provided across disciplines as well as in production of theatrical arts. An overarching goal of peace education is enabling recognition of and proactive responses to oppression. The skills of conflict-source identification that the Standards for Peace Education list as a capability include recognition of oppression as a source of violence. Theatrical arts can advance skills of conflict analysis and facilitate responses such as praxis and decolonizing practices. Recognition of globalization initiatives that sustain or renew colonialism, such as exclusion of local, inclusive, and organic performances by and for oppressed populations, is a crucial component of instruction in peacebuilding theatrical arts. Oppression occurs through exclusion or marginalization of local practices that do not promote violence in or between populations (Scharinger, 2013). Inclusion of local worldviews and cultures are peacebuilding as well as anti-oppressive, especially in regions with diverse populations where social-economic hierarchies or neocolonialism have constrained representation and participation in theatrical arts. The liminality (third space) in performance-making enables creation of reimagined relationships and interactions that exemplify peace. There is need for preparation of educators' and performance directors' provision of peacebuilding instruction through arts facilitation.

Various resources exist for preparation of peacebuilding instruction through theatrical arts. Yet, more resources for preparation and practice are needed, especially in the disciplines where integration of this interdisciplinary instruction has been very limited. Educator-preparation programs can include experience with this instructional partnership in applications of the common theories that have comprised its foundation and practice with the learning components which performativity activates, as mentioned above (Cahnmann-Taylor & Souto-Manning, 2010). The suggestions of Prendergast and Saxton (2020) for preparation of students demonstrate possibilities for instruction throughout programs of higher education.

> In an effort to broaden undergraduate applied theatre curricula, we suggest prerequisite or elective courses in leadership and facilitation offered

in other disciplines (as in educational leadership, social work, and child and youth care). We also see real value in courses that address cross-cultural understanding and experience. For instance, a course on Indigenous studies, or (even better) Indigenous theatre.

(Prendergast & Saxton (2020, p. 10)

A table in their article describes university courses related to applied theatre in schools and communities. A program for the program Bachelor of Arts in Drama Education and Community, for example, "Offers a range of drama education in classroom and community contexts. Courses cover principles, theory, and application, and electives include Theatre for Social Action, Theatre for Young Audiences, or a project-based course in Drama and Community" (Prendergast & Saxton, 2020, p. 9). The expansion of programs and resources for peacebuilding education through theatrical arts expresses hope and demonstrates commitment to making change through education.

There is much inspiration from awareness of new, revised, and sustained initiatives in education, and throughout the cultures of the Anthropocene, for developing, building, and preserving peace. The theatrical arts will continue its legacy of inspiring the imagination of humans through performances created for, by, and of peace. Provision of this holistic pedagogy in peace studies and all levels of education will do more than demonstrate hope. It will expand capabilities of peacebuilding that are critically needed.

References

Boal, A. (2000). *Theatre of the oppressed*. London: Pluto Press.
Cahnmann-Taylor, M., & Souto-Manning, Mariana. (2010). *Teachers act up!: Creating multicultural learning communities through theatre*. New York: Teachers College.
Carter, C. C. (2006). Peace education standards. *Research Gate*. Retrieved at www.researchgate.net/profile/Candice-Carter
Carter, C. C. (2008). Voluntary standards for peace education. *Journal of Peace Education, 5*(2), 141–155.
Chappell, P., & Clough, S. (2019). Peace literacy lesson plan 1: Understanding and healing aggression. *Our Curriculum, Peace Literacy*. Retrieved at www.peaceliteracy.org/curriculum
Freire, P. (1970). *Pedagogy of the oppressed*. New York: Seabury.
Galtung, J. (2004). *Transcend and transform*. Boulder, CO: Paradigm.
Kelly, V. (2019). Indigenous poiesis: Medicine for Mother Earth. *Artizein: Arts and Teaching Journal, 4*(1), Article 3. Retrieved at https://opensiuc.lib.siu.edu/atj/vol4/iss1/3/
Lederach, J. P. (2003). *The little book of conflict transformation*. Intercourse, PA: Good Books.
Prendergast, M. & Saxton, J. (2020). Applied theatre and education: We are not-yet... *Canadian Theatre Review, 181 Winter*, 8–12.
Rosenberg, M. (2000). *Nonviolent communication: A language of compassion*. Del Mar, CA: PuddleDancer Press.
Scharinger, J. (2013). Participatory theater, is it really? A critical examination of practices in Timor-Leste. *Australian Journal of South-East Asian Studies, 6*(1), 102–119.

Appendix

Standards for Peace Education

Students of peace education exhibit the following developmentally appropriate knowledge, skills, and dispositions.

Knowledge

Self-awareness
    Evidence: Recognize own values, emotional tendencies, peace capabilities.
Contextual awareness
    Evidence: Knowledge of history and current needs of people in the community.
Multiculturalism
    Evidence: Describe commonalities with and experiences of peoples having different cultural norms and histories.
Intersubjectivity
    Evidence: Identify how more than one person's ideas about something give it meaning.
Human rights
    Evidence: Identify the rights of children that were delineated by the UN and ratified by most nations.
History of peace accomplishments
    Evidence: Analyze accomplishments of people, organizations, and societies.
Non-violent service
    Evidence: Identify peace-service options in conscription, government, and non-governmental agencies.
Peace strategies
    Evidence: Recognize the difference between negative and positive methods of peace.
Conflict sources
    Evidence: Identify roots of violence that have led to local and global conflicts.

Pro-active communication
   Evidence: Identify positively transformative communication techniques.
Methods of non-violent conflict resolution
   Evidence: Describe appropriate methods for different situations.
Conflict style
   Evidence: Identify own conflict-response style and alternative methods for resolving disputes.
Democratic processes
   Evidence: Identify methods of democratic decision-making.
Environmental stewardship
   Evidence: Explain rationale for ecological care of the physical environment.
Consumerism
   Evidence: Explain reasons for socially and environmentally responsible consumerism.

Skills

Self-concept expression
   Evidence: Express a balanced self-concept using affirmation for valuing, as well as critique for self-improvement.
Analysis of communication
   Evidence: Identify techniques including representation, bias, balance, multiple perspectives, and active listening skills.
Communication enactment
   Evidence: Use multiple-perspective, cross-cultural, and compassionate discourse.
Empathy
   Evidence: Show understanding of and concern for the suffering of others, whether it was caused by one-self or someone in one's own identity group.
Inclusion
   Evidence: Choose to include in personal and group activities people with diverse social, intellectual, and physical characteristics.
Community partnerships
   Evidence: Collaborate with people and organizations that promote peace without harm.
Cooperation
   Evidence: Demonstrate ability to cooperate with others who have different goals.
Analysis of violence sources
   Evidence: Identify disrespect, discrimination, deprivation, power imbalance and destruction; thereby recognizing intrapersonal, interpersonal, and structural causes.

Perspective diversity
   Evidence: Learn from and explain three or more perspectives in conflict analysis.
Legitimize others
   Evidence: Validate the point of view, narrative, and aspirations of an adversary; one with a different goal.
Engagement
   Evidence: Demonstrate thoughts and actions for bringing about and building peace.
Accommodations
   Evidence: Accept and adapt to diverse cultural and cognitive norms of other people.
Collective and individual responsibility
   Evidence: Acknowledge and explain own group or self-contribution to conflict.
Positive recognition
   Evidence: Acknowledge all efforts and accomplishments of disputants in a conflict.
Envision peace
   Evidence: Develop and express visions of a peaceful presence and future.
Commitment
   Evidence: Commit to work for a peaceful presence and future through nonviolent conflict transformation and resolution.
Adaptation
   Evidence: Practice peace development within cultural contexts using culturally appropriate methods.
Environmental stewardship
   Evidence: Participate in ecological care of the physical environment.
Restoration
   Evidence: Use culturally responsive methods for repairing damage after harm to humans or nature.
Consumerism
   Evidence: Identify or participate in socially and environmentally responsible consumerism.

Dispositions

Acceptance
   Evidence: Display acceptance of oneself and of human diversity.
Mutuality
   Evidence: Show identification with all humanity and life forms while recognizing their distinct needs.

Respect
: Evidence: Exhibit positive regard for others, regardless of their differences from oneself.

Concern
: Evidence: Demonstrate a conscience that monitors activities for protection of life and its environment.

Empathy
: Evidence: Show compassion for those who suffer and have needs to fulfill.

Service
: Evidence: Demonstrate an interest in providing assistance to anyone, including people with diverse characteristics, when it is needed.

Optimism
: Evidence: Show belief that peace can grow out of pro-active conflict resolution.

Involvement
: Evidence: Realize personal and collective responsibility to bring about change by peaceful means where it is needed.

Courage
: Evidence: Show willingness to disrupt or stop antecedents of, as well as existing, violence.

Commitment
: Evidence: Demonstrate desire to work for a peaceful presence and future.

Humility
: Evidence: Demonstrate modesty about oneself and own achievements.

Patience
: Evidence: Show ability to wait for completion of steps in a peace process.

©2006 Candice C. Carter

Index of Names

Abramovic, M. 15–16, 24
Adichie, C. 62
Aguilar, Y. 95
Altruz, M. 142
Amir, L. 187
Anagondahalli, D. 195
Anguita, N. 93
Anjani, A. 127
Antilla, E. 147
Apat, T. 110
Apollinaire 136
Arias, L. 5
Aristizabal, H. 160
Aristophanes 192
Arts Building Peace: Creative Approaches to Transformation 110
Arusha Peace Agreement 134
Ashbrook, J. B. 49, 67
Aspera, H. 127
Astman, J. A. 8
Athens 192
Athlone 149
Atkinson 48
Austria 71–72, 78, 80–81, 88
Ayindo, B. 9, 109–110, 112–113

Bahrain 190
Bakar, F. 189
Baker, B. D. 189
Balfour, M. 4
Bamidele, O. 143
Banas-Malang, M. 129
Bang, A. H. 159
Bangayimbaga, A. 145
Bassett, C. 165
Baxter Theatre 150
Begin, M. 138
Bell, L. A. 160
Bell, C. M. 20

Bender, S. 54, 167
Benet-Martínez, V. 89
Benjamin K. 194
Bennathan, J. 76
Benza, R. 7, 10
Bergen-Belsen 42
Bernecker, R. 23
Berlinsky, N. 67
Bhabha, H. K. 23
Bharucha, R. 150
Bieg, S. 189
Bird, L. 143
Blackburn Miller, J. 9, 163, 167
Boal, A. 6, 14, 41, 43, 67, 112–113, 117, 121, 160, 167, 197, 202
Bonilla, A. 94
Bonomi, B. 190
Bourdieu, P. 25
Bourriaud, N. 151
Boyce-Tillman, J. 186
Brantmeier, E. J. 72–73, 77–79, 87, 137
Brazil 133
Breed, A. 5
Brock-Utne, B. 142
Broekman, K. 112
Brown, B. 72, 77, 79
Brownell, S. E. 189
Brumfit, C. 134
Buber, M. 46–48, 51, 67
Burgoyne, S. 133
Butler, J. 20
Butterwick, S. 160, 166

Cabedo-Mas, A. 4
Cahnmann-Taylor, M. 204
California 58
Cameroon 127
Canada 114
Cape Town 9, 146–147, 149, 153, 155

Chappell, P. 202
Carter, C. C. 3–4, 13–14, 23–24, 57, 74, 137, 142, 159, 170, 204
Carter, J. 138
Castoriadis, C. 38
Cavanagh, T. 137
Chaplin, C. 193
Chavez, C. 56
Chiang, Y. 189
Chowdhury, D. 127
Clark, M. C. 164
Claycomb, R. M. 161
Cloete, N. 23
Clough, S. 202
Cohen, C. 4, 159–160
Cohen-Cruz, J. 67
Coles, R. 48
Colley, B. M. 4
Collins, K. A. 193
Convention on the Rights of the Child 50
Comen, E. 169
Cooper, C. D. 188
Cooper, K. M. 189
Corcoran, R. 169
COVID-19 Pandemic 49, 81–82, 110, 116, 128, 146, 154, 157, 186
Crossley, C. D. 188
Cuba 133
Culbertson, H. 90
Cyrus the Great 61–62

Daloz, L. A. 161–164, 167
Danish 149–150, 154
Dávila, A. C. 6
Davie, E. 149
Davis, B. 133
Dawson, G. F. 161
Dawson, K. 52–53
Dean, R. A. 189
DeGloma, T. 142
Delors, J. 104
Denmark 147, 151–154
Democratic Republic of Congo 120, 133–134
Desai, D. 160
Dewey, J. 3, 45, 48, 167
Diamond, D. 86
Diebel, J. 169
Dietrich, W. 72–73, 76–78, 186
Dinesh, N. 23
Dirkx, J. 161, 163–164, 167
Ditzel Facci 72, 76, 78
Doat, J. 103

Doidge, N. 80
Dresel, M. 189
Duckworth, C. 3
Dunne, T. C. 188
Dupuy, K. 68

East Africa Community Language Learning 135
East African Federation 134
Egypt 138, 190, 195, 197
Eisler, R. 2
Eisner, E. 3, 63, 165, 167
Ehrenreich, B. 85
Ehrenspeck, Y. 34
Elliott, J. 96
Ellis, A. P. J. 188
Emerson, R. W. 190
Engel, J. 27
Esteva, G. 186
Estonia 17
Evans, J. B. 188
Evans, M. 170

Facer, K. 143
Fesette, N. 143
Finlay, K. 159, 165
Fisas, V. 95
Flores, A. 7
Folami, O. M. 143
Fordred, L. 120
Forgasz, R. 160
Forsyth, A. 161
Foucault, M. 28
Fox, C. L. 92–93
Fox, J. 127
Frazer, J. G. 25
Freetong Players International 127
Freire, P. 8, 41, 43–45, 47, 66, 113, 117, 121, 133, 139, 167, 202
Freud, S. 23
Friedman, E. 52

Gardner, H. 161, 165, 167
Galenzoga, R. 128
Gallagher, K. 49
Galtung, J. 2, 14, 44, 45, 91, 117, 159, 186, 202
Gandhi, E. 198
Gandhi, M. 63, 184, 187
Garcia, M. E. P. 186
Garcia-Mateus, S. 50
Gebauer, G. 20–21, 32
Genesis 47
Germany 28–29

Index of Names

Gernika 186, 196
Gibson, J. M. 198
Giguiento, D. 109, 110, 112
Glenberg, A. M. 14
Gobodo-Madikizela, M. 157
Goffman, E. 19
Göhlich, M. 27
Goleman, D. 164
Gómez, J. 92–93, 96
González, M. 102
Grätz, R. 23
Greece 192
Greene, M. 2, 161, 165, 167
Gremigni, P. 189
Grenzenlos 80–82
Gullotta, T. P. 169
Grumet, M. 49
Guteiérrez Varea, R. 10

Haffner, C. 127
Hammond, R. L. 161
Hampton, R. 169
Haraldsen, H. M. 75
Harlap, Y. 160
Harris, I. M. 183, 187
Harris, M. 46, 49
Härtel, C. 188
Hawksley, T. 90
Hayes, S. 159
Hazel Barnes, H 142
Hazou, R. T. 23
Heddon, D. 76
Heintz, S. 189
Hitler, A. 184, 193
Hoffa, J. 59
Hoffmeyer-Zlotnik, P. 38
Hoggan, C. 161, 165, 168
Holman, D. K. 133
hooks, b. 50
Horita, M. 189
Horton, M. 178
Huerta, D. 58
Hughes, J. 4
Humboldt, W. 33, 35
Hunter, M. 4
Hutu 131
Huynh, Q.-L. 75
Hussong, D. K. 189

Ingul, S. 75
Irani, K. 160
Iun, J. 188
Ivala, E. 142

Jackson, A. 43
Jamison, K. R. 50
Japan 109–110
Jech, C. J. 47
Jeffrey, D. 26
Jellicoe, A. 160
Jirata, T. J. 142
Johnson, D. 133
Johnson, R. 133
Johnston, C. 80
Johnston, K. 75
Joshee, R. 2

Khan, A. G. 187
Kaliwat Theatre Collective 117
Kandil, Y. 142
Kant, I. 34
Karen, R. 53
Karkou, V. 4
Karnieli-Miller, O. 170
Kasat, P. 143
Kasl, E. 4
Kauffman, M. 67
Kees, N. 137
Kelly, V. 203
Kennedy, R. 57
Kenya 110
Keskin, S. C. 4
Keskin, Y. 4
Kessel, M. 187–188, 197
Khamis, S. 197
King Jr., M. L. 187
Kirtel, A. 4
Kitchenham, A. 162–163
Koen, M. 189
Kokemohr, R. 28, 32
Koller, H.-C. 34–35, 37
Kong, D. 188
Koppensteiner, N. 72–73, 76–80, 83–84
Kotin, A. 44
Kramer, K. P. 47
Kress, G. 14
Kretchmer, O. 169
Kumar, R. 14
Kumar, V. 189

Labadi, S. 75
Labos, S. 118
Lagarde, M. 94
Lamas, M. 95
Lamm, C. 159, 165
Lance, K. M. 4, 10
Lapierre, S. S. 189

Index of Names   213

Latorre, A. 96
Latvia 17
Lawrence, R. L. 161, 164–168
Lawrence-Lightfoot, S. 52
Lebanon 127
Lederach A. J. 73
Lederach, J. P. 72–73, 76–77
Lee, C. 189
Leguro, M. 109–110, 112
Leupin, R. 75
Levitt, B. 143
Libya 190
Liebmann, M. 110
Lim, A. E. H. 75
Lim, F. 188
Lithuania 17
Löfgren, H. 11
Loots, L. 154
Lottering, M. 150
Lowman, J. 133
Liu, S. 75
Lum, B. J. 184–185

Mackay, S. 67
Maedza, P. 161
Maemura, Y. 189
Major, J. E. 198
Malm, B. 4
Mani, R. 111
Marovah, T. 2
Martin, R. A. 195
Martínez, I. 94
Matchett, S. 25
Mattenklott, G. 40
May, R. 50, 53
McCreaddie, M. 189
McDonough, S. 160
McElwee, J. 92–93
McFarren, C. K. 195
McGlynn, C. 137
McKeachie, W. 133
McKenna, M. K. 72
Mecheril, P. 35–36
Megson, C. 161
Mehdi, S. S. 9, 183, 197
Meisner, S. 67
Mendiburo-Seguel, A. 189
Merchant, M. 196
Mexico 91, 94, 96, 100–101
Mezirow, J. 161–164, 167
Michaels, A. 14
Micucci, J. A. 189
Midgley, M. 85

Milan, K. 118
Miller, R. 2
Milling, J. 76
Milošević, S. 196
Mindanao 110, 112–113, 117
Mindanao Peacebuilding Institute 9, 109, 111, 114
Minuchin, S. 82
Mitchell, J. 74
Modirzadeh, L. 179
Möller, E. 27
Monterona, B. 110, 113–114
Montessori, M. 2–3, 14–15
Morrin, S. 32–33
Mubarak, H. 195
Muñoz, F. A. 73, 77–78, 85, 95
Museum of Memory and Tolerance in Mexico City 100
Myanmar 127

Nadile, E. M. 189
Nathan, L. F. 49
National Centre for Peace and Conflict Studies 187
Ndura, E. 135, 137
Neck, C. P. 200
Netherlands 42
Nicaragua 133
Nicholson, H. 6, 74
Neimeyer, R. A. 4
Nisengwe, G. 9, 139
Nguyen, A.-M 89
Noddings, N. 4, 45, 48, 54, 66
Norda, J. 169
Northeast Asia Regional Peacebuilding Institute 115
Northern Ireland 159–160, 169–170, 175
Nzang, J. 127

Oakwood School 54, 67, 68
Obrillant, D. 13
Oddey, A. 76
Odom, G. 142
Okri, B. 121
Okumoto, K. 9, 115, 124, 129
Olaiya, T. A. 143
Oltra Albiach, M. A. 75
Oseroff-Varnell, D. 2
Ospina, C. 92–93, 95
Ospina, D. 92–93, 95

Paget, D. 161
Palmer, P. J. 45

214 Index of Names

Panniker, R. 186, 194
Parks, R. 187
Pao, A. 75
Paterson, D. 43, 67
Patterson, O. 169
Patton, M. Q. 170
Pavett, D. 170
Peimer, D. 142
Perry, W. G. 163
Peru 3
Pessach, L. 170
Peukert, H. 34–35
Picasso, P. 50, 186, 196
Philippine Educational Theatre Association 114
Philippines 109–112, 114
Piaget, J. 41
Pickett, L. 24, 142
Pietersen, T. 150
Plessner, H. 30–32
Posso, P. 93
Pradena, Y. 93
Premaratna, N. 74
Prendergast, M. 205
Prentki, T. 5
Pretorius, J. 189
Pruitt, L. 4

Quayle, A. 143
Quesada Palm, D. 9, 110, 114

Ramsden, P. 133
Read, H. 2, 54
Reardon, B. 45–46
Republic of Ireland 170
Resina, J. R. 20–21
Rhoades, R. 41, 44
Riessman, C. K. 171–172
Rimbaud, J. 23
Risner, D. 150–151
Rivin, J. M. 188
Robert, C. 188
Roosevelt, E. 60–61
Rora, C. 40
Rosenberg, M. 202
Rosenstock-Huessy, E. 53
Rosenzweig, F. 53
Roy, A. 40
Ruddick, S 49
Ryan, C. 68

Sadat, A. 138
Saint-Fleur, J. P. 28
Saint Phalle, N. de 15–16, 24

Sahar, K. 195
Sahlins, M. 20
Said, E. 26
Saljö, R. 14, 26
Salomon, G. 44
Saksa, J. 169
Samaratunge, R. 188
Sampedro, L. 102, 104
Samuel, G. M. 9, 158
Save the Children 66
Saw Phoe Kwar 127
Saxton, J. 204
Schall, R. 189
Schechner, R. 22
Scheler, M. 30–31
Scher, A. 159
Scherr, A. 28
Schiller, F. 33–34, 37
Schore, A 45, 53
Sekimoto, S. 188
Selander, S. 14
Sclavi, M. 189
Sepinuck, T. 164, 168–171,175
Schambeck, M. 36
Scharinger, J. 204
Sedano-Solís, A. 92
Segato, R. L. 92
Selman, J. 160
Sen, A. 182
Serbia 192, 196
Serret, E. 94
Shapiro, S. B. 49, 51, 157
Shearer, J. M. 169
Sheets-Johnstone, M. 147
Shirvell, S. 2
Shutzman, M. 67
Siegel, D. 45, 62
Sierra Leone 127
Simpson, S. 161, 165, 167–168
Singer, T. 159, 165
Skyllsted, K. 186
Slaughter, J. E. 188
Slim, H. 68
Smith, K. 133
Smith, W. J. 189
Snauwaert, D. 45
Society for Women Against Aids 139
Sombatphūnsiri, C. 196
Sone, E. 142
Sonn, C. 143
South Africa 147–154
Souto-Manning, M. 204
Sparta 192
Stake, R. E. 167

Index of Names 215

Stephan, W. G. 159, 165
Stern, D. N. 46, 48, 52–53
Stevenston Noh Project 75
Stevens, P. A. J. 189
Steward, D. 161
Stewart, K. D. 145
Sting, W. 34
Stinson, S. W. 147, 150–151
Strier, R. 170
Stuckey, H. 161, 165, 167–168
South Sudan 123, 133
Svendler Nielsen, C. 9, 146
Syria 127, 190

Tambiah, S. J. 22
Tanaka, H. 189
Tangermann, J. 38
Taylor, D. 96
Taylor, K. 165
The Metropolitan Museum of Art 120
Timpson, W. 9, 133, 135, 137
The Playhouse 169–172
Thiong'o, N. 111
Thompson, J. 11
Thompson, B. E. 4
Tjersland, H. 8, 72, 76–78
Tonge, J. 170
Trozzo E. 102, 104
Tsolaki, G. C. 75
Tuan, H-C. 75
Tubino, F. 7
Tunisia 190
Turner, V. W. 22
Tutsi 131
Twizerimana, F. 9, 130, 134–136
Tyler, J. A. 166

Ubuntu 2
Ubuntu Arts 115
Uganda 133, 135
United Farm Workers 56–58
United Nations 13
United Nations Educational, Scientific, and Cultural Organization 15, 26, 142
United Nations Commission on the Status of Women 67
United States of America 114, 150
Universal Declaration of Human Rights 60
University of Ngozi 134, 136
Urbain, O. 186

Valdez-Medina, J. 94
Van den Dungen, P. 185
Van Houtte, M. 189
Van Manen, M. 147
Van Praag, L. 189
Varea, R. G. 4, 159–160
Vedel, K. 158
Vellino, B. C. 75
Velthuizen, A. G. 142
Vernard Harrington, K. 189
Veterans of Foreign Wars 41
Victoria, M. 189
Vienna 71–72, 80–81, 88
Vilar, R. 118
Vincett, G. 90
Von Humboldt, W. 33, 35
Vrecer, N. 165
Vucetic, S. 188

Wagner B. J. 50
Waisvisz, S. 75
Waldenfels, B. 28
Walker, P. O. 10
Wallenhorst, N. 25
Wang, H. 189
Wasserman, I. C. 166
Welwood, J. 77
Weston, S. 160
Whitehead, B. 186
Wiggins, S. 189
Wijewardena, N. 188
Wilson, L. 43
Wintrobe, R. 196
Wisler, A. 189
Wolf, B. 187
Wulf, C. 8, 13–16, 18–21, 24–25

Yeats, W. B. 49
Yemen 190
Yin, R. K. 167
Yorks, L.4, 159
Younes, A. 127
Yordit 123
Yorks, L. 4, 159
Yüksel, S. 2
Yurén, T. 104

Zambia 115
Zeitz Museum of Contemporary Art Africa 155
Zelizer, C. 188
Žídek N. 5
Zimbabwe 114
Zinn, H. 109
Zirfas, J. 31–32, 36

Index of Terms

action: cultural 20; deconstruction 5; direct 111; dramatic 121, 122; educational 91–94, 208; informed 160; nonviolent 187; performative 31; protest 196; *see also* research; series 120; social 54, 165, 166, 205; teacher 151; transformative 11, 138
aesthetics: applied 15; projects 35
age 4, 54, 61, 98, 154
agency: borderless 191; educational 182; local 112; moral 8, 46, 51; skills 104; social change 44, 160
aggression 93, 202
ahimsa 2
animals 123, 197
architecture 18
artists 2, 4, 8; capabilities 19, 21, 52; citizen- 109, 110, 117, 126–128; comic 193; dance- 154; innate 116; peacebuilder- 111, 113
art: applied 8; cultural 22, 23; education 149; dynamic 126; holistic 203; integration 44; performative 8; violence 16, 17, 116, 124
attachment 53, 86
audience 5, 8, 9, 14, 81, 121, 163, 166, 168, 172, 189
autonomy 21

behavior 13, 20–22, 25, 53, 125, 140, 141, 188, 201
beliefs 93, 94, 100, 103, 119, 150
Bildung 33
bridging 44
borders 32, 35, 36, 191
boundary 154
bullying 93, 121
business 58, 133–135, 185

capacities 8, 13–15, 72, 85, 88, 117, 118
camp 81
care 45, 56, 59, 66, 85, 103, 105, 151, 157, 160, 203, 207
case study 9, 137, 159, 166, 167
catharsis 121
celebration 117, 121, 122, 143, 147
ceremony 99
chant 15, 59, 118
chaos 120, 121
childhood 4, 123, 132, 202
children 8, 9, 14, 31–36, 66; migrant 29, 30; rights 50
circles 168, 193
citizenship: comprehensive 2, 74; political 65; social 23, 74, 75; transcultural 23
coexistence 5, 7, 91, 95–97, 105
collaboration 15, 53, 59, 72, 76, 97, 118
coloniality 147
comedy 185, 192–196
commitment 59, 66, 135, 157, 205
communication 4, 7–9, 18, 19, 22, 52, 86, 135, 137, 187–189, 202
community: arts programs 159; connections 170, 207; education 168, 205, 206; imaginary 37; learner 50; memory 143; participants 112; shared 2, 17, 23, 81, 82, 188; social justice 163; solidarity 128; symbolic 22; *see also* theatre
conflict: intergroup 143; levels 124; moral 43; poetics 113; resolution 5, 42, 44, 188, 189; responses to 1–4, 57, 195, 196, 201, 202; systemic 75, 169, 206; transformation 76, 78, 93, 113, 117, 159
confidence 9, 41, 137, 174, 190, 195, 202

conformism 191
connection: audience 163; cross-age 170; crosscultural 4, 15; distant 116; interpersonal 48, 189, 202; participant 93, 102; past 21; perceptions 36, 203
consciousness 2, 35, 37, 196
constraint 2, 14
context 1, 5, 7, 20, 34, 36, 93, 112, 130, 142, 159, 206
continuity 21, 75
courage 53, 65, 77, 78, 191, 201, 209
courses 110, 111, 117, 202, 204, 205
creativity 14, 75–78, 80, 117, 118, 126, 186, 189, 203
crime 146, 147, 157, 169
crisis 9, 116
culture: expression 1, 111, 113; indigenous 109, 123; inter- 15, 23, 75; Luba 120; of peace 18, 92–95, 184; subaltern 7
curriculum: age-appropriate 68; applied 139; gender 105; hidden 2, 91; informal 9, 202; lived 86, 87; official 92; relevancy 66, 143, 203; social justice 51

dance 6, 9, 21, 46, 111, 147, 150, 155, 201
deliberation 8, 93, 94
desiderata 147, 154, 155
design 14, 30, 32, 36, 86, 98, 110
destruction 16, 50, 119, 120, 207
development: citizenship 75, 104; empathy 165, 166, 172; human 4, 20, 24, 96, 163, 189, 201; peace 25, 95, 208; relations 18
dialogue 13, 15, 41, 43–48, 116, 126, 146, 163, 203
dilemma 123, 162
disciplines 3, 133, 135, 203–205
dificultator 43
director 202
dispositions 3, 118, 120, 204, 208
dissent 32, 35, 37, 182
diversity 8, 15, 23, 24, 34, 73–76, 86, 208
dove 113
drama 7, 93, 96, 130, 205; practitioner 29
dramaturgy 121
drive 33, 34, 37, 93, 96

education: adult 163–165; aesthetic 27, 33–37; culturally responsive 143, 208; experiential 3, 4, 92, 117, 202; gender 105; holistic 14, 104; neoliberal 2; nonformal 182; peace 2, 13, 51, 73–79, 93, 111–116, 142, 185, 186, 192, 193, 201–205; performance 4, 6–8; secular 3; transcultural 23, 24; transdisciplinary 142, 185, 202; whiteness in 150
educator preparation 45, 185, 188, 204
emotion 4, 7, 8, 22, 32, 61, 78, 96, 104, 120, 143, 163–168, 189, 201, 202, 206
empathy 9, 41, 44, 93, 97, 121, 159, 160, 163, 165, 166, 172, 179, 207
enabler 72, 76, 77
enchantment 27, 29
equality 66, 94, 97, 105, 116
experience: aesthetic 4, 14, 30–33; direct 14; emotional 14, 49, 188, 189, 195; extrarational 7, 14; otherness and difference 23, 36, 85, 114, 143, 159, 206; physical 49, 160; practical 105; sensorial 13, 118

facilitator 31, 74–76, 80, 84, 113, 167, 186
fantasy 6
femicide 9, 99, 104
flexibility 114
force 45, 188, 195
frameworks 115, 164, 202
freedom 17, 45, 66, 82, 127, 182, 191
future 20, 21, 44, 136, 148, 182, 208

games 7, 14, 83, 118, 127
gender: pedagogy 105; perspective 94, 188, 189, 105; relationships 8, 9, 65, 91–105; violence 100, 161

harmony 2, 7, 17, 33–35, 37
harassment 8, 97, 121
healing 2, 4, 8, 34, 46, 48, 51–53, 111, 142, 143, 163, 173, 203
hegemony 8
heritage 13, 15, 18, 49, 195
heterogeneity 34, 95
hierarchy 151
history 44, 58, 59, 105, 119–121, 168, 191, 206
hope 41–44, 49, 57, 124, 143, 156, 160, 205
human: condition 6, 16, 24, 31, 45, 77–80, 92, 94, 157, 166, 187, 203; rights 1, 42–44, 50, 54, 59–63, 95, 206

Index of Terms

humor: comedy 192, 193; jokes 195; language 189; manager 188; political 9, 10, 186, 187; strategies 59, 62, 189, 195; *see also* stories

inclusion 2, 48, 97, 136, 138, 142, 143, 203, 204
identity 8, 9, 14, 202; collective 15, 17, 37, 147–151, 188, 195; emotional 16, 171; intercultural 75, 202; reduction 7, 62
inspiration 41, 61, 132, 206
interdependence 2, 3, 7, 103
instruction: cross-grade 61, 62; digital 110, 116, 117, 142; dominator-style 2, 133; embodied 187; integration 201, 204; humor in 189; mimetic 202; motivation 130; performance 143; sensorial 14; standardized 3; wordless 155
intersectionality 1
imagination 2, 6, 8, 19, 20, 22, 30–33, 36, 93, 122, 143, 160, 165, 202, 205
imperfection 77, 85, 87, 88
improvisation 97, 118, 195
ingenuity 14
intervention 5, 91, 92, 96, 97, 105, 117, 186
intuition 9, 50, 164
issues 54, 93, 102, 110, 112, 132, 136, 191, 194

joy 45, 50, 53
justice 1, 13, 45, 113, 123, 137, 157, 161, 194; restorative 111; social 51, 59, 161, 163

knowing: affective 166; artistic 4, 21, 22, 161, 165, 167, 203; embodied 160, 166; imaginal 27, 164, 165; not 8, 43, 48, 77, 88, 168
knowledge: diversity 24, 74, 76, 164; educator 72–74, 82, 83; intuitive 117, 118, 161; learner 3, 48, 202, 206, 207; practical 20; self- 24, 165, 187; symbolic 19

language: common 134; cultural heritage 18; *see also* dance; diversity 7, 103; instruction 149; *see also* humor; marginalization 150; new 8, 28, 128; performative 21
leader 113, 133, 185, 188, 204, 205

learning: ambivalent 28, 29, 32; cognitive 4, 13, 93, 163, 188, 203, 208; co- 72, 111; deep 78, 87, 133; domains 74; embodied 50; emotional 113; experiential 3, 117; holistic 8, 14, 24, 83, 203; interdisciplinary 1, 92; mimetic 18; performance-based 15; sensorial 3, 4; spiritual 161, 167, 202; transformative 163–167; transrational 1
liminality 204
limits 36, 42, 81
Lukasa 120
listening 48, 53, 93, 140, 143, 157, 168, 175, 207
literacy 133; peace 202; storytelling 132

machismo 100
magic 29–37
manifesto 147
mediation 18, 95, 133
memory 16, 21, 42, 100, 120, 143, 172
mentor 160, 163
militarism 112, 113; anti- 193
mimesis 20, 21, 32, 117
mise en scene 19, 20, 75
mistakes 160
monologue 43, 45, 47
movement: performance 19, 31, 92, 98, 104, 147, 154; social 2, 7, 56
museography 98
misogyny 100

nature 1, 18, 25, 111, 203
needs 2, 33, 46, 77, 79, 104, 142, 143, 193, 202, 203, 206; special 81
negotiation 7, 13, 133
nonviolence 117, 140, 187; *see also* violence

obedience 191, 196
openness 80, 117, 143, 154
oppression 1, 43, 160, 166, 196, 20, 204
otherness 7, 18, 23, 24, 28, 43, 143, 163, 173, 195, 202

patience 84, 85, 157, 209
peace: authentic 45; body 6, 19, 49; building 25, 93, 111–113, 117, 142, 161, 176; commitment 66; conflictive 78; construal 1; critical 125; culture of 13, 92, 95, 109, 185; disposition 202; disturb 41; humor 188; *see also*

peace education; making 2; negative 52; peaces 78, 82; political 192, 195; positive 45, 46, 66, 116, 124; well-being 2, 27, 34, 189; work 14
peace education: agency 104, 112; critical 4, 7, 41, 93, 102, 136, 196; elicitive 76, 77; disciplines 24, 54, 74, 202; distance 118; goals 1, 2, 44, 94, 202–204; holistic 4, 24, 78, 161; imperfect 73; nonformal 195, 201; performative 109, 112, 142; standards 204, 206–209; *see also* values
pedagogy: critical 147; of cruelty 92; culturally relevant 9, 142; dialogical 44, 66, 202; of dance 147; embodied 49; Montessori 3, 14; of the oppressed 113, 139, 202; relational 46, 66; of vulnerability 77–80
performativity 8, 14, 18, 21, 24, 201
performers 8, 75, 112, 142, 143, 168
perspective 4, 10, 16, 21, 23, 35, 37, 63, 93, 104, 137, 143, 162, 173, 208
play 4, 7, 8, 15, 31, 32, 120, 156
poetry 119, 127, 182, 185
police 169, 171, 173, 175
politician 137, 175
positionality 30–32, 150, 167
power: asymmetry 7, 10, 151; confrontation 15, 45, 57, 95; imagination 27; instructional 34, 66, 73; shared 2; transformation 161
practices: aesthetic 17, 21; bodily 49; communication 19; cultural 13, 15, 18, 24, 142, 143; decolonizing 204; discriminatory 104; performance 5; sexist 91; school 96; tourist 119; violent 93
praxis 2, 9, 74, 96, 112, 117, 127, 160, 204
presence 19, 47, 48, 53, 80, 84, 124, 202
privilege 45, 56, 79, 150, 151, 53
psychology 45, 111
puppetry 75
purpose 41, 42, 46, 52, 62, 72, 92, 142, 164, 188, 201

racism 24, 45, 160, 169
rational 6, 14, 33, 79, 93, 164, 165, 202
reconciliation 5, 113, 114, 123, 137, 140, 141, 157, 169
relations 4, 7, 18, 50, 72, 93, 101, 140, 159, 169, 185
religion 191

remembering 52, 105, 119, 142
research: action 96; ritual 18, 31, 36, 111, 118, 161
reality 4, 6, 21, 22, 35, 102, 103, 143
reflection 1, 3, 37, 72, 96, 100, 101, 117, 150, 162, 171
refugee 28, 29, 36, 37, 160
relationality 72, 78, 203
repair 9, 45, 46, 51–53
resistance 2, 17, 18, 24, 33, 57, 128, 160, 190, 191, 202
resonance 5; aesthetic 29–33, 37–39
restoration 132, 208
revolution 17, 18, 139, 195
role-play 154, 165, 166
risk 45, 53, 77, 113, 160, 161, 166

safety 118, 153, 160, 188, 195
school: boarding 132; club 9, 135–137; community 66; compulsory 151; courtyard 101; elementary 44, 46, 59, 137; future 148; graduate 51, 133; independent 54; relationships 52; secondary 91, 96, 97, 121, 122, 146, 151; university 111; whole 104
script 55, 57, 76, 101, 117, 168, 171, 174
self-image 14, 17, 23, 50
self-initiative 36
senses 2, 6, 14, 24, 118, 160, 188
sensitivity 23, 42, 54, 175
settlers 113, 169
sex 21, 65, 91, 94, 95, 104, 105, 136, 186, 192
silence 45, 52, 59, 102, 119
social: action 165, 195; alternatives 95; capacities 15; change 5, 17, 44, 49, 115, 164; consumerism 208; citizenship 23, 75; cohesion 94, 146; distancing 149; exchange 19; justice 51, 59, 151, 157, 159–161, 166; media 127, 190; memories 21; pro- 2; relations 18, 202; structures 13, 118, 204; transformation 174; wounds 1
social studies 8, 42, 54
society 5, 7, 8, 13, 21, 24, 45, 91, 109, 118, 121, 125, 137, 171, 172
solidarity 19, 56, 59, 113, 115, 128
space: boundedness 80; constraint-free 14; creation 74, 128; digital 116; dynamics 19; glocalized 27; heterotopic 28; holder 76, 88; homeless 63; imaginary 7, 31;

inclusive 105, 143; liminal 28, 37; negative 154; sacred 41; socialization 104
spect-actor 121, 122, 196
spectators 51, 92, 121, 196
states: authoritarian 183, 196; militarized 123, 192; of mind 59, 93, 128, 202
stereotype 62, 91, 94, 95, 105, 176
stories: back- 117; constructive 143; counter- 75, 142, 143, 160; creation 97, 98; engaging 140; embodied 65; hegemonizing 127; participants' 72, 73, 77, 86, 119, 142; patients' 48
structure 31–33, 35–37, 80, 82, 83, 93, 114, 116, 121
student: all 4; purpose 52; *see also* resistance; teacher 47; traumatized 4; whole 46, 84
subjectivity 121, 206
sustainability 13, 24, 130, 137, 142, 143
system: education 137, 170, 185; family 52; political 17, 182, 196; sex-gender 94, 95

teacher: artist 64, 146, 147
theatre: applied 5, 37, 44, 66, 75, 112; community 5, 9, 113, 142; devised 54, 76, 77, 104; forum 115, 121, 122, 196; image 114; Indigenous 205; making 80; street 195; testimonial 167
theory: arts 124; attachment 53; education 33–35; learning 3, 161; peacebuilding 117; role of 48
thinking: body 49, 187, 196; creative 136, 201; critical 104, 118, 133, 142; character 52; parental 153; social 181; theory 30
time 85, 157
tradition 1, 13, 17, 18, 21, 23, 45, 87, 93, 97, 98, 102, 105, 113, 119, 126, 135, 142, 143, 203
transformation: agent 5, 95; barrier 121; cycle 93; education 45; *see also* conflict; personal 4, 187; perspective 159; relational 78
trauma: healing 4, 6, 111, 126, 142, 143, 172

trust 31, 45, 47, 48, 50–53, 66, 84, 85, 168, 195

Ubuntu 2, 115
understanding: aesthetics 34, 203; characters 41; *see also* conflict; correctional facility 153; critical 94; diverse 74; history 59; identity 150; intercultural 15, 205; migrated children 28; mis- 7; oneself 102, 202; otherness 23; peace 2; performance features 97; injustice resistance 57; sensorial 14; transrational 78
universities 111, 181, 187
utopia 36, 44

values: cultural 49; educational leadership 185; expression 118; intrinsic 124, 206; programs 44; peace education 6, 7, 187; peace work 127; systems 137
violence: body 6; confronting 15, 18, 24, 140, 182, 202; cultural 92, 116, 125; cyber 196; denaturalization 103, 104; direct 3, 116, 125; domestic 122; femicidal 100; gender 99; implicit 50; invisible 101, 102; involuntary 192; *see also* conflict response; performance 4, 16, 17; reduction 18, 125, 132; structural 13, 44, 116, 125, 204, 206, 209
voice 29, 41, 45, 57, 59, 95, 98, 104, 118, 142, 143, 148, 160, 164, 194
vulnerability 19, 53, 65, 77–79, 86, 87, 202

war 2–6, 27, 41, 130, 134, 135, 140, 184, 187, 192–194
wellbeing: collective 2, 27, 44, 51, 142, 143, 195; enchantment of 34, 35; individual 45, 66, 188, 189
Weltoffenheit 30–33
whiteness 150, 202
world: alien 28, 32; cultural 30; imaginary 7, 35; heritage 18; inner 20, 22; nest- 183; objective 47; regions 2, 3, 65, 109–114; view 15, 118, 139, 162, 163, 203